D1524598

First published in 1990 by Motorbooks International Publishers & Wholesalers, PO Box 2, 729 Prospect Avenue, Osceola, WI 54020 USA

Created by Tex Smith Publishing Co. PO Box 726, 29 East Wallace, Driggs, ID 83422

The information in this book is true and complete to the best of our knowledge. All recommendations are made without any guarantee on the part of the author or publisher, who also disclaim any liability incurred in connection with the use of this data or specific details

We recognize that some words, model names and designations, for example, mentioned herein are the property of the trademark holder. We use them for identification purposes only. This is not an official publication

Motorbooks International books are also available at discounts in bulk quantity for industrial or sales-promotional use. For details write to Special Sales Manager at the Publisher's address.

Library of Congress Cataloging-in-Publication Data

Johnson, Rich
    How to build Chevy hot rods / from the editors of Hot rod mechanix.
       p.   cm.
    ISBN 0-87938-458-1 :
    1. Hot rods—Design and construction. 2. Chevrolet automobile-
-Modification.   I. Title.
TL236.3.J65 1990
629.28 ' 78—dc20   90-31172

Printed and bound in the United States of America

Contents

Publisher	LEROI TEX SMITH
Editor	RICHARD JOHNSON
Tech. Editor	RON CERIDONO
Art Director	BOB REECE
Art Assistant	VICKY DAVIDSON
Copy Editor	BECKY JAYE
Circulation	JANET SMITH

Foreword

Chevy and Ford. Stovebolts and T-bones. Any time you start to write a definitive history of American hot rodding, you simply have to use both trade names. And if you dig back far enough, you find that the Chevrolet brothers made Ford speed equipment before embarking on the project of their own car.

There was a time, during the 1920s and 1930s, that the Chevrolet 4-cylinder engine could take on the best four-bangers that Ford had (assuming that both were in the hands of hot rodders, of course). For years, on circle tracks and at southern California dry lakes, the Chevrolet four raced heads up with everything that came along. It won as many as it lost. But then, when the Ford flathead V8 was introduced in 1932, it would be years before the Chevy inline six would emerge again as a serious competitor.

While there were a few Chevy sixes running in competition during the late 1930s, real performance didn't come along until after World War II. When aftermarket speed equipment for the Ford V8 began to appear in quantity, a small amount of performance parts was being produced for both the Chevrolet six and GMC six. The introduction of the OHV V8 engine in the late 1940s would short circuit rapid development of the Chevy six, however. Finally, when the Chevrolet V8 came along in 1955, that was the virtual end of any kind of widespread popularity the six might have attained. Of course, since the small block Chevy V8 came on the scene, it has literally dominated hot rodding and many forms of racing.

But there is much more to the Chevrolet as a hot rodding foundation than the engine. Much, much more.

If you go back to those depression years of the '30s, and scan America as a whole, you find some interesting things about Chevrolet. It was, and to a large extent still is, a workhorse car. It was considered an everyday car for the masses. It was simple to work on, it was almost bulletproof, and it would run under extremely difficult conditions. But in some parts of the country, it offered something unique. In the south, where most roads were either mudbogs or sandtraps, the Chevy six of the '30s offered unusual torque. The engine was a stump puller, and the chassis had semi-elliptic suspension — springs at all four corners. Here was a car that farmers could relate to. And, it used stovebolts in its construction. Those square nuts that every farm wagon was built with. Never mind that the car used a wood base for the body. So did wagons, and they held up just fine. Those wooden foundation bodies, when still new and tight, even had a more substantial feel than did the Fords.

So, if you talk to old-timers today about cars, they'll tell you that it was Ford in the upper Midwest, bigger expensive cars in the East, MoPars in the Rocky Mountains, but Chev-uh-lay in the South. Which may explain, in part, why the modern hot rod sport, especially street rodding, includes so many Chevrolets from southern states. They simply have a greater supply to work with, possibly.

Whatever the case, Chevrolet makes a great foundation for a hot rod. Obviously, from 1955 on, the car has been the staple of hot rod building. The 1955-'57 Chevy, often called Classic Chevy, even has its own club. And there are Camaro clubs, and Impala clubs, and Stepside pickup clubs. But, by and large, the pre-1955 Chevy has been overlooked by the media as a solid hot rod base. Partly because it uses wood in the pre-1937 versions, and partly because there have been so many more Ford products on the road. Much of that is changing, thanks to contemporary rod runs and big events like the NSRA Street Rod Nats.

More and more rod equipment builders are putting Chevrolet parts on the market. There have been several large restoration suppliers serving the Chevrolet market for three decades now, but it has only been during the late '80s that the rod equipment companies have started to offer suspension and body parts for Chevy.

This is an especially welcome sign, however, since with the advent of street rod interest in the "fat fender" hot rod, the 1936-'48 Chevy is gaining real momentum as a hot rod favorite.

There are many who will argue that from 1937 through 1948, the Chevrolet styling leaves Ford in the dust. While it may be necessary to chop the top of that era Ford to get a sleeker look, Chevy buffs argue that all the 'Bolt needs is a suspension lowering. From 1939 on, it had independent front suspension, and hydraulic brakes earlier. And, with some attention to engine power, the inline sixes of modern year can easily give the earlier cars outstanding road performance. In short, it is said, the Chevrolet offers the hot rod enthusiast more to work with than Ford ever did. So, who's to argue?

The only way to find out is to build a Chevrolet hot rod. And that is what this book is about. No, it isn't a total, absolute definitive "last word" on the subject. It isn't intended to be. This is Book One of what we see as an ongoing series of books. After we have published several books in this series, perhaps we will realize that everything necessary has been printed. We don't know. And the only way to find out is to start with How To Build CHEVY HOT RODS, Book One.

If you have experience building Chevys and want to share your hard-won information, please drop us a line. If you happen to have taken photographs of a project as you went along, send the pix and information. Don't worry that what you did seems too amateur. Don't worry about being a writer, that's our job. And if you don't have photos, make up some sketches. We'll polish it all up, and we'll put it in the files for Book Two.

Enjoy this book, and share your experiences. That way, there will be some Chevy hot rod builders well into the next century.

LeRoi Tex Smith
Editor/Publisher

by Tex Smith

What To Build
(and where to find it!)

So, you have decided you want to build a Chevrolet hot rod. You want something for the street, but in addition to appearance and comfortable reliability, you want some engine performance. Maybe a car that goes 180 mph, has the ride of a new Chevy, and gets 40 mpg. Well, a guy can dream.

When deciding on a Chevrolet to build, there is more to the question than whether to make a traditional street rod (something produced before 1949), a late model hot rod, or a custom. The decision has to do with wood. Up through the 1936 model year, Chevrolet (most GM divisions as well) used wood as the body framework. There is little wrong with such a practice, except that wood does not have the lifespan as a body material that metal does. For this reason, anytime you consider a 1936 or older Chevy, you have to assume that you are going to do some amount of wood repair/replacement.

It is for this reason that so many Chevy enthusiasts prefer to build 1937 and later Stovebolts. For racing as well as for the street. While the decision will be yours, money and effort will be less a factor with a post-'37 than an earlier Chevrolet.

Also, there will be the problem of front suspension. Chevrolet offered a special factory option for the front suspension, called Knee Action, throughout most of the Thirties. These are bulky appendages that are supposed to be a form of independent front suspension. When brand new, they worked OK at best. Worn, they are terrible. The basic Chevy front end included semi-elliptic springs and a beam axle, into 1939. If you find a Chevy with the knee action assembly, just plan on bolting in a replacement of some kind (you can use stock semi-elliptic springs, or one of the late model IFS units, such as kits from hot rod shops, or the popular Mustang/Pinto type). If you use a 1940-'48 Chevy, you will have a good independent front suspension to start with. The brakes won't be discs, but they will be good

units. In this case, you'll probably want to change the drums to the more popular 5-bolt wheel pattern, which is not difficult. And, you can get kits to install late model discs on the early spindles. Rebuild kits for the Chevy IFS are available through restoration parts suppliers.

Because all the Chevys have semi-elliptic rear springs through 1948, it is a simple matter to substitute a later model Chevy rearend. But we'll tell you again, some of the '48 and earlier rear springs have the centerbolt ahead of the axle centerline. If you just drop a different rearend in place, it will locate about 2 inches ahead of where it should be. Center the spring perch on the stock rearend to see if this is the case, and all you have to do is drill a new centerbolt hole in the later model rearend perch to compensate.

Putting a late model OHV V8 into any of the early Chevys is really simple, compared to other types of cars. In the 1949-'54 Chevy, such a swap usually entails cutting clearance in the firewall gussets (uprights between frame and firewall). Transmission swaps are equally simple, and most Chevy radiators (all years) seem to handle V8s easily. Late model inline 6-cylinder engines can be installed in virtually all Chevys, from the late Twenties through 1954, without much hassle. Sometimes, the late model engines are just a tad longer than original. On 1936 and later Chevys, extra clearance is available by simply moving the radiator to the front edge of its support.

The frames of all Chevrolet cars are plenty strong, especially if you want to add an IFS to one of the pre-1940 cars. Torsional rigidity is great.

Trying to select between a coupe/sedan/open car might be frustrating. Just remember that any kind of open Chevy (roadster, phaeton, or convertible) is rare and getting rarer. But, so are the 4-door sedans. Since rodders and restorers have given the coupe and 2-door bodies more attention the last 3 decades, the 4-doors have been going to the crushers. Now, they are getting rare, and might be a fun choice. But, a 4-door sedan will not bring as much resale as other body styles. It will cost just as much to build/restore, however.

Replacement parts are not as difficult to find for Chevrolet as you may think. There are plenty of restoration parts suppliers, and several of the hot rod parts manufacturers are beginning to stock Chevy units. Your key here is to search our list of sources, get as many catalogs as you can find, and pour through the pages. Sometimes you'll find that this kind of pre-selection "inventory" will show some years/models to be much better to build.

Finally, trying to find the Chevy of your choice may prove much easier than something more popular. There are lots of Chevys around, especially 1937 and later (thanks to that wood body problem, again). If you start considering the 1941-'48 Chevrolet, when you start looking you seem to find them everywhere. But the 4-door sedan will seem more prevalent than the 2-door, which is natural because there were more of the quad-doors produced, and the restorers/rodders will have found the 2-doors and coupes already.

Chevys are prone to rust, just like other cars, so you'll find better basic building machines if you conduct your search outside of the rust-belt areas. But, since the Chevrolet is still not perceived as a "popular" car by the general public, if you look around you will find exactly what you want at a really reasonable price. Well, that is unless you're hung up on an open car. You'll be surprised at the number of old Chevys that are still lurking in long-established wrecking yards. Chevrolet is a great car for hot rodding.

by John Lee

Identification Guide
How to know Wha'cha Got When Ya' Get It

Not too long ago, we noticed an ad in the paper offering a '57 Impala for sale. We were really tempted to go look at this thing, 'cause if it was for real it would be a one-of-a-kind. Chevy didn't start making the Impala until 1958.

There are lots of Chevys out there that make great hot rodding material. Millions. The 50-millionth car built by General Motors was a '55 Chevy, and they claimed that nearly 60% of the 50 million were Chevys. Who knows how many million more have been built since then!

To help you identify what you have or what you're looking for, we offer this identification guide. It's not complete; to show every year and model would take an entire book twice the size of this one. (Incidentally, Krause Publications, 700 State Street, Iola, WI 54990, has just published such a book — the Standard Catalog of Chevrolet — which gives specifications, production figures and other historical facts for all Chevrolets.) Here, we intend only to give you a quick reference and point out some of the identifying characteristics.

During much of its history, Chevrolet has followed three-year styling cycles. Sometimes longer, sometimes shorter, but knowing the styling cycle can help you identify interchangeable parts.

A new body style generally got a new name, which usually was elevated to a series name within a few

The 1922 touring was a pretty basic car, four-cylinder with wood spoke wheels.

years. Thus, the first two-door hardtop in 1950 was a Bel Air, which became a series in '53. The Impala sub-series of '58 became a full series in '59, and so on with Caprice, Malibu, Nova and others.

Chevy could be identified in many years by its round taillights. Three lights per side meant the highest level of trim, lesser series were assigned two per side. After V8 engine production began in 1955, Chevy always placed some kind of V emblem on the car to distinguish it from a six-cylinder model, which sometimes had an identifying emblem but more often didn't.

We hope this identification guide will be helpful.

By 1927, Chevy had disc wheels. This is the Capitol roadster.

The 1928 roadster still had a four-cylinder engine.

This 1931 Chevy cabriolet was turned into a street rod in the 1970s.

What was a 5-passenger coupe for Chevy in '31, was called a Victoria by Ford.

Vent doors on the hood replaced louvers for 1932. This is a 5-passenger coupe street rod.

Stock 1932 coach has chromed hood vent doors and sidemount spare.

There was a new V'd grille and one less hood vent per side for '33.

Styling was little changed for '34. This 2-door street rod has an integral trunk.

Here's a 1935 Chevy street rod with a chopped top. Stock hood sides have three horizontal windsplit-type louvers.

Entire '36 Chevy line had new, rounded styling introduced on the '35 Master Deluxe.

New, crisper lines were featured for 1937.

Horizontal grille bars distinguish '38 Chevy from similar '37s which had vertical bars.

Restyled '39 front end had the GM "prow" grille and more squared fender trailing lines.

1940 models were all new again with more blunt grille, rounder lines.

Head and parking lights were finally integrated into the fenders for '41.

1941 started the almost-rectangular taillights that became popular for customs.

Before production stopped for WWII, '42 Chevy trim was painted, which makes this chopped fastback in style again now.

Curved top grille bar surrounding horizontal bars distinguishes the '46 Chevy.

Fleetline fastback 2-door for '46 had stainless steel stripes on fenders and optional skirts, too.

Grille of the '47 has horizontal bars extending beyond the opening. A Fleetline 4-door was also offered.

This '48 has a vertical center grille bar to set it off from the '47.

All-new styling came for '49 with integrated front fenders. Grille of '49 has seven equal-size vertical bars, trunk has a T-handle.

Bel Air was a series by '53. Hardtop design was new, as was three-tooth grille in an oval opening.

Heavier slotted vertical bars below parking lights and revised hood emblem help spot a '50. This was also the first 2-door hardtop Bel Air.

Revised '54 grille extended full width with five teeth.

The 1951 grille bar is smooth, and air intake grilles appear next to parking lights.

Taillights were new for '54 with red lens above, white below. 1953 had a round lens between upper and lower.

Five teeth on the center grille bar, wider parking lights and horizontal rear fender spears mark this Bel Air as a '52.

Famous Ferrari-inspired egg-crate grille and hooded headlights introduced the all-new '55. This is a Bel Air 2-door sedan.

Tire-in-a-basket spare mount was a popular accessory for '55 Chevys. Bel Air convertible also has skirts.

Sporty Nomad station wagon added to the '55 Bel Air line, descended from a Corvette-based dream car.

Base series for Chevy was the 150; '56 model had trim strip ending just aft of door. Large hood emblem indicated a 6-cylinder engine.

One step up, 210 series has full-length sweep spear, optional two-toning. V on deck with small emblem denotes V8 engine.

The 1956 Bel Air series had double trim strips making a natural two-tone break.

The 1957 210 trim was the same as Bel Air but without fluted rear quarter insert and trim on front fender louvers. Chevrolet script on hood indicates 6-cylinder engine.

Bel Air for '57 had more trim, although skirts and bumper guards on this hardtop are options. Note hood V for V8 power.

Low line for '58 was called Del Ray and had single side spear. Emblems have been removed from this two-door.

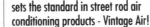

Sporty Nomad 2-door wagon was gone, but Yeoman was a cheap, basic station wagon alternative. V8 power was optional, as hood V indicates.

Impala was a Bel Air sub-series embracing a convertible and hardtop. Top and rear quarters were completely different.

Impala was already a series for 1959. This is the 2-door hardtop with wild gull-wing rear fender fins.

Fins were toned down somewhat for 1960. The El Camino car-pickup inaugurated in 1959 was popular.

Restyle for 1961 was much more conservative. Impala had a two-tone color insert in the side trim.

The 1961 Bel Air 4-door hardtop has less lavish trim than Impala, double taillights per side rather than triple.

While Impala got a new, squared top for '62, hot rodders preferred the slipperier "bubble" hardtop of the Bel Air carried over from '61, especially for a 409 drag performer like this one.

The new Chevy II for 1962 was a more conventional compact than the Corvair. This is the top line Nova hardtop.

Lighter in weight and trim, '63 Biscayne was chosen by many performance enthusiasts.

1963 Impala convertible was luxurious. Super Sport option with bucket seats and console was popular.

With 283 or 327 V8 power available, light '66 Chevy II Nova hardtop was a hot performer.

The latest in luxury was the Caprice, distinguished for '66 by its squared quarter windows.

With a wheelbase of 115 inches, the intermediate '66 Chevelle was about the same size as a '55 Bel Air. Four-door hardtop was cleanly styled.

In 1967, the Chevelle Malibu convertible offered power from six cylinders up to the SS 396 big block option.

Families found the '67 Malibu station wagon to be a reasonable compromise between too big and too small.

Luxury was stressed in the '68 Caprice 4-door hardtop with hidden headlights.

Chevy's answer to the Mustang was Camaro. This '69 convertible has the Rally Sport trim package.

Nova got bigger and rounder for '69, but is a hot performer with either small or big block power.

1970 brought the cleanly styled Monte Carlo personal luxury coupe on the Chevelle chassis. This '72 model represents the last of that initial styling cycle, with revised grille, headlights and taillights.

Chevrolet went into sports car production in 1953 with the fiberglass Corvette, powered by a modified six-cylinder.

By 1956, Corvette had a dual-quad 265 V8 under its reverse-opening hood and was building a performance image.

Quad headlights, started in '58, didn't help the 'Vette's looks. Some trim was changed for this '59.

Styling remained similar through 1962. Ducktail rear treatment came in '61, this '62 is the same except for revised trim.

Famous split-window fastback coupe highlighted the all-new Stingray for 1963, but the feature lasted only one year. Hide-away headlights were part of the new '63 Stingray front end treatment.

Light truck styling echoed that of the passenger car line during the 1930s. This half-ton is a '36.

Pickup was restyled for 1941, and the series carried through 1947 with no noticeable change.

Chevy pickup body introduced in 1948 was still around in '54, when it got a new grille and one-piece windshield.

The 1954 pickup with prominent vertical center grille bar was carried over into the first part of the 1955 model year.

New-styled '55 pickups came along several weeks after the passenger cars. Grille and headlight themes are similar.

This '55 pickup has a '57 hood with its twin windsplits. An accessory sunvisor has been added.

1956 pickup is the same as '55 except bar of hood ornament is below, rather than above. Emblem and fender trim is above character line.

1957 pickup carried on the same styling with a new grille.

Cameo was the name Chevy gave its Sunday dress-up version with fiberglass styleside quarters and upgraded trim. This is the '57 edition.

Stepside pickups like this '68 are popular for customizing because of their straight-forward style.

Chevy designated its new V8 engine for '55 with V and bowtie emblems on the rear fenders.

A V with crossed racing flags designated the 348-inch big block on '59 through '61 models.

23

by Geoff Carter

Chassis

Virtually everything attached to the chassis — suspension, steering, body and all — depends on the frame's strength and straightness. There's more to starting a street rod project than finding a good frame, though, especially in the case of early General Motors cars.

The chassis chapter may seem like a strange place to be discussing bodies, but they make up one of the biggest differences between Chevy and Ford street rods. The difference is spelled, WOOD. Prior to 1937, General Motors used it in mass quantities. GM bodies of the 1920s and early '30s tend to look like they were made of wood, then covered with a few pieces of metal to keep out the weather. As late as 1936, wood was still being used in the door jambs and elsewhere. Because of this, the chassis of a Chevy hot rod needs to be rigid enough to support the body.

To illustrate the point, imagine you were entering a driveway at an angle. With a lot of cars you can feel the car twist as first one corner of the car goes up the drive way, and then the next. The chassis must be built in a manner that makes the suspension, not the frame, compensate for extremes in uneven surfaces, eliminating excessive twisting forces on the body. When considering early models up through 1936, inspect the wood in the body carefully for structural integrity. If replacement is deemed necessary, see the chapter on body wood.

It is usually easier to start with a car of reasonable condition. You can rebuild a fairly complete car with a succession of repairs and replacements. Although one of the reasons you were attracted to hot rodding was the wide-open atmosphere of uniqueness, ease of building is one of the biggest reasons you see so many 1937 and newer Chevys and their brothers at rod runs. This popularity has led to a slightly greater list of sources of advice and parts for these later years.

If you read the ads in rod magazines, you have probably noticed that many front end kits are offered for 1936 through 1948 passenger cars. That's because the front of these frames is virtually identical. The rear parts changed over the years up through 1939, so don't expect to switch 1936-'39 frames at random. If you locate separate passenger car bodies and frames of 1940-'48 manufacture, however, you will find that they vary only within factory tolerances. You can't swap frames between cars and pickup trucks, but due to the similarity of their frames, 1936-'53 trucks will accept most of the same front end kits.

Most all GM cars were factory equipped with strong frames, so chances of finding a nearly complete car, 1937 and up, is fairly good. Ideally, start with a body and a chassis unit. Though some years are interchangeable with a minimum of fuss, there is less difficulty reassembling components that were meant for each other.

It is rare to find a "cherry" original frame. Most of them will have imperfections. One of the most common defects is the classic hacked-out center crossmember. Check out brackets that extend beneath the frame. They threaten speed bump damage.

Sight down the rails from top to bottom along their length to check for twisting. Now sight down each rail from the end. If any damage is evident, such as warped or bent rails, pass on it unless it's the best frame available. Otherwise it may have to go to a frame repair shop for straightening.

If initial inspection uncovers no major damage, set the frame on jackstands and level it. Measure for squareness by dropping plumb bobs to the floor from corresponding points (bolt holes or marks that are in exactly the same places on each rail) around the frame. This can be done with the body on or off, as your situation dictates. Measure in an X pattern between the points where the plumbs touch the floor. The length of both legs of each X must be within 1/8-inch; 1/16-inch is even better. Use this procedure for bare frames or complete cars.

Aside from damage, the biggest problem with any old frame is rust. Water and dirt hunt for places where they can hide undisturbed for generations, eating holes through the steel. Anywhere the body overlaps the frame is also a troublesome spot. If rust is limited to surface damage, it can be sandblasted away. If a hole has developed, however, it must be cut out and filled with new metal.

This is the time to be realistic about your own level of ability. How much time, money and labor can you afford to invest in building your hot rod? The better frame you start with, the sooner it will cease to be a drain on the budget. These considerations are the major selling points for reproduction frames. Initial purchase price may be more than a complete original car, but they do reduce garage time considerably.

Getting Started

There is no reason to believe that only the professional rod builder has the tools and skill needed to build a real hot rod. While it is true that the pro's experience, equipment and manpower does see him through some awe-inspiring projects, each builder is still just an individual working with his hands and his ideas.

One such thinker is Orv Elgie. It seems that each car out of Elgie's garage is more unusual and more creative than the one before it. He farms out upholstery and some other specialized operations (after applying a few money-saving tricks of his own). He has a good welder, paint gun and compressor, but little else. His greatest asset is his patient dedication to perfection. His wife Shirley and son Myles assist with the construction of every car he builds, which are usually cars no one else would dream of making into a street rod.

With no pattern to follow, and no aftermarket kit to buy and bolt on, how does he do it? He starts by getting out the carpenters' tools: tape measure, chalk line, framing square, and level.

Before dismantling the car (or temporarily reinstalling the body), figure out where it should ride when finished, and also keep the wheels centered in the openings. Here's how Orv does it.

Before he modifies a frame, a chalk line is made on the floor down the center of the car and across the center of the spindles and rear axle. Reference marks for the front and rear of each fender opening are also laid out on the floor. To establish ride height, Orv determines how far he wants the fenders off the ground, and records that distance on the reference points established earlier. The diameter of the wheel and tire combination to be used is determined and the centerline distance from the floor to the spindles and rear axle is measured, and recorded. These ride height measurements allow the position of a subframe to be determined, or the amount of drop necessary in an axle, or spring arch required to obtain the desired ride height.

If major modifications are being made, the next task is to establish the wheelbase. Orv simply locates the centerline of the spindles and the rear axle in the middle of the the fender opening reference points, and that determines the wheelbase. The centerline is used for side to side measurement, and to "square" to. One caution should be observed in the case of doing a subframe; as the suspension compresses, the wheels move to the rear slightly. Orv compresses the suspension during his subframe installations by removing the shock and replacing it with a long threaded rod with big washers and nuts at each end. He then compresses the suspension to ride height before completing the subframe swap. It's that simple, but it's a necessary trick.

To keep from scuffing his chalk marks off the floor, Orv makes them permanent with Keep Track bottle markers. They're lacquer (he uses yellow, but five colors are available) in a "ballpoint" bottle for less than $2.00 each.

According to Orv, "You need a flat floor, although a little tilt is OK if you know just how much it is. But you have to hold the chassis down." What he does is set the frame on jackstands, and use shims of wood to get everything level. He then cuts a 4x4 to length, wedging it between a beam in the ceiling and the frame so the frame can't move. "That's how I put the new suspension where it was on the original car," he explains.

This may sound crude, but stop and think about what it is he's doing. With all of the critical positions located, he now has a frame jig, of sorts. Frame jigs are worth their weight in billet aluminum to the professional production shop, but you can make do with what you have. Set up your floor and use it like a hot rod shop uses its tables and fixtures.

Most of the cars we're talking about here have, or will have, independent front suspension. Unless you're building a traditional hiboy, there's almost no reason to think of retaining a solid front axle. The ride and handling benefits of independent front suspension far outweigh the effort required to install it.

Now, we must prepare a rigid frame. Fortunately, boxing is not a necessity for most Chevy chassis. With the exception of the commercial frames, and the very early models, Chevy frames were made from box-shaped material. If you plan to build a blown big block strip stomper, however, you should reinforce accordingly.

One thing that should be done, in any case, is weld all crossmembers that were originally riveted to the side rails. This is usually all you have to do to reinforce a Chevy frame in preparation for receiving modern suspension and drivetrain.

Some builders prefer to work with a clean frame, while others would rather grind the areas to be welded, tack weld the components in place, then disassemble and send the whole frame out for sandblasting before finishing the welding.

Dip stripping is another good way to fight rust, but it can't be done at home. It is most useful when you can't blast, as in the case of sheetmetal. With sandblasting you have a choice: farm it out or do it at home. If you have a

compressor and an enclosed place to work, your investment will be minimal.

If you've ever spent time under a car with a wire brush, you don't need to be sold on the merits of sandblasting. It can reach into the smallest cracks and crevices. Dirt, grease and rust blow away, leaving a bare metal surface ready for primer. However, bare metal rusts quickly, so don't start to sandblast until you're ready to throw a coat of primer on the frame right away.

You can't sandblast everything, sheetmetal for example. Every abrasive particle that strikes a metal surface creates a small crater, like thousands of tiny hammers. This has the effect of stretching the surface being blasted. With sheetmetal, this causes warpage that is virtually irreparable

During this stage of chassis preparation is the time to plan for the air conditioning system and other accessories you will want to install later. Before welding in motor, transmission, steering, and other mounts, make sure you have allowed enough space for the proper radiator, condenser, fan and compressor drives. This may necessitate the purchase of some of these items earlier than you anticipated. But if you guess wrong now, you'll have a real headache trying to force it all to fit later.

No matter what car you are building, time dedicated to chassis development is time well spent. This is particularly true with early Chevys, because their wood body structure requires extra strength in the frame. But beyond that, there are many of us who believe that a well finished chassis is where the true beauty of a hot rod is.

by Tex Smith

Suspensions

Until the mid 1930s, Chevrolets used a basic ladder frame, with semi-elliptic springs at each corner. The basic dimensions of frame and suspension members remained fairly constant during this period, and many late model components (pickup truck beam front axles, late model rearends, etc.) often interchange with little or no modifications necessary.

During the mid '30s, a knee action independent front suspension was tried, but this unit was not a success. Chevrolet produced the traditional leaf spring/beam

axle during the same period. During the late '30s, a true A-arm independent front suspension was introduced, with the lower A-arm longer than the top. The top A-arm attached directly to a double-action shock absorber. These shocks are usually worn out on older Chevys. Rebuilt double-action shocks are available through 5-Points Shocks, 7471-G Slater St., Huntington Beach, CA 92647. When these shocks are good, and all the bushings, rod ends, etc. are in fine shape, these pre-1949 Chevy suspensions are excellent. The basic design was not changed much through 1954, so about the only thing rod builders are after for these IFS units are dropped spindles and disc brake conversion kits. Fat Man Fabrications, 8621-C Fairview Rd., Hwy 218, Charlotte, NC 28227 (phone 704-545-0369) has been designing dropped spindles, and advertisers in this book have brake kits.

The rear springs have been semi-elliptic for all popular hot rod Chevys, but the distance apart at the spring rearend mounting point has changed slightly. For this reason, it is sometimes necessary to relocate a late model rearend spring mount pad to align with the older springs. Spring lengths, widths, rates, and mounting methods have changed, but with a bit of thinking it is usually possible to swap late model springs to earlier frames. Most builders prefer to use the original springs and modify the rates by removing or adding spring leaves. Always, the old spring is taken apart, each leaf carefully cleaned and painted, and during reassembly strips of Teflon are inserted between each leaf for reduced friction. New special-built springs are available from Posies, Hummlestown, Pennsylvania, with Teflon inserts in each spring tip.

Some springs, such as those under the pickups of the '40s and '50s, do not have the spring centerbolt aligned with the axle housing centerline. Instead, the centerbolt is about 2 inches forward. In this case, a different rearend housing should have a new centerbolt hole drilled in the mount map, to keep the axle centerline in the center of the wheel housing.

Some builders do not change the rearend of pickups when they are trying to get a 5-bolt wheel. The 1955 passenger car rear axles and hubs will fit the pickup housings, as will the center section. This gives the 5-bolt wheel pattern, as well as an open drive rear axle. Similar swaps work for the passenger cars.

The front spring design and measurements for Chevys of the late '20 and '30s (beam axle) is almost identical to Chevy pickups through the '50s. For this reason, it is possible to use later pickup front axles and steering components on the older car chassis.

It has become popular recently to swap the entire front suspension on Chevys. Frame clip swaps are popular on 1937 and later Chevys (through the 1954 model year), and the mustang/Pinto front suspension that is so popular with lightweight Fords is not uncommon. One note of caution with the Mustang unit: These are not made for heavy cars. Before using such a system, whether you modify a wrecking yard unit or use a component kit from a hot rod shop, check that your Chevy is not heavier overall than a Mustang, and that the front end weight is not greater than a Mustang. Often, special front end kits made by hot rod suppliers will include heavier duty ball joints and other parts for the Chevy kits.

The bottom line is that, with the exception of the knee action front end, all Chevy suspension components seem to be more than adequate for hot rod use.

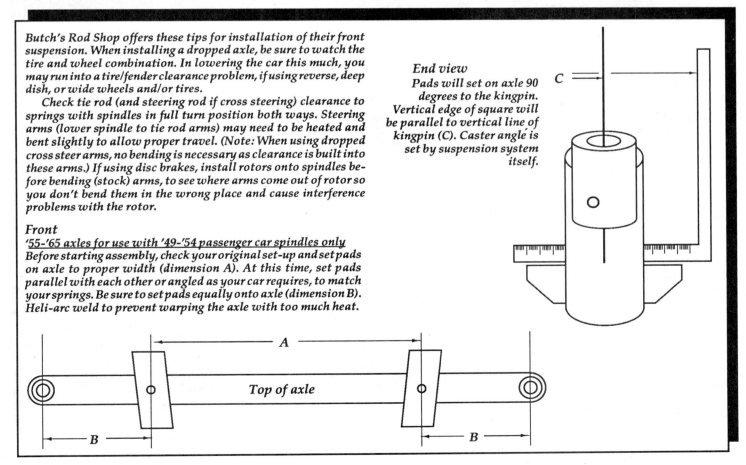

Butch's Rod Shop offers these tips for installation of their front suspension. When installing a dropped axle, be sure to watch the tire and wheel combination. In lowering the car this much, you may run into a tire/fender clearance problem, if using reverse, deep dish, or wide wheels and/or tires.

Check tie rod (and steering rod if cross steering) clearance to springs with spindles in full turn position both ways. Steering arms (lower spindle to tie rod arms) may need to be heated and bent slightly to allow proper travel. (Note: When using dropped cross steer arms, no bending is necessary as clearance is built into these arms.) If using disc brakes, install rotors onto spindles before bending (stock) arms, to see where arms come out of rotor so you don't bend them in the wrong place and cause interference problems with the rotor.

Front
'55-'65 axles for use with '49-'54 passenger car spindles only
Before starting assembly, check your original set-up and set pads on axle to proper width (dimension A). At this time, set pads parallel with each other or angled as your car requires, to match your springs. Be sure to set pads equally onto axle (dimension B). Heli-arc weld to prevent warping the axle with too much heat.

End view
Pads will set on axle 90 degrees to the kingpin. Vertical edge of square will be parallel to vertical line of kingpin (C). Caster angle is set by suspension system itself.

Top of axle

27

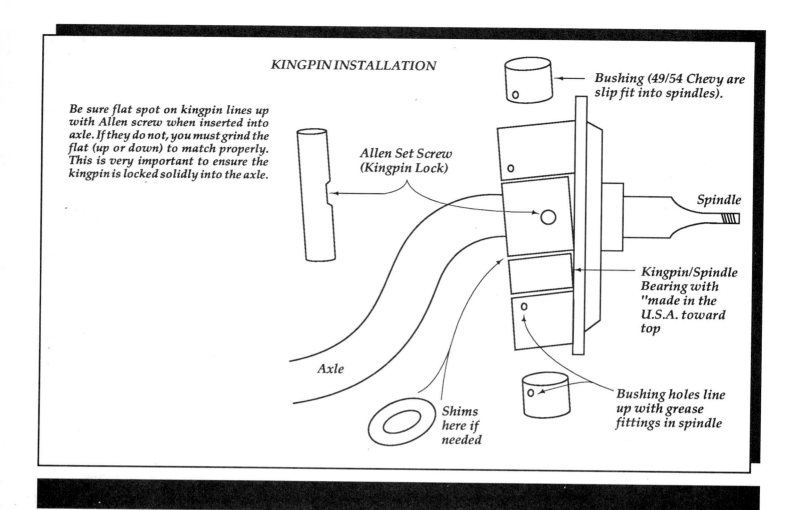

KINGPIN INSTALLATION

Bushing (49/54 Chevy are slip fit into spindles).

Be sure flat spot on kingpin lines up with Allen screw when inserted into axle. If they do not, you must grind the flat (up or down) to match properly. This is very important to ensure the kingpin is locked solidly into the axle.

Allen Set Screw (Kingpin Lock)

Spindle

Kingpin/Spindle Bearing with "made in the U.S.A. toward top

Axle

Bushing holes line up with grease fittings in spindle

Shims here if needed

1936-'39 Chevy Chassis

Although Butch's Rod Shop has lots of chassis components for all Chevys from 1928 on, it is the 1937 and later Chevy that is getting most of the attention from builders. So, we asked Butch for information on a typical 1938 chassis, to give you an idea of what is available.

Yes, you can build most of these parts yourself, if you want to take the time. Or you can order just a few ready-mades. Doesn't matter. These frames are of the hat-section design, a kind of inverted U-shape with a brim, and a lower plate welded on. The result is a rectangular tubing cross-section that is very strong. For this reason, a beefy X-member is not usually incorporated in the design.

The 1936-'39 Chevy frames are very similar, with a kickup at both front and rear.

CONTE ENTERPRISES • 28002 110 AVE. E., DEPT. MX., GRAHAM, WA 98338
(206) 847-4666

INDEPENDENCE FOR ALL

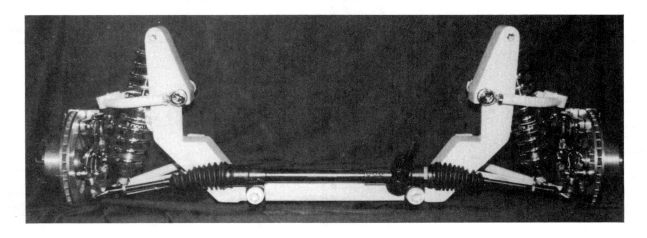

This is one of several new front suspension kits for the heavier street rods and pro-street rides. This new design uses a longer 4-inch stroke coil over shock that lets the suspension work properly, giving you a much better ride, excellent handling, and greatly reduces bump steer. The crossmember and A-arms are hand-built, we use GM spindles, rotors and calipers (or JFZ calipers) and pinto rack and pinion. The 28-31 Ford uses a rear-mounted rack and sway bar. Complete front suspension weight is approximately 180lbs. with rotors and calipers.

The suspension unit pictured was designed for the 35-40 Ford's. Below is a list of what we have designed suspension kits for. If your car is not included it may be in the planning stages or one of the crossmembers we have may be very close to fitting your car if your frame rails are 24"-35" wide outside. If you have any questions about your application please call. We also guarantee final spring rate on the finished car. Thank you for your interest in my product.

READY FIT APPLICATIONS ARE:

**ALDAN
SHOCKS**

37-39 Chevy car
40-48 Chevy car (bolt in)
55-57 Chevy (sub frame)
28-31 Ford
35-40 Ford

40-54 Chevy Pick-up
55-59 Chevy Pick-up
48-52 Ford F-1
53-56 Ford F-100
57-66 Ford F-100

**JFZ
BRAKES**

Base kit price: $1,150   *Chevy bolt-in kit: $1,250*

FOR FULL INFORMATION, PLEASE SEND $2.00 TO HELP COVER COST.

The 6-inch drop Butch's Rod Shop tubing axle in place. The axle is 2-inch o.d. with .250-inch wall thickness (seamless).

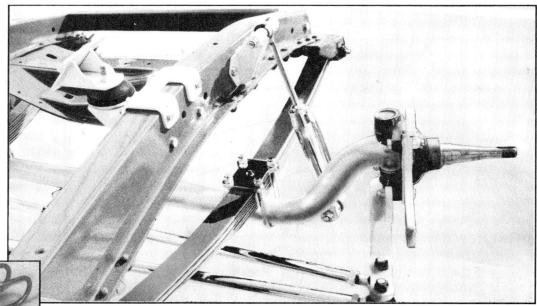

1949-'54 Chevy passenger car spindles are used. Disc brake kit replaces drums. Shock kit allows use of contemporary adjustable shocks. Dropped spindle steering arms allow tie rod and drag link to clear spring when dropped axle is used.

Above-Suppliers have new U-bolt and king pin kits for 1928 and later Chevys. Follow their installation instructions carefully.

Kits are available in you-select form, including center crossmember for late model TurboHydramatic 350 and 400 transmissions, and motor mounts for small block Chevy V8s. Saginaw and Vega cross steering brackets update the steering gearboxes. Brake pedal kits bolt directly to the frame rail.

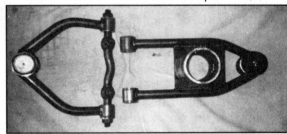

by Scott Smith

Conte *Front Ends*

There are a number of front end kits available today to help the hands-on hot rodder put his car on the road under the influence of improved ride quality and superior handling characteristics. The beauty of using a kit as opposed to scrounging around in the local wrecking yard is that the kits are ready to bolt on or weld to the chassis.

Conte Enterprises (28002 110th Ave. E., Graham, WA 98338; 206-847-4666) has front end kits available for just about every type of car and truck dating from the late '20s to the mid '50s, with steel tubing A-arms as well as aluminum A-arms. Of special interest to late '40s Chevy hot rodders is the Conte kit featured on these pages.

We stopped by Mike Conte's shop one day to shoot some photos of the crew doing an installation of this kit on a '46 Chevy. Follow along with the photos, and see just how simple the procedure is.

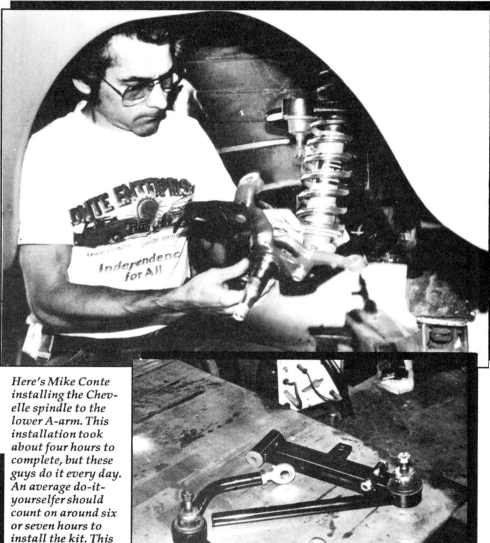

Here's Mike Conte installing the Chevelle spindle to the lower A-arm. This installation took about four hours to complete, but these guys do it every day. An average do-it-yourselfer should count on around six or seven hours to install the kit. This kit is a weld-in type, and as with most front ends available today, the engineering and workmanship are of high quality.

Spindles are stock 1968-'72 Chevrolet Chevelle items. Mike has dropped spindles available as well.

A-arms for large later model cars are made from 1-inch diameter carbon steel tubing, and the ball joint bases are machined from the same material. Greasable Aurora rod ends are employed, and the ball joints are stock GM items.

Right-After the main crossmember is welded in place, the lower A-arm is installed. Here, the strut rod bracket is cut to fit and welded into position. The biggest value of the strut rod type A-arm is that it spreads the stress load of bumps and hard braking to a larger area of the frame.

Below-Mike used Aldan coil-over shocks on all of his kits. They are adjustable, and can come with a variety of options such as chrome springs, chrome shocks, and aluminum shocks.

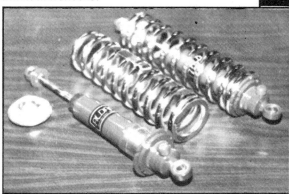

Right-This front end kit can be installed without removing the front sheetmetal clip. However, Mike recommends that you remove the sheetmetal to make life easier and to prevent the possibility of damage.

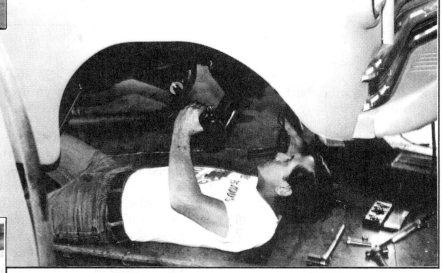

Below-This is the car, back on the ground at about ride height. As with most front end kits available today, this one is fully adjustable in ride height and handling.

Right-Here is what the front end looks like before installation. Notice the long coil-over shocks. This is to increase spring travel, thereby giving a better ride. The front end uses stock 1968-'72 Chevrolet Chevelle type rotors and calipers. Mike also has an adapter kit so you can use JFZ calipers, if desired. The small crossmember below the front end is for mounting the radiator and front sheetmetal.

33

by Tex Smith

Subframes

LATE MODEL IFS — Firewall — Mark frame — Cut frame — Beam Axle — Distance A — New Clip — Cut — A

Subframing is very much a topic of every bench racing conversation, which is strange, since the process took so long to catch on. The first subframe swaps happened way back in the early 1960s, but it has taken many years for the hot rod builders to accept the fact that subframes can be fit to most any car. Of course, appearance being a vital part of any chassis modification, subframes are usually restricted to fat fender cars, from about 1935 and later. This is because the larger cars run fenders, and the fenders cover the bulk of the independent suspension components. Also, from 1935 on, most American cars have the engines moved forward over the front crossmember.

For Chevrolet, the starting point for useful chassis subframing would be 1936. Since Chevys have always had a very strong frame, due mostly to the semi-elliptic springs all around, subframes work fine. But, since Chevrolet also switched to independent front suspension in the late Thirties, it is not always necessary (or wise) to subframe any passenger car after the 1939 model year. On the other hand, Chevy trucks through the 1961 model year continued to use the beam axle, so subframes there are extremely popular.

A subframe swap is not a front suspension swap, in the manner of a Mustang/Pinto or Fiero swap. When the frame gets a subframe graft, the original frame is cut off. If you can do arc welding, or if you have a friend who is a good welder, you can do a subframe job.

The vital secret to a successful subframe graft is in careful measurement and alignment. Get it right. Check, recheck, and check again on all measurements and levels. And, buy at least one special tool. A degree level indicator. This is a hand-size plumb-bob with a degreed circular face. Set the magnetic base on a metal surface and read the degrees off horizontal or perpendicular. Inexpensive, this tool is available at most tool supplies and all Sears tool outlets. Get one.

So, start with measurement. First, measure the track of your original vehicle. This is the distance between the two front wheels, as measured at the center of each tire. Obviously, if you use offset wheels or wide tires, the track width will vary. Compare this measurement to that of the donor vehicle. The late model car track will usually be wider, often about 3 inches. This wider track can be critical in two areas: front fender clearance, and steering ackerman.

Fender clearance can be increased by the use of positive offset wheels, that is, wheels that offset toward the middle of the car. Ackerman is a different story, however. Refer to the section in this book about Ackerman principle, and note that if the wheelbase of the donor car is substantially longer than on the rod, the Ackerman will probably be out of whack. Some builders narrow the front crossmember of the IFS to make the track nearly the same as the original car (the rod being built).

If the crossmember is going to be narrowed, do this before anything else. Assuming that you use the most popular subframe, something from a 1971-79 Chevelle, etc., you will cut the subframe from the donor car right at the firewall. This is the area where the perimeter frame starts to widen. To narrow the crossmember, first remove the tie rod, and anti-sway bar. Make the necessary narrowing cut at the center of the crossmember. As a general rule, no more than 5 inches is taken out. It is essential that this cut be perfectly parallel, so that when the crossmember halves are put back together and arc welded, the wheels are in the same symmetry. It doesn't hurt to fishplate the welded joint, to insure maximum strength. The tie rod center section must be shortened the same amount, and the anti-sway bar will need to be replaced with a narrower unit, or be heated/reshaped and shortened.

Before starting on the hot rod frame, get an absolute measurement of the wheelbase and wheel track. Mark this on the cement with chalk for convenience. Measure the centerline of the solid axle vertically to the frame, and mark the frame for reference. Now, the rod's engine and front sheetmetal can be removed, and the original front suspension taken out.

Before cutting the subframe from the donor car, set the car level so that the frame beneath the doors is level. Using the degree level indicator on the front crossmember, determine what the crossmember level is. It may be tilted slightly up, or slightly down, just record this amount, because you will duplicate it on the hot rod frame. Degree the flat top portion of the crossmember, or the adjacent frame, not the top of the A-arms.

Once you have the subframe cut from the donor car, measure from the axle centerline (a line drawn across the frame from spindle to spindle) to the rear, and cut away the frame just where it starts to widen out.

Set the hot rod so the frame is exactly level (find some section of the frame that is parallel to the ground), and check it several times. Make sure it is level side to side as well as fore/aft. Block the car so it won't roll around. Measure from the new IFS frame centerline back to where the frame has been cut off. Transfer this measurement to the hot rod frame, using the axle centerline you put on before disassembly of the car. This tells you how much to cut off the hot rod frame. HOWEVER: Here is a tip that lots of builders overlook. When an older frame gets a late model subframe, because of the kick-up in the later frame, the vehicle will sit lower. Also, because of the built in angle of the late model upper A-arms (to counteract brake dive), the front wheel centerline will be slightly behind the original wheel centerline unless some careful compensation is made.

To get a better idea of exactly where the spindle centerline will be when the front end is at exact ride height (as the wheel goes up, the centerline moves rearward, because of caster and A-arm tilt), it works best to collapse the front springs to ride height during the swap. Get a large diameter threaded rod from the hardware store. Run this through the spring center, add a thick steel plate top and bottom, and a couple of nuts. Tighten the nuts to pull the spring down to "normal ride" position. This is the correct place so you can get a good axle centerline measurement. In addition, since the wheels will tend to angle backward slightly, you can compensate slightly more. Simply add 1/2" to the cut-off mark on the hot rod frame. This will move the wheels slightly forward in the fender wheel opening, but when everything is assembled, it will make the wheel fit the opening. When this problem is not ad-dressed, the end result is a wheel that seems to be aft in the opening. The more the front end is dropped, the more pronounced this rearward offset. In some cases, such as the pickup trucks, where there is considerable drop with the subframe swap, builders compensate an inch or more.

So, now you know where to cut off the hot rod frame. It will be somewhere near the firewall. Again, make sure the frame is on jackstands, with the entire front part clear. The frame must be level, side to side and fore/aft. Make a vertical cut of each frame rail. This cut must be clean, either with a hacksaw/powersaw, or with a torch. Use a grinder to smooth the cut face. The cut on the subframe should be equally clean.

Now, block up the trimmed subframe to fit snugly against the hot rod frame. Likely, only a small area of the rod frame will mate against the new frame clip. Even if it looks impossible to mate the two frames, it will work. Depending upon the frame, the rod frame may be slightly wider or slightly narrower than the clip. Just get common points to match.

Measure the wheelbase again, noting that the new wheelbase may be about 1/2" longer than the rod original. Use the degree level to set the front crossmember at the same angle as it was in the donor car (which will often be dead level), and level the new clip side to side. Measure diagonally from a common point on the hot rod frame to a common point on the new clip, to insure that everything is going in "square." If you're not sure that the rod's frame was "square," measure from a common point on the new clip diagonally to some point near the rear of the frame. If you are within 1/8-inch, you are closer than the original factory tolerances. Adjust the front clip until everything is level and square.

Tack weld the clip to the frame at any points where there is a mating fit. Tack weld one side, then the other. Alternate from side to side, measuring often to make sure the weld heat is not causing the clip to crawl out of alignment. After the clip is tack welded in place, make gussets between the clip and frame, so that considerable strength is added at critical points. When in doubt, add more strength. Use plate, not thin sheet metal. Box the entire area, so that you end up with a stronger joint than the original frames had.

Interesting thing about a subframe graft is that you end up with motor mounts in place, as well as steering. Bolt the hot rod's front sheetmetal together, and set it in place. The clip frame horns will have to be trimmed for clearance, and the fender splash aprons will need to be trimmed to fit the new IFS system. With the sheetmetal in place as a unit, you can see where a plate must be welded to the new clip crossmember to serve as a mount for the radiator yoke.

Not nearly as difficult as it might seem, and the result is a ride and handling superior to the older beam axle. And, parts are updated.

by Tex Smith

Dropped Beams
Better Brakes

Although there is a minor amount of machine work necessary with this dropped axle/spindle swap, it is a job that the average person can do at home with minimal tools. Plan a weekend for time.

Some years ago, I had a 1954 Chevrolet half-ton pickup with a big-inch Olds engine and trans. I wanted to drop the front end, and wanted to get rid of the Chevy 6-lug wheels in front. It was all a fairly straight forward bit of swapping, so when we scheduled this book, I asked around if the same things held true for the swap. Answer: Yep.

So, rather than reinvent the wheel, herewith is how I accomplished that particular swap. The result was a beam axle front end (just in case you want to keep one, rather than go with a subframe swap, which is really common now). That got the truck down, and the brakes were much better.

Since the idea is to get the truck in the weeds, aftermarket helper springs may not be wanted or needed. If the stock springs are in bad condition, the local spring shop can make replacements. Fully loaded, there should be at least 4 inches of operating room between the top of the axle and the frame. A 1-inch clearance notch can be cut in the frame. If so, the frame area should be boxed on the inside.

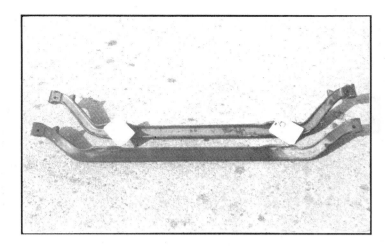

You can get dropped axles for Chevy products from several sources, including tubing units from SuperBell and Butch's Rod Shop. This beam unit comes from Mor-Drop, 600 29th Ave., Oakland, CA 94601, and has an effective drop of 2-1/2 inches.

No matter what axle is used, always carefully check fit of the desired spindle to the axle boss. Do this checking with a new kingpin kit, so that you have spindle-to-boss bearing and shims on hand. In this case, the axle boss had to be cut down slightly. To use Olds/Pontiac brake drums and wheels, use 1941-'52 Oldsmobile or 1941-'54 Pontiac backing plates and drums with the stock pickup spindles. The '52 and later Chevy truck will accept just the '50-'54 Chevy passenger car drums as a way to get the 5-bolt wheel pattern. Mounting the Olds/Pontiac backing plates is done the same way that we show here.

Bearings on the passenger car for Chevy/Olds/Pontiac should check out the same, but if you run into a problem, use the new spindle bearing spacer and your local bearing supplier can find an inner bearing that has the correct inner/outer diameters.

The stock Chevy truck backing plate at left, compared to the passenger car unit at right. Note the offset on the car backing plate. Brake hoses all interchange.

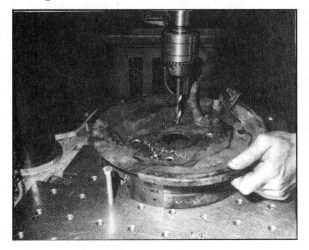

Hold the passenger car backing plate to the spindle. The two upper mounting holes will align, but the two lower holes will be off. Mark the backing plate (backside, through the spindle mount) and drill new lower mounting holes.

Now, set the backing plate on the spindle. The center register hole is the same for Chevy/Olds/Pontiac. Measure through the backing plate mounting hole to the spindle mount. This is the length of the new spacers.

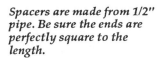

Spacers are made from 1/2" pipe. Be sure the ends are perfectly square to the length.

The modified backing plate is in front, with spacers in place. Note the lower holes, with spacers in position for Chevy truck spindle.

Use donor car backing plate bolts, or get new ones that are at least grade 8.

Spindle in place, note that the kingpin bearing goes between the bottom of the axle boss and the spindle.

If you come up with an inner bearing race that does not fit the spindle snugly (as shown here), use the stock inner race and get bearings to fit race/hub inner bearing.

Rebuild or get new wheel master cylinders. Brake hoses will fit.

It is essential to take the finished conversion straight to the front end alignment shop, especially if a dropped axle is used. In the case of a beam axle, bending it to fit factory specs is no big deal. We haven't confirmed the rumor that 1957 and later Corvette drum brakes will fit 3/4-ton Chevy truck spindles. Worth looking into perhaps.

If the stock steering arms are to be used, check the shape of the arm ball. If it is out of round, get another arm. Usually, the arms do not need to be bent for tie rod-to-spring clearance.

by Bill Buxton

Bolt-On Chassis
Up-date kits for Chevy builders

For backyard builders, there's something special about hauling an old hulk into the garage, thrashing on it in the evenings and weekends and finally driving the completed car out for its first test run.

Like most '30s, '40s, and even '50s cars, the ride, handling and stopping power of a vintage Chevrolet can be greatly improved with the installation of modern suspension components. This used to mean major surgery for the old Chevy, in the form of a late model frame clip or a welded-in Mustang II or similar crossmember. Doing it right takes the proper welding equipment and a fair amount of welding skill.

RB's Obsolete Automotive has changed all that. They're dedicated to helping hobbyists build quality cars, but also understand the desire to keep the projects at home. This led RB's to offer a line of bolt-on chassis kits that update 1937-'54 Chevy passenger car front and rear suspensions with modern components and do not require any chassis welding. They're designed with the do-it-yourself rodder in mind, and are perfect for those handy enough to build their own cars — though they may not be welders or may not have the welding equipment needed to install the usual components.

RB's front Chevy crossmembers are completely bolt-on units. They're designed for easy installation, and they use Mustang II components that the hobbyist can buy separately from RB's or other suppliers, or find used at a wrecking yard. The kits include detailed instructions and accurate templates for determining where to drill the mounting bolt holes in the frame. For improved handling, a one-inch sway bar without the stock Mustang bulge, is also available.

The front end is just part of a modern chassis update. While the stock parallel leaf springs used at the rear of Chevys work better than the Ford transverse springs, they're usually worn, resulting in a stiffer ride. The

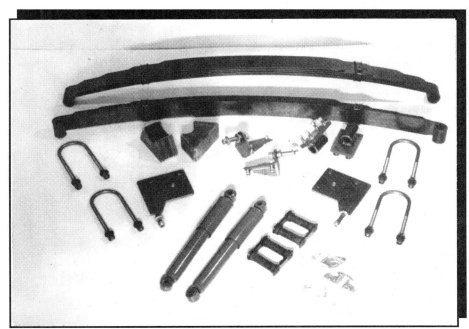

RB's rear suspension kits give Chevys that "just right" stance. The '37 to '48 kits include upper shock mount brackets. The '49 to '54 kits utilize stock shock mounts.

stock rear shocks are simply inadequate, and when a later model transmission is used, the closed driveline rearend must be swapped for an open unit. The closed driveline stock rearends are mounted to rock in the spring pads, and are offset 1-3/4 inches from the spring bolt. When mounting an open driveline rear, this offset must be maintained so the wheels will fit the fender wells properly.

As with the front end, RB's has taken care of these problems with a mostly bolt-on kit that updates 1937-'54 Chevys to a modern open driveline. Springs and shock mounts are bolt-on units, but the housing mounts must still be welded to the rearend housing. The good news is that everything can be installed, the rearend positioned, and housing mounts marked for welding. Then only the rearend and the housing mounts need be sent out to a welder. It's important that this be done by a competent welder who will be careful not to warp the housing. Otherwise, axle bearings won't last.

The rear suspension kit includes new springs with Teflon pads for easy slide, shackles, shackle mounts,

39

lower spring plates and shock mounts, upper shock mounts, gas shocks, and the weld-on housing mounts. These housing mounts place the rearend 2" lower than stock. Additional lowering blocks can be added to get the car even lower to the ground. Builders can use a variety of rearends, and excellent instructions and accurate templates are provided.

For those who are installing a Chevy V8, there are more bolt-on kits. Front and rear bolt-on motor mounts make that task an easy project. And for steering, RB's can supply the steering joints needed to connect the steering column to the rack.

Why trailer your project to a chassis shop, when you can install a modern chassis yourself at home in your own garage, with the help of easily installed kits?

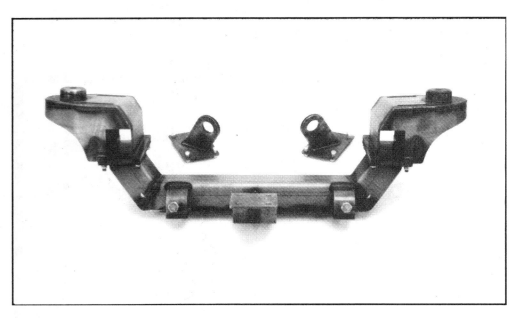

The 1937-'39 front crossmember, shown here, bolts in with no welding necessary. It uses Mustang II components, sold separately.

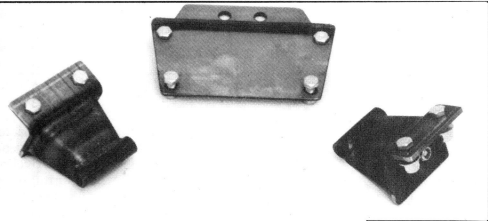

The bolt-on motor mounts are for installing a Chevy V8 and a selection of Chevy transmissions. Mounts pictured are 1949 to '54. There are two kinds of rear mounts for these Chevys. RB's will help you determine which is correct for your car.

Unlike the Stock Mustang units, the RB's sway bar has a straight center. It features a 1" bar, heim ends and urethane bushings.

For more information, call (206)568-5669 or write RB's Obsolete Automotive, 7130 Bickford Avenue, Snohomish, WA 98290. Order toll free 1-800-426-6607; in Washington, 1-800-922-5339. The $5.00 catalog is free with any order.

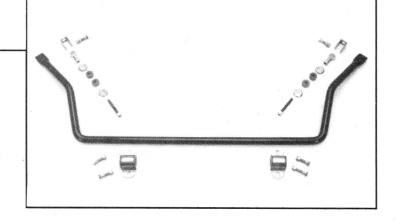

by Warren Gilliland

Brakes

When building a brake system, the following concerns should be considered. First, the system must be capable of meeting the performance characteristics you intend to build into the car. Second, the system must be well balanced and allow the car to stop safely and consistently from all speeds. In order to accomplish this, it is necessary to examine the system and all components closely to make sure the chosen components match well for your application.

To reach our goal, we must make sure that we put all the pieces in place to give us an adequate brake system. We will need to put a pedal in the car with the correct pedal ratio, so that we can develop sufficient push on the master cylinder. We need a master cylinder with sufficient volume to handle the system requirements but not too large to defeat our line pressure requirements. Finally, we need components adequate to handle the vehicle stopping requirements without undue strain.

By far, the most widely accepted way of obtaining brake components for a street rod is to head for the old reliable salvage yard, where an abundance of "previously owned" treasure awaits at modest prices. Where the novice builder first gets into trouble is that he makes an assumption that since the disc/drum system worked well on the '68 Camaro, it will work just as well on a '32 sedan. This is not true, and he has laid the groundwork for assembling a brake system that will be virtually impossible to balance.

General Motors fans have a very broad selection of suitable, easy to get components with which to work. In the '60s, GM manufactured two basic systems; one for intermediate cars, and one for full size cars. In the '70s, they repeated the same basic idea, using a disc/drum combination system. The wrecking yards are full of these cars, so piecing together a suitable set of components should not be a problem. The problem is, which to use with which?

In order to help explain the factors that go into determining brake components, let's take a look at two very different cars in the process of having their brake systems improved.

The first car is a '35 Chevy roadster that is being

modified to have a 427 cu.in. motor with a turbo 400 transmission. The car will be outfitted with 165x14" front tires and 255.15" tires in the rear. Although the car originally had a curb weight of less than 2500 pounds, it is expected that it will probably gain a few hundred pounds when complete. This car will be used for both street and nostalgia drag enjoyment.

From this information, we have the key factors to assemble a very respectable match of components for a disc/drum brake system. Using a '68 Camaro (curb weight approximately 2900 pounds) for comparison, we can see that the components from that car should be more than adequate for the weight in the car to be built.

But wait, there are some substantial differences in the two applications that need to be addressed. In the case of the '35 Chevy, the large rear tires constitute a major change to the balance of the car. The amount of braking energy required to stop a large wheel from turning is greater than that required for a small wheel with the same amount of weight on it. This means that in the case of any automobile that is using substantially larger tires on the rear than on the front, more of the responsibility for stopping the car has been shifted to those larger tires. For this reason, there is going to have to be a compensating factor plugged in somewhere to deal with this change. In our example, because of the extreme difference in the size of the tires, the best choice would be to replace the rear 10" brakes that came on the Camaro, to 11" brakes found on the full size cars. This will allow the rear brakes to share more of the braking responsibility, especially in low-speed stops common to around town driving. Since drum brakes are self energizing, it is necessary to limit their performance in high-speed stops so rear wheel lockup does not occur. This will be covered later, while discussing valving.

Other possibilities for balancing the system include smaller front calipers, smaller front rotors, bigger rear wheel cylinders in the 10" brakes, and using a proportioning valve to reduce the system pressure to the front brakes. Our choice would be to use 11" rear brakes because they require no modification, and it is always preferred to make as few modifications as possible.

In another example, let's consider the updating of the brake system to a disc/drum combination on a totally stock '48 Cadillac. In this case, the owner only wants to improve the stopping characteristics of the car so that it can be driven with confidence in the current environment. The car has a curb weight of over 4800 pounds, however we will be using stock tires and the maximum speeds will be 65 mph. Since the weight proportions of the car will remain similar to a later model car, it will be OK to adapt components from cars of similar weight, or even a slightly lighter car such as a full size Chevrolet from the '70s. This will still give considerable improvement over the stock system, especially in the area of fade recovery and wet weather stops. The system pressure can be improved by changing the pedal ratio and using a large power booster. This will be discussed under master cylinders and power boosters. For this example, we would choose the readily available components from a '72 Cadillac Deville.

The important thing to remember in both cases is that the car must have balance to the brake system to prevent lockup of either the front or rear wheels during braking application. This must be true through the entire range of stopping speeds encountered under all circumstances. For instance, if the brakes work well in a high speed stop when exiting a freeway off ramp, it does not mean that the brake system is correct. In fact, it could very well be that in all other driving instances the front brakes are doing all the work, causing excessive wear and damage to those components. It is not unusual to talk with street rodders who are constantly replacing front pads, but the rear brakes look like new.

When selecting components, consider the actual clearances and room available in the car being modified, as well as any similarities in such things as wheel bearings, spindles, steering arms, and axle hole spacing for mounting the new components. It is common to see similar bolt patterns used from one car to another, and it is also common to see that the size of the old spindles for the inner and outer wheel bearings are the same. In these cases, removing the old ball bearings and replacing them with roller bearings is all that is necessary to make the complete new disc brake spindle fit right onto the car. It is best to check with someone who has experience, whenever changing components. Steering geometry must also be watched to ensure safe handling.

MASTER CYLINDER AND POWER UNITS

Selection of the master cylinder seems to be the biggest problem for many builders. There may be some misunderstanding about the factors that make a master cylinder acceptable for the application. Let's take a look at those requirements and pick master cylinders for our two sample cars.

The most important element of the master cylinder to be selected is volume. The master cylinder must be capable of supplying sufficient fluid to all of the chosen components in less than 2/3 of its total stroke, thus allowing a suitable reserve. The reservoir must also be able to supply fluid to the bore as the brake linings wear down. To determine the size of the reservoir, when the linings are fully worn, the reservoir must still have about 25% of its total capacity remaining in the tank.

The second factor is bore size. Master cylinders come in a variety of sizes, most commonly 15/16" to 1-1/4". If you have chosen to use all four wheels of brake components from the donor car, the choice is easy — use the master cylinder from the car that supplied the rest of the brake components. If it does not fit the available space, limit your choices of other master cylinders to those with the same size bore.

Next, consider internal valving. Does the master cylinder have an internal residual valve? If so, can it be removed without harming the master cylinder? In most cases, the answer is that it can. When we get into the section on valving, we'll explain why this is so important.

Finally, other things that should be considered are the mounting hole position, outlet hole size, where the lines enter the master cylinder to ensure clearance, and the pushrod. The closer you get these items to meet your needs, the less adaptation that will be necessary later on.

General Motors fans have an extremely large selection from which to choose. It should not be a problem to find a cylinder just right for your application. They are available in all sizes, shapes, and with or without power assist. This leads us to the next subject. Do you need power assist? On most street rods that weigh less than 2700 pounds, it will not be necessary to have a power assist unit. On heavier cars, it is recommended to help keep the pedal effort within an easy operating range. The most common reason for excessive pedal effort is an incorrect pedal ratio. The ideal pedal ratio for a disc/drum, non-power system is 6:1. If your pedal is not already that ratio, you can drill another hole closer to the pivot point to increase the ratio. The only time I would add a power booster would be to ease the pedal effort on a heavier car, or when space does not allow the necessary ratio. If you choose to use a power booster, stay with a GM unit if possible. Many

aftermarket units, although more compact, do not have the output of the GM units. If you are going to put one on, use one that will do some good.

On early '30s rods, the master cylinder is often placed under the floor. If you place the master cylinder there, be sure to watch for some potential problems. First, avoid running the exhaust system within a foot of the master cylinder. If you must, place a heat shield between the exhaust and the master cylinder. Use either a metal barrier or a suitable non-flammable material approved for this use. There are some new wrapping materials available for exhaust systems that are used for racing applications which might be worth exploring for this purpose. Second, keep in mind that periodic maintenance dictates that you should check the master cylinder level regularly, so make sure you have access to do so. It also becomes necessary to put a 2-pound residual valve in the line to stop fluid from rolling back to the master.

BRAKE SYSTEM VALVING

After all of the components necessary to stop the car have been selected, the problem still remains to keep the system as balanced as possible throughout all possible types of stops.

As speed increases, the energy required to stop the vehicle increases as well. The problem is that the energy required for stopping increases with the square of the speed. In other words, if you are cruising at 30 mph, and then increase the speed to 60 mph, the

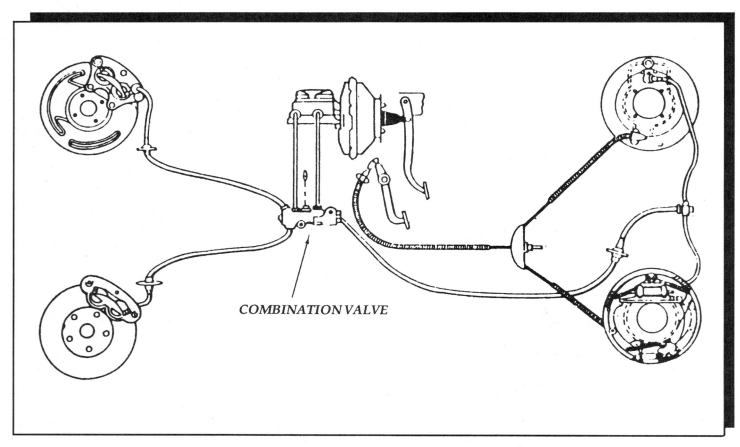

COMBINATION VALVE

energy required to stop the car is four times as great. If you increase speed to 120 mph, it now becomes 16 times as great. Many people are surprised at how long it takes to stop a car from high speed, but that is the reason why.

Another situation occurs as well. The harder you push on the brake pedal, the higher the rate of deceleration. As the deceleration rate increases, more of the weight on the rear wheels moves forward. This decreases the weight on the rear wheels and makes it easier for the rear wheels to lock up. Unfortunately, when this happens, you not only cannot stop as quickly, but the rear of the car wants to go faster than the front. The result is a spin-out and loss of control. In order to avoid this, it is important to decrease rear braking effectiveness at high deceleration rates of disc/drum systems. This is not necessary in disc/disc systems or in drum/drum systems.

On the accompanying charts, it is shown that the rear drum brake curve is climbing faster than the front disc line. Eventually it puts the system out of balance. By installing a proportioning valve, the effect is to reduce the amount of line pressure to the rear drum brakes. Kelsey Hayes manufactures an in-line proportioning valve that can be adjusted to suit various needs. It is the best choice if a proportioning valve is needed. In the case of the '35 Chevy street rod, a series of test stops under safe, controlled conditions should be made to see if premature locking occurs. Because the rear tires are so large, it is possible that no locking will take place. If any occurs at all, a proportioning valve should be installed and adjusted to stop rear wheel lock up. If the system is going to have any axle locking up before the other, it should be the front and not the rear. This at least allows the car to stop in a straight line.

A proportioning valve is the most misused valve on a street rod and should never be installed unless the need has been clearly established. A proportioning valve only reduces brake effort, it never gives you more, and seldom is there a problem with too much brake. If, for some reason, you have too much brake on the front (premature lock up), it is possible to plumb a proportioning valve to the front. Make sure there is not another reason for your imbalance, and explore other alternatives before you install the valve.

If you are adapting disc brakes to a 1950 - 1970 non-disc brake car, for the purpose of improved stopping ability from higher speed,

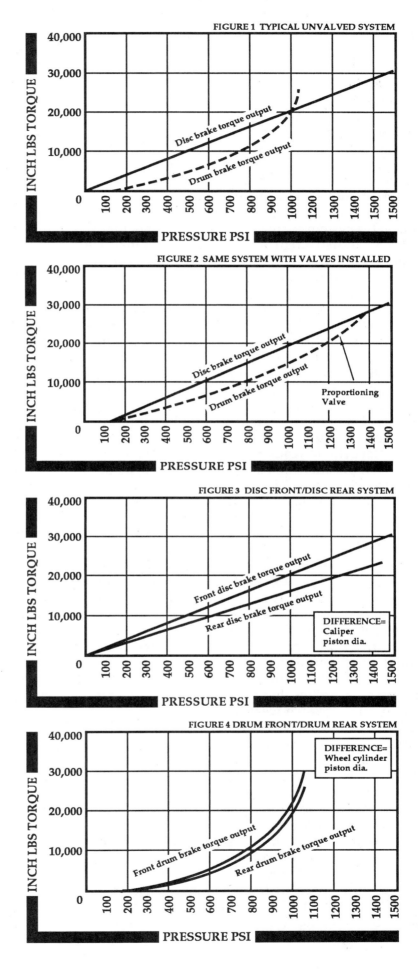

try to use all the components from a similar late model car of the same weight. This will assure you that all valves are used in the proper mix.

In most GM cars, starting in the late '60s, a combination valve was employed. This valve contained the residual pressure valve for the rear brakes, the proportioning valve for the rear brakes, and the metering valve for the front brakes. We have already explained the proportioning valve, but the other two are just as important under certain circumstances.

The residual valve is a valve that keeps slight pressure on the system even when the brake is not in use. Drum brakes have return springs of substantial size and strength and are easily able to return a shoe to rest, even if a residual valve is present. A drum brake always requires a 10-pound residual valve to keep the system from using excessive pedal travel. A disc brake, on the other hand, will have the piston push the pads into the rotor with even the slightest residual pressure. If you have a 10-pound valve present in a disc system, expect severe drag and excessive wear to the disc pads. The only time a residual valve should be present in a disc system is when the master cylinder is mounted lower than the calipers it feeds. In this case, when the brake is not being used, fluid will return to the master cylinder, causing excessive pedal travel on the next application. To resolve the situation, use a 2-pound residual valve. The 10-pound drum brake valve is too severe for this application. Brake loss could result if a residual valve is not in the system, and it is recommended that you do not attempt to drive the car without it.

The metering valve is in the system for the benefit of the front disc brakes, and is the valve most often overlooked in a street rod. This valve delays the first 50 pounds of line pressure from reaching the front brakes until the rear shoes have a chance to overcome the return spring tension. This allows all four brakes to apply simultaneously. Without this valve, the front brakes begin stopping the car before there is sufficient line pressure to allow the rear drum brakes to operate. Not only is excessive wear a problem, but in rainy weather, you are much safer to have all four tires helping decelerate the vehicle at the same time.

In the case of our two example cars, the Cadillac is fairly simple. Use all the components from the donor car brake system. The only addition would be a 2-pound residual valve if the master cylinder is below the level of the calipers. Changing older stock cars to disc/drum combination systems from newer cars usually does not involve selecting correct components as much as it does picking components that adapt themselves easily to the project vehicle. In the case of the modified '35 Chevy, both component selection and adaptation are problems. For example, a proportioning valve may not be necessary but a me-

tering valve, a 10-pound residual valve for the rear drum brakes, and a 2-pound residual valve for the front brakes (remember the master cylinder is below the floorboard), are absolutely necessary for a quality system.

PLUMBING THE BRAKE SYSTEM

Many people think that if there is any one thing about this project that they can do right, it's run the brake lines. Unbelievable as it may seem, this is one of the biggest problems in street rod brake systems. Use of improper materials, incorrect sizes and improper routing of brake lines are a few of the potential traps awaiting the builder.

Always use approved steel brake line. Do not use plastic hose that is used on many go karts, and don't plumb the car entirely with steel braided line. Plastic line is extremely unsafe and will fatigue from vibration. The flex line will grow when pressurized and will cause spongy pedal feel. Steel line may be either 3/16" or 1/4" diameter, or a combination of both. On factory GM products, both sizes are used so that the resulting fitting sizes are different. This makes it virtually impossible for a mechanic to mistakenly hook up the front line to the rear and vice versa.

If brake pedal sponginess is one of your concerns, use 3/16" brake lines instead of 1/4". As stated before, pressure will cause the hoses to grow, so use of a smaller hose keeps that to a minimum. Let's correct a major fallacy right now. The size of the brake line has no impact on the effectiveness or pressure of the brake system. Once the system has been bled, you are basically just pressurizing what is already there. Use factory brake hoses whenever possible, but if you intend to run steel braided line, make sure you purchase them from a reliable source to ensure that the ends have been fastened securely. This is one place where you want to be sure you are doing it right.

Routing the brake lines requires much care and consideration. In addition to making sure you keep it away from heat sources, you want to make sure it is placed safely away from potential damage from rocks, undercarriage scraping and the like. Make sure that all runs are kept straight, and avoid making loops and U-shaped bends such as those over the rear axle. Air inside the brake lines during bleeding likes to move uphill, but at the top of the loop it is hard to force the air downhill. Unless you want to create a bleeding nightmare, check with professionals, or at least observe how it is done on other cars before attempting this.

BRAKE FLUID

A hydraulic brake system will not operate without brake fluid. To a large degree, the level at which it does operate is dependent on the choice of fluid.

Among other things, the more important elements of brake fluid are high boiling point, consistent viscosity, and good lubricating ability.

All brake fluids commonly used in automobiles sold in the United States are regulated by the Department of Transportation (DOT). The brake fluid container will have a number such as DOT 3, which refers to the test designation that the fluid meets.

DOT Minimum Boiling Points

Dry Boiling Point	Wet Boiling Point
DOT 3 401 F	284 F
DOT 4 446 F	311 F
DOT 5 500 F	356 F

DOT 3 and DOT 4 fluids are normally polyglycol base products and are hygroscopic, which means that they absorb moisture. As the amount of moisture absorbed increases, the point at which the brake fluid boils decreases. In a well sealed brake system, these fluids require changing approximatly every 1 or 2 years, depending upon the severity of use. Unfortunately, street rodders have access to master cylinders that do not have diaphragms capable of tightly sealing the brake fluid from the air. Using this type of master cylinder is out of the question, since moisture in the air will be assimilated by the brake fluid immediately.

This is also why you should never buy brake fluid by the gallon, because once you have opened the container to put a little fluid in your master cylinder, moisture in the air inside the can will ruin the remaining fluid. Also, never reuse old fluid that has been removed from the brake system. Once the system has been filled, replace the cap immediately to avoid affecting the fresh fluid.

Never put any fluid in your system except brake fluid. Damage to the seals in the entire system could result if you mistakenly add transmission fluid or oil. Polyglycol DOT 3 or 4 is highly recommended, and can be mixed with each other without adverse effects.

Both DOT 3 and DOT 4 fluids attack paint. Since most street rodders have invested a great deal in their paint jobs, caution must be employed when using these products. If brake fluid is accidentally spilled on the paint, flushing with water and quickly wiping up the mess will prevent damage.

DOT 5 silicone brake fluid will not absorb moisture, nor will it attack paint. Unfortunately, it does have some undesirable characteristics. First, it is extremely expensive, costing as much as 10 times more than polyglycol fluids. Second, and more important, the compressibility of silicone fluid is very unstable throughout the temperature range encountered under normal driving conditions. As the temperature increases, the pedal travel necessary to compress the fluid changes, resulting in unpredictable pedal height.

Silicone fluid is not compatible with other fluids, and it is affected by changes in atmospheric pressure (altitude). This would not be such a problem except that we must not only be able to develop pressure in a brake system, we must also be able to remove that pressure. In the case of silicone fluid, the expansion can be so severe that even when you take your foot off the brake, excessive drag can continue heating the fluid and increase the expansion until the entire brake system locks up.

If you are one of the many street rodders who have experienced sponginess in the pedal after the car is used for a while, you now know the most likely reason. You may also be shortening the life of the brake pads due to excessive dragging. The other factor is that silicone brake fluid affects the seals found in standard systems. Ethylene proplyene rubber looses its hardness when exposed to silicone, resulting in a change in the size and an increase in the wear rate of all rubber components in the system.

In essence, both types of fluid have advantages and disadvantages to consider. The bottom line, however, is that safety and reliability must be of paramount importance in a brake system. There is no fear worse than that caused by stepping on the brake pedal and finding nothing there. Make sure your car meets all the requirements for safe braking.

by John Lee

Rear Disc Brake *Conversion*

Converting to rear disc brakes is fairly simple on '55 and later Chevys, or earlier models with late rear axles. A kit for the bolt-on swap is made by Street Rod Manufacturing Co. They make the brackets to mount JSM brake parts on various Chevy rearends. Calipers, rotors, brackets, bolts and hoses for the switch all come in the complete kit, or you can buy any of the components individually.

In these photos, Street Rod Manufacturing's brackets and rotors are being used along with '78 Monte Carlo front calipers. Other GM parts will work, including '79 Cadillac Seville rear units with a parking brake built in. For a stock '55-'57 rearend, JSM makes a bolt-on parking brake kit that attaches to the driveshaft.

Installation is shown on Kip Larson's '56 Chevy, which has a '69-'73 Nova 10-bolt rearend. The Nova rear will bolt up to '55-'57 springs if the spring pads are moved out. Kip wisely had 1/8" longer studs installed to make up for the thickness of the rotors. A double-reservoir master cylinder is required for disc brakes. A '78 Monza master cylinder bolts in the stock '56 location.

Get in touch with Street Rod Manufacturing Co. Inc., at 9635 Hwy. 85, Littleton, CO 80125-9729, or call (303)791-1881.

Far Left- Rear disc brakes for Chevys are a bolt-on conversion with an available kit.

Caliper bracket bolts to the back of the backing plate flange on the Nova rearend.

View from the back shows caliper bracket bolted up to the backing plate flange. Brackets are ordered according to the rearend used.

Nova axle has 1/8" longer studs installed to make up for the rotor's thickness. Complete kit includes brackets, calipers, rotors, hoses and bolts.

1978 Monte Carlo front calipers were used on this installation. Several other GM units will work.

Installing new hoses and bolting a '78 Monza master cylinder in the stock '56 location completes the conversion.

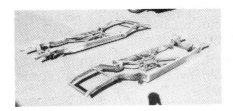

by Tex Smith

Steering

Interestingly, most of the original Chevrolet steering systems were of a good design, one that could take abuse and last for years. This held true for the side drag link versions of the early years as well as the cross steering that came later.

But, the ravages of time will have destroyed most of these steering gearboxes. And, improvements in steering during the Fifties and later makes installation of later gearboxes almost a foregone conclusion. Especially for any of the side drag link versions, and almost especially for the cross steering units.

Adapting later steering to any pre-1949 Chevrolet is almost exclusively a matter of making an adapter plate to fit the gearbox to the Chevy frame. Not at all difficult, if you have

With Chevrolet semi-elliptic springs and early side mounted gearbox steering, an interesting problem of bump steer correction happens. The spring pivots at point A, and the spindle bolt swings through an arc at point B. If the drag link mounting points are correct between points B and C (at the pitman arm), the arc caused by the drag link connection will exactly counteract the arc caused by the spring, eliminating bump steer. This self-cancelling feature would not be involved with a cross steering system.

done any metal cutting and welding. It becomes slightly more detailed if you change the front suspension or use a dropped axle.

If you use a dropped axle, using original spindle steering arms will result in a tie rod that is higher than original (relative to the frame), and this will cause misalignment between the tie rod and the steering rod (the link from pitman arm to steering arm). Invariably, the result will be bump steer.

If you are using a side steering unit, the steering rod angle will increase, but it usually will not cause enough bump steer to be a major problem. Getting the correct geometry with a side steering box and semi-elliptic springs is not as easy as with a Ford type cross spring. The centerpoint of the spindle bolt swings through an arc, up and down, as the axle moves about the spring front attachment bolt. But, the spindle bolt is also

connected to the pitman arm via the drag link, and since the pitman arm is behind the axle, the arc it causes can actually cancel out that caused by the spring rotation. As designed by the factory, this cancellation is fine. But, when using a dropped axle, the spindle bolt pivot point is raised, changing the arc. A good rule of thumb is to raise the pitman arm/drag link pivot point as well. This usually means raising the gearbox mounting, shortening the pitman arm (in the case of an arm that hangs downward), or using a gearbox that has the pitman arm point upward (like a Mustang).

But, it is also possible to reduce the arc differential by modifying the spindle steering arm that accepts the pitman arm so that the drag link forward mounting point is lower than the stock location.

While you can figure all this arc business out with the actual components (you'll need 5 hands!), it is easier to draw everything lifesize on the garage floor. From this, you can figure where the side steering pitman/drag link connection should be.

The dropped axle (or any front end geometry change caused by using a non-stock assembly) also causes problems for the cross steering. The dropped axle raises the spindle steering arms, and the tie rod. If the steering gearbox location remains stock, the cross steering drag link will usually run uphill, so that the linkage arc at the right front wheel is now drastically different. The arc no longer swings through a neutral point. Bad bump steer is the result. The gearbox can be moved upward, the pitman arm can be bent upward, the drag link end can be moved from mounting below the pitman arm to mounting above the pitman arm, or the spindle steering arms can be reshaped so that they are lower, back to original position. The latter choice is the way hot rod parts manufacturers go with steering correction kits.

Essentially, with any form of steering linkage, the idea is to have the spindle bolt swing through a neutral arc as the wheel goes up and down throughout normal travel. So, at rest, the spindle bolt arc would be at the normal limit one way. As the wheel goes up, the bolt (centerpoint of the wheel) passes through neutral after about 2-1/2" to 3-1/2" of wheel travel, and it reaches the normal limit of opposite arc at the top of normal travel (another 2-1/2" to 3-1/2"). If this doesn't happen, and there is more arc differential at one end of travel than the other, the steering linkage will cause the wheels to swing one direction significantly. This bump steer makes a good car miserable to drive, and dangerous.

While we have been talking about using dropped axles, the same kind of steering problems come into play if you use dropped spindles on an independent front suspension, or if you use a different IFS. Any change in front end components can lead to bump steer problems.

You can go to the wrecking yard and get different steering gearboxes, and you can make up your own adapters, but many rodders prefer to leave all this engineering and fabrication up to a hot rod supplier. But, not a lot of Chevy component suppliers are available. In this respect, Butch's Rod Shop (Dayton, Ohio, phone 513-298-2665) has long been a leading supplier in the field. Butch's has steering kits to adapt Mustang steering to 1928-'35 Chevy frames (drag link side steering, for use with or without a dropped axle), Vega steering kits for cross steering in the same model years, and kits to mount the GM Saginaw standard or power steering gearbox (or Vega) in 1936-'39 passenger cars with beam axles.

The Chevy gearboxes used on independent front suspensions through 1948 are quite good, but getting rebuild parts can be a problem. They can be replaced by the Vega or Saginaw power steering units. If the front end is lowered, via dropped spindles, spring work, or A-arm relocation, the spindle steering arms must also be relocated. It is far simpler to use the arms supplied by Butch's than to make up your own components.

If there is any confusion about getting the correct front end components in place, and the steering, call in a knowledgeable friend, or get guidance from a professional rod builder like Butch's.

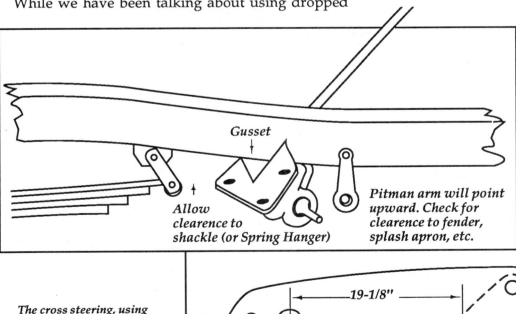

Gusset

Allow clearance to shackle (or Spring Hanger)

Pitman arm will point upward. Check for clearance to fender, splash apron, etc.

It is possible to mount a Mustang gearbox below the early Chevy frame, which gives a modern box and a pitman arm that points upward. This drawing from Butch's Rod Shop instruction sheet shows how it is done.

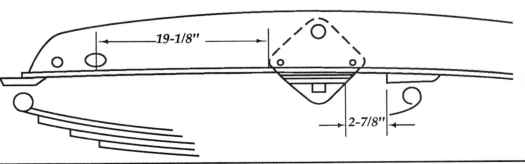

The cross steering, using Saginaw gearbox on the 1936-'39 "hat section" frames, has an adapter plate on the inside part of the frame.

19-1/8"

2-7/8"

Right-Special dropped spindle steering arms are available for use with a dropped axle to get the tie rod and drag link in correct positions.

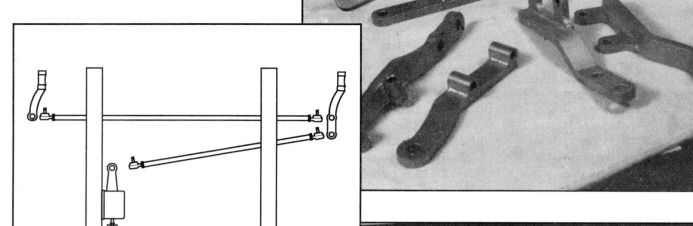

Cross steering components must be in correct relation, or bump steer will result.

On 1928-'35 Chevys, and 1928-'46 pickups, a cross steering system is available using the Vega gearbox and these components from Butch's Rod Shop.

On 1936-'39 Chevys with a beam axle, a kit is available to use the Saginaw/Vega cross steering gearboxes. A kit to use GM power steering will soon be available from Butch's for 1940-'48 Chevys.

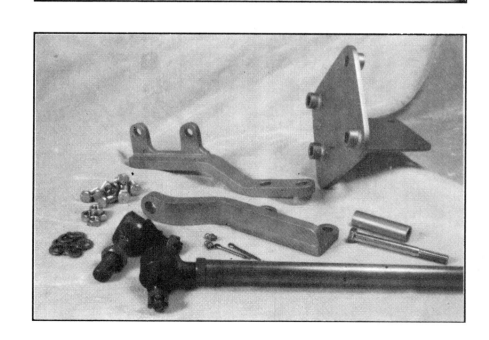

BORGESON UNIVERSAL COMPANY INC.

Borgeson offers a variety of universal joints, splined intermediate shafting, and couplers which fit almost every Mopar application. The joints can be furnished with both ends unsplined for welding and are also spot drilled for pinning, with one end splined and one end plain, or with both ends splined in any of the available sizes we offer.

We also offer "Double D" configuration (a round shaft with two parallel flats) in both the 3/4" and 1" sizes (this will fit the collapsible Chevy system).

For the serious street rodder who wants to have a "driver" as opposed to having the car trailered, we recommend the needle bearing style joint. Our joints use the same bearings as those used by General Motors.

Our splined shafting is stocked in 2" increments up to 36" in length and is very easy to measure, easy to install, safe, and removable if necessary. This allows your steering to be a bolt-together system. Our shafting is 3/4" OD which is stronger than the 5/8" OD shafting.

Borgeson universal joints have less than 1/1000" of backlash, are made exclusively for steering in high performance vehicles, and are the strongest for their size.

Borgeson offers a smaller (1-1/4" OD) non-needle bearing style joint for those who do not intend to drive their cars much or where size is restricted.

Borgeson offers a double universal joint in either style for those who have up to 60° of misalignment.

Please call Borgeson Universal Company, Inc. at (203) 482-8283 and our competent sales staff will be happy to assist you with any technical questions.

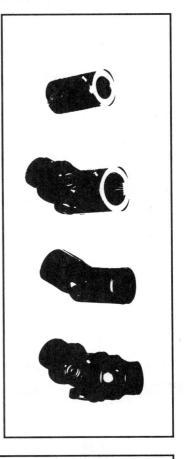

BORGESON UNIVERSAL COMPANY INC.
1050 South Main Street
Torrington, CT 06790
(203) 482-8283

53

Ackerman
Principle

Consider the car as it turns in a constant circle. The inside front wheel is turning a smaller-radius circle than the outside front wheel. Something must be done in the front steering mechanism to allow this to happen. This something is called the Ackerman principle, and if you look at a set of spindles you see that the steering arms on the spindles have the tie rod end holes closer to the center of the car than the kingpin holes.

If you draw a line from the center of the kingpin to the center of the rear axle, the line should pass directly through the steering arm rod end holes. If not, the car does not have perfect Ackerman effect. Current mass production technology is beginning to ignore this principle somewhat. Some new cars with rack and pinion steering ahead of the front axle centerline actually have the outer tire turning tighter than the inner wheel. Tire technology is offsetting some of this problem and so is wheel offset, but for our purposes, stick with making a pure Ackerman effect on your rod.

If it is necessary to bend a spindle steering arm for any reason, be sure and set it so that the Ackerman check line described is obtained. Sometimes, when a crossleaf spring is used on a frame with a suicide spring perch, the tie rod runs into frame interference. Rodders have cured the problem by reversing the spindles side-for-side. This puts the tie rod in front of the axle. And the Ackerman goes out the window, resulting in very poor turning control at higher speeds. If there were enough room, the spindles could be heated and bent outward so that the tie rod holes would again line up for the Ackerman check. Not really conceivable, so better to find another way and keep the tie rod behind the axle.

One method is to mount a rack and pinion steering gear directly to the solid axle. This is usually a simple matter of two sturdy brackets between the rack and pinion unit and the axle. This creates a problem with the steering shaft, however. As the axle travels up and down, the effective length of the steering shaft changes. Some new cars use spline sections in the steering shaft, and rodders cure the variable-length problem this way.

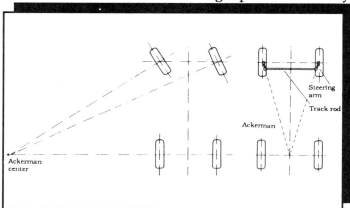

Srub Line

One of the more important checks in any vehicle safety test would be that of the scrub line. That is, any part of the chassis/body that hangs below the wheel's diameter. Unfortunately, a large percentage of hot rod builders violate this basic safety tenet, with both early and late model vehicles.

The reason for not wanting to have anything hanging lower than the bottom wheel lip is obvious. Given a flat tire, the offending part(s) can cause serious problems. One example would be a steering pitman arm that is too low. It digs into the pavement and the car can go out of control instantly. A bracket or such grinding against the pavement sends up sparks and a fire can result.

While it is true that a flat tire seldom lets the wheel rest on the road surface, good building sense says never take chances. To check for scrub line violations, have a buddy hold the end of a long string while you hold the other end. Start by running the string between the bottom edges of the two front wheel. Then move the string diagonally from one front wheel to the opposite rear wheel. If there seems to be something hanging too low, it is worth a further check, and repair if necessary.

Alignment

Once you have the suspension system installed, all would seem well and good. It is ... almost! Now, you must make the wheels roll true, and do what they should do in a turn.

Leave the final wheel alignment to the professional shop. However, there is a lot of alignment that you can do at home to get things at least in the ballpark. Since most projects are a long time from first movement to final drive-away, this initial alignment will help things considerably.

A note here: If you have an independent rear suspension, it is vital that this unit be aligned by the professional. Such systems have a lot to do with how the vehicle will handle, and they are not simply set with the wheels parallel to the chassis and vertical to the ground.

Rearend alignment is supposed to be right on the money if you have measured carefully when attaching all the mounting brackets. Quite often it is. But to find out, measure diagonally from the leading edge of the rearend housing at the outer brake backing plate flange, to some known point on the opposite frame rail, well forward. Do this on each side to the opposite rail. If the frame has measured square, this will give exact true to the rearend. Measure across the chassis from the rearend housing flange to make absolutely sure the rearend is centered under the frame. If the rearend must be moved, now is the time to do it.

Front end alignment is similar. The axle at the spindle should measure identical on a diagonal to a frame point. Adjustment at the radius rod mount(s) or the A-arm mounts will bring this into "square." Now, lay the kingpin inclination backward until there is about 5 degrees of caster in the spindle. The wishbone or 4-bar set-up can be adjusted, and shims are available to be placed between A-arm mounts and the A-arm itself. Since there are a number of different adjustments in the A-arm system, ask the front end professional for adjustment points with your particular system.

Wheel camber, or the amount the wheel leans in at

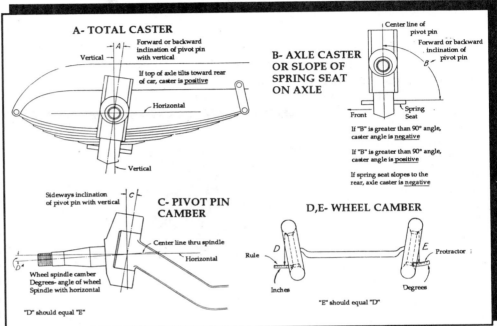

the bottom versus the top, is not important at this time, although a sighting down the wheel line from in front should show the bottom tilted in slightly from the top.

If you have decent caster, and the camber is usable, then the only other factor is toe-in/toe-out. Measure across the wheels from one side to the other, using a tire sidewall or tread mid-point as reference. Generally speaking, at this early stage, something like 3/8" toe-in will work. That is, the measurement across the front of the tires will be closer together by 3/8" than measuring the same place at the rear of the tires. If you do not have a toe-in or toe-out factor in the front end, you'll feel a lot of shimmy in the steering.

Trying to measure the rear of the tires can be a problem (as in the front if there is sheetmetal in the way). A quick solution is to tape plumb bob weights to the center of the tire, front and rear, then measure from these (near the floor).

Sometimes, no amount of toe-in work seems to remove shimmy from a front end, especially one using a solid front axle. Try as much as 1/2" toe-out. This often cures the problem. Of course, shimmy can also be caused by excessive play in the kingpin bushings, or excess play in the tie rod ends. Also check the steering gearbox for wear.

Rewooding
Early Chevy Bodies

by Dave Entler

Early General Motors bodies, up to and including 1936, were framed inside with wood. This is called composite construction. If you are lucky enough to find one of these bodies, it will usually have some or all of the wood rotted, which should be replaced.

The first step in rewooding these bodies is to remove all the upholstery, including the seats. The next step is very important for those who have never tackled this kind of job before. Get out the 35mm camera and load up with a 36-exposure roll, shoot plenty of close up shots, have them printed, and mount them on a board for ready reference.

Now, using an ice pick, poke around the wood to determine how much of it is soft. If the body is missing all the wood, skip this step. If you are fortunate enough to have some good wood, figure out what is good and what is bad, then order whatever replacement parts necessary.

If you determine that the body needs all new wood, remember that the wood structure was assembled with the screws being installed from the outside in. You will be doing the opposite during assembly. Most all accessible screws will be rusted tight. It is easy to remove them, using a 1/8" diameter drill bit, about 1/4" deep right in the center of the screw head. Then change to a 1/4" or 5/16" diameter drill bit to open up the hole, and the head will pop off. Use this technique anywhere a screw cannot be easily removed with a screwdriver.

Most of the sheetmetal is nailed to the wood. If you look carefully, you will find the nails. Using a small, sharp chisel and hammer, pop the heads off of the nails. (Wear safety glasses during this procedure.) Pry the wood out carefully, using a large screwdriver, then spread the metal tabs open with channel locks.

Once the wood is removed, clean the inside of the body by sandblasting or applying a rust remover. If a reputable sandblaster can be found, it is best to clean both sides of the body. It makes it easier to finish off the body after the wood is installed. Use a shop that specializes in sandblasting auto bodies, because an inexperienced sandman can destroy the body. An excellent alternate plan is to have the body dipped in rust remover. If you don't choose to move the body from your garage, use a rust remover available from Eastwood or other auto suppliers. I always prime and paint the inside of the body, as well as the outside, for additional rust protection.

The new wood should be preserved by using a marine spar varnish. Thin the first coat 25% with paint thinner, so it will soak into the wood. Subsequent coats should be applied full strength.

Start by assembling the front hinge pillars to the lower crossbar with the metal brackets. Set the cowl up on stands to get the front of the body up off the floor. There are Tee nuts (threaded fasteners) which fasten to the top of the hinge pillars. These must be tack welded to the inner metal panel above the windshield. An alternate plan is to use #4 sheetmetal screws, as per the diagram.

Next, slide the hinge pillars up in place and, using C-clamps or Vise Grip clamps, pull the assembly up until the crossbar touches the lower windshield metal. The hinge notches in the pillars should be centered in the notches in the metal. Fasten the metal with several nails, then hang the doors on the hinges and make sure the body moldings line up. If they don't align well, pull the nails back out and adjust the metal up or down to get perfect alignment.

Next, install the side roof rails and body lock pillars. Secure these in place with several nails. Slip in the main body floor sills and attach floor brackets to the hinge pillars and lock pillars.

Install the floor cross bars and triangulate the floor assembly by measuring the left-front floor bolt hole to the right-rear floor bolt hole, and the right-front floor hole to the left-rear floor hole. Then, install screws in the cross bars. The holes in the floor sills will match the holes in the frame.

Now, install the rear window assembly and rear roof rail by fastening them to the roof side rails. Install the roof side rails after sliding the front header into place. Install the roof bows, starting at the front and working your way back.

Next, install the rear bow and fasten it with nails. Sill kickups are used in the Master series and should be positioned next, along with the trunk floor support.

Use the rocker panel for a length gauge at the door bottom, and place a few nails in the metal under the kickups. This should provide about 1/8" gap at the rear of the door. The rocker panel provides the clearance. Place the two front floor sill bolts through the wood and the frame, and fasten them with nuts and lock washers. You should use 1/8" body anti-squeak between the wood and the frame. It may be necessary to place a shim between the sill and frame to raise the rear of the door.

After the major wood parts are installed and you are satisfied with the way the body looks, install the remainder of the nails and screws. Finally, install the remainder of the wood, and align the sheetmetal as necessary.

Once the wood is all installed, the body will be very strong and as good as new.

Complete Wood Kits:

David J. Entler Restorations
R.D. 2, Box 479C
Glen Rock, PA   17327
Phone: (717) 235-2112

Pillar mounting holes are drilled in the proper location. Use the existing Tee nuts or buy new hardware from Auto Hardware Specialties (catalog available from RR 1, Box 12A, Sheldon, Iowa 51201). Drill two 9/64" diameter clearance holes in the sheetmetal stamping for two #4 x 3/8" sheetmetal screws. This will keep the Tee nuts in place while installing the pillars to the crossbar with the cowl, after using pliers to spread open the sheetmetal above the top hinges and up to the curve area. This will allow the pillar unit to be installed easily. Center the hinge cutouts in the body hinge cutout area, and nail the metal to the wood. Only use a half dozen nails until everything is aligned.

Drill 9/64 "diameter clearance hole in sheet metal for #4 x 3/8" sheet metal screws.

Tee Nuts

When installing the floor sills, place new webbing between sill and frame. Then install new bolts in front of sills and tighten at A. Placing shims under bolt B will pick up the rear of the door, align belt rail molding at D, and close the gap at E. If the door is tight at E, forget shim at B, and shim the C bolt. There are excellent instructions for aligning 4-door sedans in the Fisher Body Service Manual, 1933-1936, available from Crank-En-Hope Publications, Blairsville, PA 15717.

This 1931 coupe shows how the wood was replaced in the rear sill assembly and door frame. New top slats are partially visible.

Moving in to take a look at the interior of the '31 coupe, the floor assembly and door frame are seen. Note the trap door in the floor for access to the battery.

Restoring the wood in this 1933 Chevy 4-door involved working on both the front and rear doors. These photos show how the door frames and body pillars interface as the wood is replaced.

This 1934 Chevy roadster needed a complete re-wood job. The photo shows how wood was replaced for the seat frame and top compartment.

Front hinge pillars and floor assembly in this '34 roadster were replaced with new wood. When everything is aligned and fastened down, the body will be as solid as when it was new.

Here's a photo of how the door framework is put together for the '34 roadster. Careful alignment, and possibly a bit of shimming, are necessary to make the car look as it did the day it rolled off the production line.

ROOF ASSEMBLY

A. Three flathead machine screws 1/4" 20 x 3/4" long at each end. Three Tee nuts at each end.

B. 1/4" 20 x 4" long step bolts, two required.

C. Trim to length at rear of slats.

D. Use a metal dolly to back up bows when nailing slats to bows.

E. 1/4" 20 x 2" long carriage bolts. Sixteen required. Also sixteen 1/4" lock washers and sixteen 1/4" flat washers.

F. Seat square end of slat at front.

G. 3/4" long flathead wood screws (metal plate to front roof rail) need about sixteen, also used at rear roof bow.

H. 1/4" 20 x 3-1/2" long roundhead machine screws, two required.

I. Top installation requires approximately 2 dozen stainless steel nails.

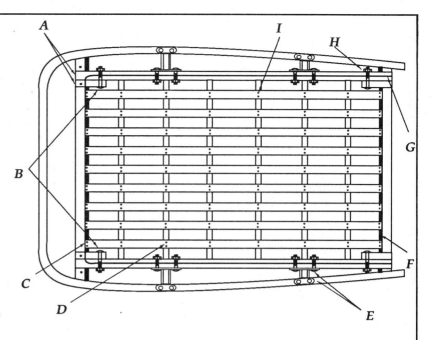

4-DOOR SEDAN BODY WOOD

(This illustration shows a '33 Master sedan. Not all parts apply to '35-'36 Master sedan and '36 Standard sedan.)
A - Main sill
B - Main sill cross bars, 2-piece set
C - Rear end sill
D - Front body pillar
E - Body hinge pillar
F - Dog leg
G - Rear quarter pillar
H - Windshield header trim
I - Windshield lower cross bar
J - Rear belt rail
K - Rear quarter belt rail
L - Rear window frame assembly
M - Trunk floor board
N - Sill kickup (Master)
O - Sill kickup cross bar
P - Rear quarter frame top
Q - Rear quarter radius block

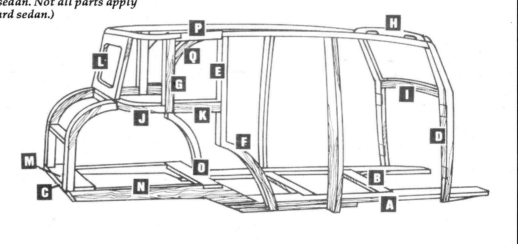

COUPE BODY WOOD

(This illustration shows a '34-'35 coupe. Not all parts apply to '35-'36 Master coupes and '36 Standard coupes.)
A - Master main sill
B - Main sill cross bars
C - Rear end sill
D - Front body pillar
E - Body lock pillar
F - Windshield header
G - Windshield lower bar
H - Belt rail
I - Rear window frame
J - Deck opening side rail
K - Deck opening upper bar
L - Deck opening lower bar
M - Deck lid kit
N - Trunk floor support
P - Sill kickup (Master)
R - Quarter pillar (Master)

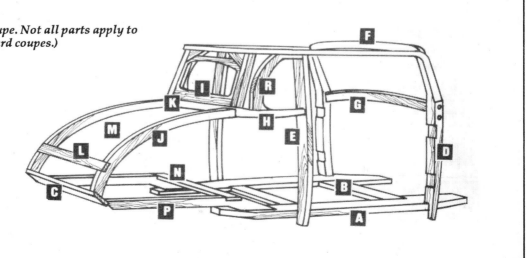

2-DOOR SEDAN BODY WOOD

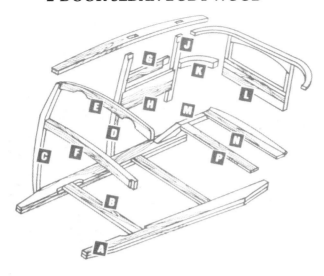

*(This illustration shows a '33-'34 Standard 2-door coach struc-
ture. Not all parts apply to '35-'36 Master and '36 Standard
bodies.)*
A - Main sills
B - Main sill cross bars
C - Front body pillar
D - Body lock pillar
E - Windshield header
F - Windshield lower bar
G - Belt bar
H - Window regulator board

J - Rear quarter pillar
K - Belt rail
L - Rear window frame
M - Sill kickup (Master)
N - Rear sill (2 pieces)
P - Floor support

SEDAN DELIVERY BODY WOOD

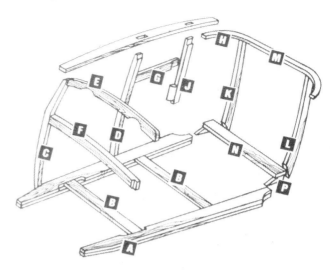

A - Main sills
B - Main sill cross bars
C - Front body pillar
D - Body lock pillar
E - Windshield header
F - Windshield lower bar
G - Belt bar
H - Roof rail corner

J - Quarter pillar
K - Rear door lock pillar
L - Rear door hinge pillar
M - Rear door header
N - Rear sill
P - Rear sill spacer

CABRIOLET AND ROADSTER BODY WOOD

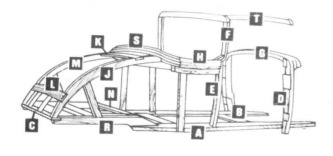

A - Main sills
B - Main sill cross bar
C - Rear sill
D - Front body pillar
E - Body lock pillar
F - Roof bow
G - Windshield lower bar
H - Belt rail
J - Deck opening side rail

K - Deck opening upper bar
L - Decking opening lower bar
M - Deck lid kit
N - Trunk floor support
R - Sill kickup
S - Rear body top compartment
T - Front top bow

COUPE AND SEDAN ROOF WOOD PARTS

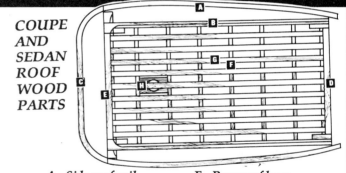

A - Side roof rail
B - Crown roof rail
C - Rear roof rail
D - Front roof rail

E - Rear roof bow
F - Roof bows
G - Roof slats
H - Dome block

DOOR WOOD

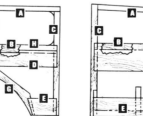
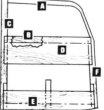
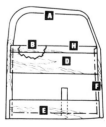

A - Top header
A - Top header and door
lock pillar (coupe style)
B - Cross bar
C - Door lock pillar
(sedan style)

D - Lock board (window regulator)
E - Door bottom
F - Hinge pillar
G - Dog leg
H - Regulator board, top

**The Only Company Devoted Exclusively
To Manufacturing Power Window Kits For Older Vehicles**

 **Specialty
Power
Windows**

(912) 994-9248 Technical Information
1-800-634-9801 Factory Sales Desk
1-800-728-3881 West Coast Sales (CA)
FAX (912) 994-3124

Route 2, Goodwyne Road, Forsyth, Georgia 31029

Doctoring Wood

In hot rodding, the words wood and Chevrolet are synonymous, and this has been one reason that the 1936 and earlier Chevy has never been an overwhelming hot rod favorite. Which is a shame, because repairing or replacing the body wood in any Chevy body is not nearly as difficult as it might seem.

Not so many years ago, when these Chevys were still in general public use, every body/fender repairman had to repair the wood. True, back then most of the wood was still in good condition. Only broken pieces, caused by wrecks, were replaced. But those repair practices are still valid today, if the original wood is in reasonable condition.

If the wood piece is really rotted away, then the entire piece must be replaced. If all the wood is in bad shape, complete re-wood kits are available. But here, we are concerned with just fixing up a basically decent wood framework.

Test the wood with an ice pick or knife blade, especially around joints and anywhere water has been present. If the wood is soft, it is rotted. Often, just a small area around a joint will be bad. This area can be repaired with a splice. Simply cut away the bad section, make a new piece, and glue/screw it in place. This would be the same as repairing the section if the car had been in a wreck.

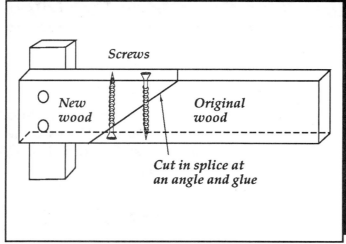

Selection of wood for any repairs starts with good hardwood. Do not use a soft wood such as pine.

There is an unusual product available that eliminates this need of making a splice, however. Originally marketed under the name RSP, and now called Kwik-Poly, this resin/catalyst first showed up in the early 1980s at restored-car events. Restorers learned that they could repair wooden steering wheels with the stuff, and it was even used on wooden spoke wheels (which we do not recommend).

The product is a two-part chemical that will soak into the wood. If you have an area that is essentially complete, but dry rotted, you can apply the thin chemical and it will completely soak into the rotten wood (like a sponge). But, since the chemical also works like a glue, be sure that all joints are in correct alignment before applying the material. Once Kwik-Poly has dried (which is very soon), the wood can be drilled and tapped for screws. It becomes harder than the adjacent "good" wood.

In the event that a part of the wood is missing, Kwik-Poly can be mixed with sawdust until a paste is formed, then this paste can be built up on the bad wood to the original shape (or a new shape can be formed). A piece of cardboard can be taped around the area to be filled, as a kind of form. If a filler is going to be used, the rotten wood should be soaked with regular Kwik-Poly before going to the filler, in order to get the strongest combination possible. Once the filler has been applied, it can be sanded and filed the same as regular wood.

No, this kind of repair does not give the same results as a re-wood job, but it is an alternative, and a good one.

One member of the famed Los Angeles Roadster club once found a 1934 Chevy roadster body that had good metal, but poor-to-bad wood. With all the body clamped into alignment, he spread fiberglass over the entire wood surface (from the top). Once this dried, he then turned the body upside down, and covered all remaining wood with fiberglass resin and cloth. Again, this was not the same as re-wooding the body, but it was a low-cost and very effective method of making the body rock solid. The result was a body that was much more solid than original, with a solid feel normally reserved for the most exclusive of classics. The extra weight also made the car ride better. But, and this is vital, be sure that the body is in absolute correct alignment before doing such a fiberglass bath treatment. The downside of this kind of job is that getting to sheetmetal for subsequent repair is more difficult.

When making wood repair, no special tools are needed. An ordinary table saw will make most cuts that are needed. If the wood needs a curved cut, a regular jigsaw works fine. A router can be a plus in some cases, but simple wood chisels work well. Wood rasp files and regular body grinders are used for shaping the rough cuts. Good water-resistant glues are imperative.

It is not difficult to make wood framework repairs, only time consuming.

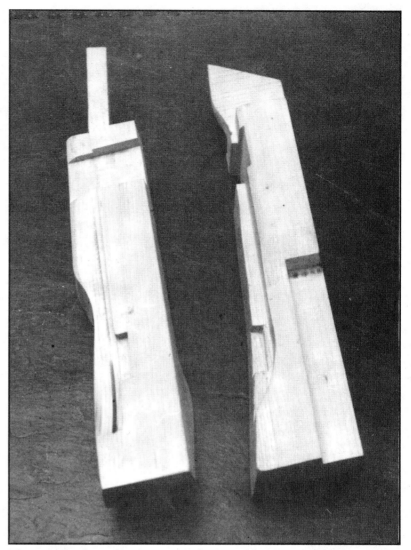

These pieces of wood were cut entirely on a table saw. Small cavities and curved areas were made with a chisel.

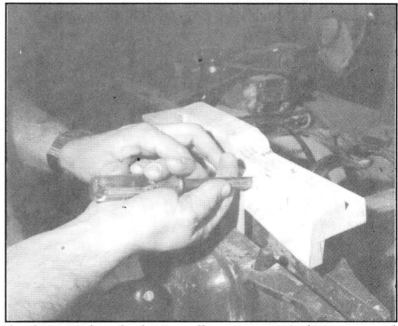

The advantage of wood is that it usually requires no more than patience and basic hand tools.

This 1932 Chevy has doors with wood that is basically good, although there is some dry rot in the lower corners. Door is held in alignment while Kwik-Poly is applied to the corners. All screws are tightened first. New screws can be added after the chemical cures.

Although it is now labeled as Kwik-Poly, an unusual wood treatment chemical is a two-part space age product originally called RSP. It mixes like any ordinary resin.

If there is any indication of slight dry rot, the entire wood surface can be coated with Kwik-Poly. Address is 24 ST. Henry Ct, ST. Charles, MO 63301, Phone (314) 724-7153.

Kwik-Poly mixed with sawdust becomes a sandable filler for anywhere wood is missing. It can be used free form, or in a cardboard form.

by Dave McNurlen

Fabricating
A '34 Hood

Building a 3-piece hood for a '34 Chevy isn't difficult. All it takes is some 18-gauge sheetmetal, a good sabresaw, some files, and a lot of patience.

Start by having the body mounted to the frame, to avoid alignment changes. Install the grille shell and align it, using a stock hood if you have one. When the new hood is cut out, the best fit will be achieved by the "put it on, mark it, take it off, file it" method.

There are several ways to get a pattern to work from. One is to make a paper pattern of the stock hood top when it is installed on the car. What I did was take half of a stock hood top, flatten it out, and trace around it directly on the new sheetmetal. Then flip it over, add some extra in the middle for the hinge, and trace the other side. A 4' x 4' piece of 18-gauge sheetmetal was used for the hood top, and another piece the same size for the sides. After making the pattern, the stock hood top was bent back to the stock shape, with no damage.

Cutting out the metal was done with a 24-tooth (per inch) blade in a standard hand-held sabresaw. I changed blades a lot, to keep a nice clean cut. (Safety glasses are essential for this job.) To maintain a straight cut, a 1/2" x 1" piece of bar stock was used as a saw guide. The blade was lined up with both ends of the cut line, and

This '34 grille shell has part of a '37 grille shell welded to it. The weld seam of the '34/'37 shell is still visible, along with the curve at the bottom of the '37 channel, which gives the '34 shell a stock appearance. The '37 metal was welded right over the top of the '34 shell, and could actually be removed if someone wanted to (gulp!) put fenders on the car. Note that the hood is attached to the frame about a foot back from the front. This was eliminated later.

the bar stock clamped to let the saw run down the bar. These cuts always came out straight and only needed file touch-up. Curves were done freehand, always with a new blade.

When the hood top was rough cut, a centerline was established on the grille shell, hood and cowl to help maintain proper alignment during final shaping and fitting. No hood lace (padding) was used between the hood and the body until after the hood was permanently mounted.

Tools for bending consisted of several thick cardboard tubes of different diameter, and an empty acetylene bottle. One thing to check for on the bottle is that some have a raised ridge around the bottom that can't be seen easily. Before bending metal around it, check the bottle or you'll end up with dents in the hood.

When fitting the hood top to the car, start at the centerline and work outward from it on both sides. I didn't start bending until the hood fit to the point of the bend. It took lots of filing, and some recutting to get the fit. Before bending, eyeball the imaginary line the bend will take, and mark it on the hood. Start the bend slowly to check the centerline of the bend. You may want to practice with some scrap sheetmetal before bending the real thing. Round up several different diameters of tubes to bend with, and go for a radius similar to the stock hood. In some cases, a tube smaller than the actual radius can be used to get a tight bend and help the hood hug the body. A piece of plywood helps to form the metal over the tube. Go easy, and don't bend too much at one time.

How the panels are attached to the car affects the shape of the top of the side panels, since most hinge set ups require a 90-degree angle at the top to attach the panel. I didn't have a brake, and didn't really want a hinged hood anyway. The solution was riveting a slot on the inside edges of the hood top, with a 3/4" deep groove. This was reinforced with 1/2" square tube, running the length of the hood, which was tapered in the cowl area for clearance. The slot was spaced with a strip of 16-gauge sheet-metal.

Next, side panels were measured, cut and fitted in the same fashion as the top. A strip of 18-gauge sheetmetal was riveted to the top of the side panels, that would fit up in the groove just enough to leave a uniform 1/4" gap between the top and the sides of the hood. The rivets can be countersunk and filled if desired. Be aware that the cowl and grille shell sides aren't parallel surfaces, and some bends will have to be made to get a good fit.

I attached everything to the body with Dzus fasteners. The top was fastened first, with two fasteners on each side. Then the sides were slipped into the slots from the bottom and fastened at the front and rear bottom with two fasteners per panel. When the hood was first mounted to the car, screws were used to attach it. Plates were attached to the body as mounting points. When the Dzus fasteners were added, the existing screw holes were simply drilled out, springs attached for the fasteners to screw into, and the hood reinstalled. Then the hood was spaced up from the cowl and grille shell with hood lace to align with the body.

One note about solid hood sides. This car has a very good cooling system with a thermostatic electric fan, so cooling problems didn't exist even with the solid hood sides. Going over a mountain pass in Wyoming did make it vapor lock once, though, so now the side panels are louvered.

Right-And here's the completed hood. Even with solid side panels, the cooling system was capable of keeping temperatures under control for normal driving conditions. However, louvers were added later after a vapor lock problem while crossing a high mountain pass.

Above-Here's the inside rear edge of the left hood side attaching strip. This is riveted flat to the side panel with a slight bend (done with pliers) to mount the strip for easier installation into the hood top groove, and to angle the side panel slightly at the top for better appearance.

Left- The shape of the hood center top is visible. Some may want to consider removing the bump in the center of the shell for a clean line across the back of the shell.

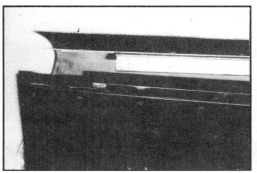

Left front edge of the hood top and side. The attachment and hood top reinforcement can be seen here. The hood top is the outer edge, with a strip of 16-gauge metal sandwiched between another strip of 16-gauge and a 1/2" square tube. Note that the sandwiched piece of 16-gauge goes all the way to the end of the hood to add support for the hood sheetmetal in the area of the Dzus fastener. The groove is 3/4" deep, with the side panel strip 1" long from the top edge of the strip to the side panel seam. This leaves 1/4" gap between the top and side when installed.

One of the mount plates for the hood panel fasteners. The spring that the fastener fits into is visible behind the plate.

Above-Here's a view of the channel on the left side of the grille shell.

67

by Dave McNurlen

Chopping
A '34 Chevy

According to most enthusiasts, a '34 Chevy looks good no matter what shape it's in, but a chopped '34 Chevy looks fantastic. Here's an example of how to make good look fantastic.

Step one was to measure and mark the top for the amount of metal to be removed. A 3" chop is about right for this car, leaving enough glass area for visibility and making the proportions pleasing. Wide strips of masking tape were used to mark the portion of sheetmetal to be removed. Note in the photos that the rear quarter section of roof is marked for cutting slightly below the midpoint of the rear window. Careful measuring revealed that this cut would allow the rear glass area to fit together fairly well after the top was lowered.

After the top had been cut away and the desired 3 inches of sheetmetal and windshield posts removed, the top was set back on the body for a trial fit. The photos show how much misalignment there was at the windshield posts with the top set on so that the rear edge of the door was in alignment at both the body and the top. This is the easiest way to calculate the amount of top stretch necessary to bring everything back into proper alignment.

The next step was to cut across the top, side to side, and add a 1-inch wide strip of sheetmetal to effectively lengthen the top. This is necessary because the overall profile configuration of this particular top is a slight trapezoid, so as it is shortened vertically, the top must stretch horizontally in order for the uprights to align. After cutting the door window uprights, the door tops were lengthened slightly for the same reason. I found that with a wire welder, I could stack beads to build up the lip on the edge of the door. If a gap was too wide, a few beads were run and then ground smooth for the desired fit.

After lengthening the top, the original insert was filled with a piece from the roof of a '75 Nova 2-door. It

was cut out with a sabre saw, and fit down in the slight recess around the roof opening. This was welded with a wire welder and .024 wire. Short beads were run on alternate sides, to keep the insert from warping.

When the interior wood was installed, the stock interior support for the roof of the Nova was installed, and that gave support that the wood couldn't provide. All the wood in the doors was installed after the metal work was done. The next time around, I will give serious consideration to using steel tubing instead of wood. The wood kit used in the '34 weighed over 200 pounds, and cost more than $1000.

When everything was fairly well aligned, the joints were tack welded. Where necessary, the sheetmetal was relief-cut and massaged into position for perfect alignment. This is especially necessary where the upper and lower radii of the rear window meet each other and must be aligned. Also, the rear quarter sheetmetal had to be slotted and moved around for alignment.

Is it all worth it? Look at the photo of the finished car, and you decide.

Before any metal work was started, the body was braced for support to maintain strength of the body once the top was removed. There was no wood in the body to begin with, so the new door jamb wood was cut and temporarily installed.

Clean metal was exposed and masking tape used to mark the 3-inch section to be cut out. On the tape is written, "Here we go."

The first cut of a first-time chopper's top chop. A hack saw and a sabre saw were used.

The scariest moment of the entire job was lifting the now-severed top off the body and realizing that I may have made a mistake in trying to do this myself. The 3 inches haven't yet been cut out.

The best moment of the job was setting the top back on and realizing what the car would look like after completion. Note the amount of misalignment at both front and rear mating points.

This is the misalignment at the front, with the top lined up at the rear edge of the door opening. It was decided to add an inch to the length of the top, rather than angle the posts.

No alignment problem at all in the windshield area. The cut was made just below the stopping point of the crease line that runs around the top of the windshield.

With the rear door edge aligned and the extra braces added, the top is cut between the two C-clamps sticking out of the roof. The leaded factory top seam is just to the left of the left C-clamp.

C-clamps are used in conjunction with a length of flat stock or angle iron to maintain alignment between the front and rear sections of the top after they are separated by cutting across.

Looking to the rear on the driver's side, the 1-inch gap is seen with temporary reinforcement, and the factory leaded seam is just in front of the cut.

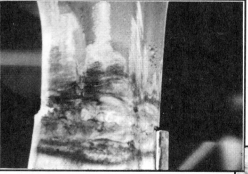

Left windshield post after oxyacetylene welding. There is still some misalignment, but it is easily taken care of.

Below-Left side of the rear window. Rather than cut some of the window opening out and move it over, it was decided to roll the metal on the bottom part out to meet the top part — like uncurling a backwards "C". A little metal work and filler restored the body line.

It took forever, but eventually all of this was welded up. Only half of these cuts need to be made. A first-timer's mistake. Wet shop rags were used to prevent heat transfer, and short tack welds were made to keep from warping the roof.

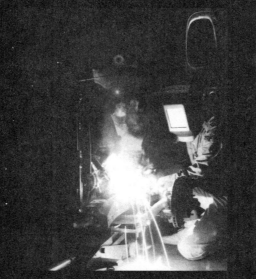

Paint
Preparing For The Car Show

Tricks of the trade that make the difference between a champion and an also-ran!

The world of true show cars is quite different from the world inhabited by your average street-driven vehicles. At first, those differences may not be obvious. The chrome is the same (almost), as is the glittering paint (almost), and the vibrant upholstery (almost). But within that different world, to be a champion may mean something as incidental as paint overspray on a hidden frame member or a spot of grease on a tie rod end.

In the restoration hobby, it is generally said that a 100-point vehicle represents the ultimate perfection, a machine that is far superior to what it was when new. And, the difference between a 95-point car and a 100-point car can equal thousands and thousands of dollars.

For the hot rod and custom car enthusiast, the ultimate vehicle is not so much a matter of money as it is of labor, assuming that the enthusiast can do the majority of his own work. But whether the builder does his own work or farms it out, there are some very specific tricks of the show trade.

The first step in building a show winner is to determine exactly how serious the vehicle will be in show competition. The assumption is that the vehicle is already constructed, or very nearly so. If show competition is to be very serious, it is wise to visit several area shows and carefully inspect similar vehicles. Talk to the vehicle owners as well as to show producers and judges. Every region of the nation will have peculiarities — types of cars that are most popular, items that the judges consider more important, show

Much of show preparation begins with an outstanding paint job. Excellent paint means removal of doors, hood, deck lid, etc. After the door is removed, finish jambs as well as outside of body.

building limitations, numbers of spectators, etc. Learn these things before showing the vehicle, if possible.

If the vehicle is to be shown only casually, chances are it will probably not win the overall top prizes. Even in the street driven classes, where the vehicle is assumed to be driven many miles a year, the vehicle that is best prepared for the show will win. Attention to detail is the first order of show preparation, once the decision is made to be competitive in show judging.

If the vehicle will only be shown locally, there may or may not be an advantage in belonging to the International Show Car Association (ISCA). However, if the vehicle is to be shown in several area shows, there is a definite advantage to being an ISCA member. Many ISCA shows pay tow money, as do some non-ISCA shows. This is usually so much per mile, one way. At ISCA shows there is also the possibility that awards will include cash prizes, so that a successful show vehicle may break even, or make a slight profit because of the show. For full information on ISCA, write to 32365 Mally Drive, Madison Heights, MI 48071.

When building a car that will be shown competitively, it is a matter of going the extra mile in preparing the overall car. Keep in mind that the show judges will consider giving show points to the vehicle as they inspect five basic categories: body, interior, undercarriage, engine, and safety. The object is to garner the maximum number of allowable points in these areas, and to do this the builder must pay maximum attention to detail in each area. As the judge looks at each area, he will keep two things uppermost in mind — degree of difficulty of making the change or restoration, and quality of execution. It is in the little things that points begin to pile up, and that is where the tie-breakers are determined.

What appears to be a dynamite vehicle might be

Pay particular attention to the imperfections that are bound to be apparent on door jambs. Use filler sparingly and finish very smooth.

Edges of all opening panels should be very carefully sanded, filled and sanded again. This is particularly true of the hood inside edges, which are readily seen by judges.

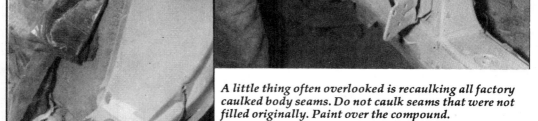

A little thing often overlooked is recaulking all factory caulked body seams. Do not caulk seams that were not filled originally. Paint over the compound.

Even the frame needs attention, as will the suspension parts.

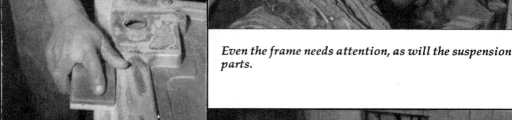

Inner edges of doors need the filling and sanding routine. Total amount of time doing this is negligible considering how many extra points this attention is worth.

Here special recessed head screws replace the more common factory items, a little plus that adds to detail.

The little nooks and crannies in the engine compartment opening should be finished just as nicely as any place on the car.

Don't overlook areas that seem to be inconsequential, such as upper overhang of recessed lights. Judges will feel in these areas to determine quality of work.

'Vette owner John Moore looks over color charts and design drawings for graphics on his show winner. Selection of color scheme is extremely important when going after the biggest prize.

Custom paint whiz Carl Brunson color sands the Corvette body. This foundation must be flawless. New acrylic paints provide superior finishes.

nothing more than a good exterior paint job. Closer inspection might reveal a lack of detailing, and such a vehicle is quickly out of contention for the big prizes. Judges will very carefully look at the finish on door jambs, under the fender wells, nooks and crannies in the engine compartment — just about every hidden area possible.

When painting the vehicle, take the extra time to prepare all the raw edges. Remove the doors so that every part of the door jambs can be filled and sanded smooth. Remove the hood and fill/sand around everything, even the areas that can't be seen readily. Smooth the edges of the fender opening, finish inside the grille cavity, don't leave any area undone. During painting, take the extra time to make sure that each of these areas gets excellent treatment. Just a small spot of overspray or unpainted surface, and the award can go elsewhere.

This attention to detail extends to the upholstery. Do not leave any frayed edge showing. Clean everything until it is spotless. Make all the trim fit exactly.

When working with vehicle accessories, whether in the engine compartment, passenger area, or on the exterior, make sure the accessories are harmonious. Don't add something just for the sake of the addition. For example, if braided stainless plumbing is used in the engine compartment, it probably should be used for everything. This keeps the theme constant. At the same time, try to keep everything uncluttered. Don't overdo, and don't underdo. Keep in mind that it is very possible to create beyond the experience of the judges (although this is highly unlikely at the better shows). For instance, a super high-tech machine may be so understated that the judges fail to see that the degree of difficulty in making something "trick" far exceeds the norm.

Paying attention to detail extends even to the nuts and bolts. In an area where there is a line of screw heads, take the time to index the screw head slots. That is, make them all line up. It is a little thing, but doing it pays dividends.

Also pay strict attention to the vehicle class rules. This is another excellent reason for joining ISCA and using their rule book as a building guide. If your particular class is allowed a set number of modifications, then if you do even a small modification extra, you can be in another classification. This might be something as innocent as filling a body seam with sealer. Incidentally, seams should always receive attention. After the body has been prepared for paint, but before paint is added, always clean out the seams and recaulk. One trick of the trade is to caulk a seam, then run a knife blade or hacksaw blade down the seam. This smooths the area and still makes it look like it is factory original. While paying attention to class rules, it is generally necessary to build to the maximum of the rules if the vehicle is to be a serious competitor. If five modifications are allowed, it may be that all five are necessary to win. Generally, though, the biggest temptation to overcome is the tendency to overbuild.

Rule of thumb for all serious show builders is that the better the car (and the more well known it becomes), the more it will be picked apart by the judges. The better you are at preparing a show car, the more that is expected!

The ISCA rulebook contains a special section on how to show a vehicle for championship points. In the show circuit, there is a championship competition, a competition that can sometimes reach heroic proportions. Even so, the first-timer can (and often does) beat the seasoned expert, especially if he has a good vehicle and has followed the ISCA advice.

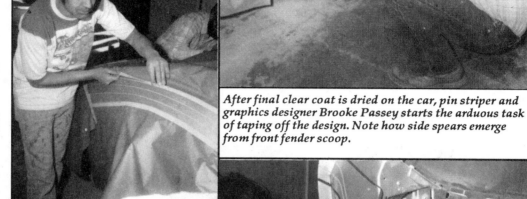
After final clear coat is dried on the car, pin striper and graphics designer Brooke Passey starts the arduous task of taping off the design. Note how side spears emerge from front fender scoop.

Brunson and Passey tape perimeter of graphics with paper. A good taping job determines how well the finished graphics will appear.

This is where attention to detail begins to show. Side graphics are carried over to the door jamb.

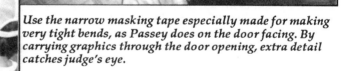
Use the narrow masking tape especially made for making very tight bends, as Passey does on the door facing. By carrying graphics through the door opening, extra detail catches judge's eye.

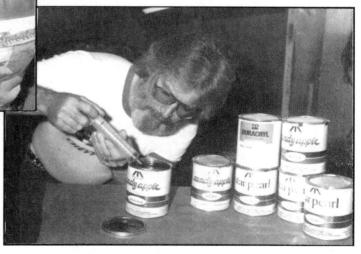
Special MetalFlake colors require absolute precision in measuring. John Moore found an animal syringe from an agriculture supply store ideal for the purpose.

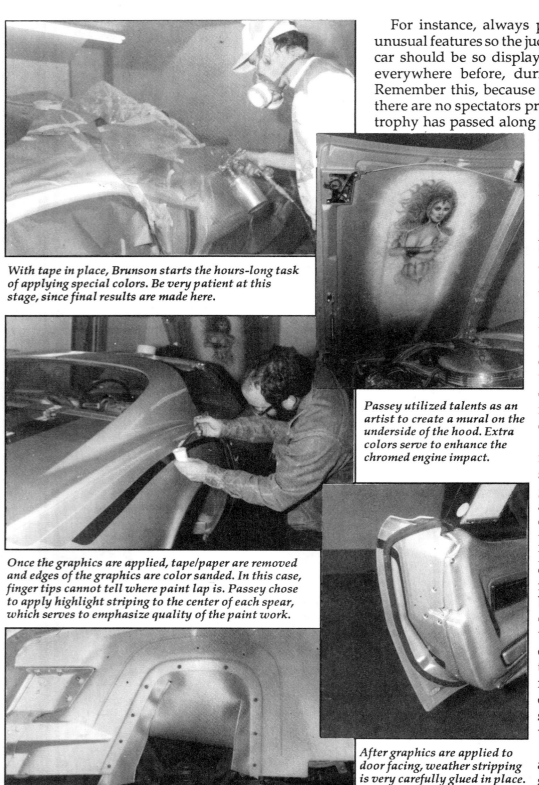

With tape in place, Brunson starts the hours-long task of applying special colors. Be very patient at this stage, since final results are made here.

Once the graphics are applied, tape/paper are removed and edges of the graphics are color sanded. In this case, finger tips cannot tell where paint lap is. Passey chose to apply highlight striping to the center of each spear, which serves to emphasize quality of the paint work.

Passey utilized talents as an artist to create a mural on the underside of the hood. Extra colors serve to enhance the chromed engine impact.

Note how frame and suspension components in another color contrast well with body colors. Even the flexible apron for upper A-arm travel is made special from silver Naugahyde. Since wheels are removed for show display, inner fender panels are also finished perfectly, then striping is added for highlights.

After graphics are applied to door facing, weather stripping is very carefully glued in place. The effect is one of maximum attention to the paint scheme.

For instance, always point out to the judges any unusual features so the judge can look at them. And the car should be so displayed that the judges can look everywhere before, during and after show hours. Remember this, because some judging is done when there are no spectators present, and many a first-place trophy has passed along because the exhibitor closed shop when the building doors were shut.

Always show the best side of the vehicle to the public, but don't try to hide any mistakes or imperfections. The judges are experienced enough to pick up on this right away. The judges give points only for what they can see, but they will deduct points for what they discover, as well. Clean the vehicle thoroughly, including the undercarriage. The exception to this would be the special Street classes, where the undercarriage is often not judged for cleanliness.

A good display is always recommended, and here is the secret to being good but not gaudy. The display draws attention to the vehicle, and can even be utilized to emphasize the vehicle's strong points. Example: Fully chromed undercarriage, so mirrors are essential. Do not build a display that overpowers and competes with the vehicle, and do not created a display that is too large for the building. When there might be concern about a display, always contact the show promoter well in advance.

Also, always enter a show as much in advance as possible. Some shows pay tow money only to the first so-many exhibitors, and in some cases the first-come best-display-spot rule applies.

Ultimately, the best advice for getting involved with building a winning show car is to enter the shows and learn the ropes. You may win the first time out, and you may not, but you will certainly know far more at the end of the show than when it began. Just beware of one thing — car shows can be habit forming!

The CLASSICS™

MOON-EYES SERIES
NEW! Ideal for the nostalgia rod! Chrome low-step bezels with mechanical pressure and temp gauges. Tach (10,000 RpM), Vacuum, Oil Temp and Amps also available. Designs are approved by Moon Equipment Company. About $295 as shown with senders!

VINTAGE SERIES™
Our most popular design series ever offered! Light-brown dial-face and red antique pointer. Available Brass or Chrome with programmable speedometer the set of five with senders is only $330 Factory Net!

NEW! FOR THE 1990's

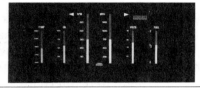

GEM★STAR™ Analog Panel
High-tech and easy to read in one beautiful panel! Requires 3⅛ x 7½" dash opening. Includes all functions pictured plus Night-Mode! About $480 plus sending units. Free descriptive brochure on request.

CLASSIC SERIES™
Our first design and we are still shipping these in record numbers! Chrome bezels, white dials, all-electric movements, programmable speedometer! The set as pictured including sending units available at most dealers for under $250.

TRADITIONAL SERIES™
Selected by more builders for Pro-Street and Resto-Rod applications. Tach, Clock, Gear Selector also available. With all required sender units, about $290 Factory Net. Also with Brass Bezels on custom order.

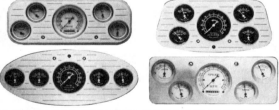

MACHINED ALUMINUM DASH INSERTS
Assembled, ready-to-install inserts for 1932 and 1940 Ford dash. Panels designed for standard 3⅜" Classic programmable speedometer and still fit the STOCK dash opening. Also shown are the 1937 Chev and 1933 Plymouth inserts. Panel with instruments, turn lights as shown plus senders, about $430.

ELÀN GT SERIES™
Use in high-performance race applications requiring 200 MpH Speedometer. Fully-adjustable speedometer and four small standard instruments with required senders, about $300. Add a 10,000 RpM Tach for only $65.

All instruments manufactured by Classic Instruments Inc. in USA and carry our exclusive Three Year Limited Warranty! The GEM★STAR Analog Panel is shipped with an 18 Month Limited Warranty.

We are low-volume, high-quality and probably the smallest instrument company you will ever deal with but you can't buy better instruments at any price! Our reputation as a leader since 1977 has depended on

our product quality, innovative designs, and customer service. Go with the BEST! Go with CLASSIC! First choice of quality car builders world-wide!

MANUFACTURED EXCLUSIVELY BY

CLASSIC INSTRUMENTS, INC

1678-P Beavercreek Road, Oregon City, Oregon 97045

TOLL FREE 1-800-828-8174
FOR ORDERS ONLY
Tech-Desk 1-503-655-3520

Full color catalog — Send $2

"Classic," Classic Series, Elàn GT Series, GEM★STAR, Traditional Series, and Vintage Series are trademarks of Classic Instruments, Inc. The Moon name and logo are registered trademarks and used by permission of Moon Equipment Company.

by Skip Readio and Dave McNurlen

Charging Systems

ALTERNATORS VS. GENERATORS

Charging systems can either be generator driven or alternator driven. There are advantages and disadvantages to each. The advantage of an alternator over a generator is that it can provide sufficient voltage to a battery even at an idle, whereas a generator must be spinning faster than it would at engine idle to produce a comparable amount of electricity. On the other hand, an alternator must have battery voltage present to operate. If the battery is dead and you were able to push start your engine to get it started spinning, the alternator still wouldn't charge the battery or provide enough electricity to fire the spark plugs. This is because without an externally applied voltage to get things going, the alternator just spins freely. Voltage must be applied to the slip rings in an alternator to produce a magnetic field in the spinning motor. This magnetic field is what will induce a current into the windings wrapped around the rotor and supply AC to the diodes. If there's no magnetic field, there's no output.

A generator, however, will start charging as soon as it's spinning fast enough. A generator needs no external voltage to get it operating.

Voltage regulators in a generator system are wired to the generator and the battery. No other wires are necessary for this charging circuit to function. Voltage regulators in alternator systems not only connect to the alternator, they also are fed by battery voltage via the ignition switch and most also employ an indicator (idiot light) as well. Without the switched power wire, the alternator cannot function.

Early GM alternator regulators are mechanical and are separate from the alternator, usually mounted on the firewall, fenderwell or radiator bulkhead in stock applications. Later model GM alternator regulators are housed right inside the alternator itself. These alternators put out more voltage than the mechanical units. This is due to the fact that these alternators are

designed to work with maintenance-free batteries which require a higher charging voltage than the older-style batteries which had to have the electrolyte topped off every once in a while. Using an older style battery with an internally regulated alternator usually results in boiling the water out of the battery faster than would be the case if an early (externally regulated) alternator were used.

EARLY GM ALTERNATORS

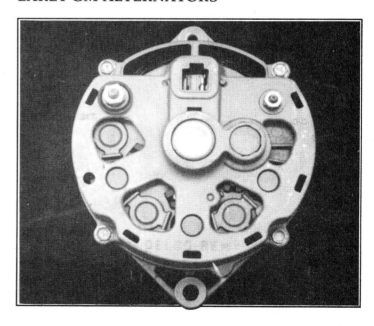

GM alternators with separate regulators can be connected in two ways. The factory configuration (with an indicator lamp) employs an external resistor (sometimes a special resistance wire instead) in parallel with the indicator lamp in the circuit. This circuit normally connects to terminal 4 on the voltage regulator. Regulator terminal 3 is connected to the ignition switch on the same terminal as that which feeds the ignition coil. Regulator terminal 2 connects to the terminal

labeled R on the alternator, and regulator terminal F connects to the terminal labeled F on the alternator. Don't forget to ground the regulator, even if you have to run a separate wire all the way back to the motor from the floor of your hot rod.

The alternative method for wiring an external GM regulator is to connect both terminals 3 and 4 to the same wire from the ignition switch and eliminate the indicator lamp (idiot light), and use an ammeter or a voltmeter instead to monitor the condition of the charging system. Connect the output lead of the alternator to the (+) terminal on your ammeter with a length of 10-gauge wire. With another length of 10-gauge wire, connect the (-) terminal of your ammeter to the same post on the starter solenoid that your battery cable is connected to.

LATE GM ALTERNATORS

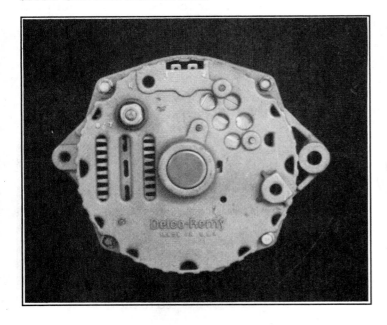

When using an internally regulated GM alternator,

you need only run one wire to the regulator to energize it. This wire, like the other alternator/regulator systems must come from the ignition switch. However, if you physically connect it to the same lead as your ignition coil, the car will not shut off once it has been started. There is another terminal on the regulator, but it is hooked to the alternator output on a long wire in GM factory configurations. In a street rod, it can be jumpered back to the output with a short length of 14-gauge wire. This terminal will be the one farthest away from the

alternator output stud.

The regulator energizing wire that runs back to the ignition switch goes to a terminal marked IGN 3. This terminal is in the lower corner of the GM column-mounted ignition switch in the smaller of the two plugs. The terminal is on the opposite end and opposite side from the coil lead on the IGN switch. The other two wires in this plug are for the key buzzer.

If you don't have a GM column, you can go out and get a replacement ignition switch for an older Corvette at an auto parts store. The '57 Corvette ignition switches have two leads that are live only when the switch is in the run position, yet are separated when the switch is turned off.

You don't want to hook this wire to the ACC position because operating the radio while the motor isn't running will drain the battery as the alternator is also being biased at the same time.

You can run the alternator's regulator-energizing wire off the same ignition switch post as your coil if you put an idiot light in series with the switch and regulator. You will need a lamp socket with two insulated connectors. Neither of the wires on the lamp socket can be connected to chassis ground. To wire the idiot light, connect a length of 14-gauge wire from the IGN post to the base of the idiot light. Connect another length of 14-gauge wire to the internal voltage regulator.

THE LATEST GM ALTERNATOR

GM has a new, smaller alternator that has been in use for the last few years. It's called the CS series and has between 80 to 120 amps of output, depending upon the model. The mounting system is close enough to the '70 and '80s style alternators that the earlier mounts will work with the new style alternators, and the pulley shaft size is the same as before. With their greater amperage output and small size, these units are ideal for rods with electric cooling fans and powerful stereo systems.

The alternator pictured here came from an '87 Olds Calais with a 2.5 liter 4-cylinder engine, and it has a 100 amp output. The alternator harness came from the same model car. Most GM models newer than '87 use this style alternator, and amperage output is clearly stamped on the case.

Hooking it up is easy if you've got the plug-in connector. Most dealers don't stock connector plugs, though some may have the "metri-pack" type terminals for the plug. A connector plug and terminal kit is available from Dr. K's for $7.50. When getting a plug at a wrecking yard, try to get as much of the wire harness as possible. This makes splicing much easier.

The best place to get an alternator is at your local GM dealer, or look in the phone book under "Automobile Electrical Service" for Delco distributors. It might be a good idea to know the model and year of the car the alternator originally came on so the counterperson will have a starting point.

Used alternators are cheaper, but don't buy one expecting to overhaul it because you can't. These things are put together to be replaced as a unit, and even under new car warranty they're replaced as an assembly. Only a minimum of disassembly should be attempted, such as swapping the drive belt pulley or reindexing the front half of the case for better connector plug alignment.

When connecting the alternator to the vehicle, you have a choice to make that depends on if a voltmeter, an idiot light, or neither of these is used. The main "Bat" terminal on the alternator connects to the main starter post, or the positive battery terminal, whichever is closer. That's the easy part. On the four-wire connector plug, three of the connector labels match the connector labels on the alternator plug-in (S, L, and P). On the last one, they got tricky and labeled the plug F, while the plug-in on the alternator is labeled I. That will be referred to as the I/F terminal.

The I/F terminal (I on the alternator, F on the plug) is hooked to an "ignition on" circuit in the car to start it charging. If an idiot light is used, hook the "ignition on" feed to the lamp (in series), and run that to the L terminal in the alternator plug. If the L terminal is used, be careful that a bulb is in the circuit, as the regulator will probably fry if the power is hooked directly there. The I/F circuit is designed for direct power, but the L circuit is not.

Some GM factory harnesses had connectors in both the I/F and L circuits so the engine harness would fit more cars. So, if you're using one of those harnesses to hook up the alternator, the one you don't use can be eliminated. The S terminal can be connected to the same spot as the "Bat" wire. This lead tells the alternator how much amperage it needs to put out in order to keep up with demand. If your used harness doesn't use it, that's okay; there's also a part of the regulator that can do that job on its own.

This leaves the P terminal, but it isn't used by any GM car at this time. Shop manuals and other information say it's for a tachometer output signal, with no other information on calibration or signal output.

So, basically, if you want to slap one of these CS series alternators on your rod, bolt it up to your old bracket, hook the I/F circuit to an "ignition on" fuse or the L circuit to an idiot light, the "Bat" terminal to the battery or starter post, and hit the road.

Voltage Regulators

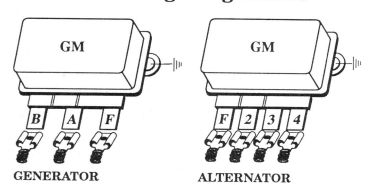

GENERATOR   ALTERNATOR

Starters & Relays

Wiring Schematic For GM "CS" Series Alternators

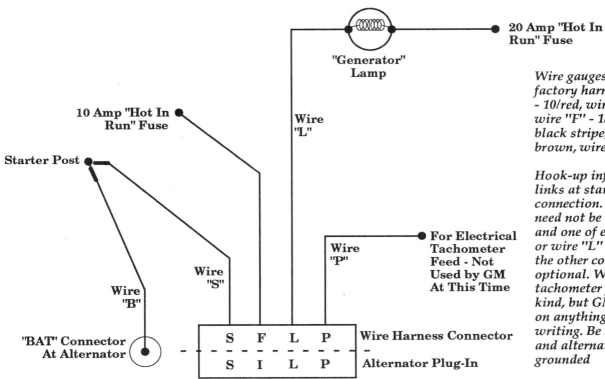

"Generator" Lamp

20 Amp "Hot In Run" Fuse

10 Amp "Hot In Run" Fuse

Wire "L"

Starter Post

Wire "S"

Wire "B"

Wire "P"

For Electrical Tachometer Feed - Not Used by GM At This Time

"BAT" Connector At Alternator

S	F	L	P	Wire Harness Connector
S	I	L	P	Alternator Plug-In

Wire gauges, and colors of factory harnesses: wire "B" - 10/red, wire "S" - 12/red, wire "F" - 18/pink with black stripe, wire "L - 18/ brown, wire "P" - not used.

Hook-up info: use fusible links at starter post connection. All connections need not be used: wire "B", and one of either wire "F", or wire "L" must be used; the other connections are optional. Wire "P" is a tachometer feed of some kind, but GM hasn't used it on anything as of this writing. Be sure the engine and alternator are solidly grounded

Notice the difference in size between the late GM (left) and CS Series GM alternator (right). Compact size and high output are two of the advantages of the newer style alternator.

Amperage rating is stamped into the front of the case. Here, 100A is equal to 100 amps of output.

Even though the drive pulleys are different, the shaft size is the same for both the late GM and the CS Series alternators.

This is the harness plug for the alternator. The hold-in clip is on the other side. Note the S, F, L, and P stamped in the plug.

Three bolts hold the front and back halves of the alternator case together. If you must rotate the housing to get the alignment you need, pull only the front half loose. Don't pull the rotor out of the back half of the case.

The CS Series alternator installed. Note the ground wire from the alternator case to the frame. This eliminates any chance of a bad ground later.

Installation of Kill Switch in Starter Circuit

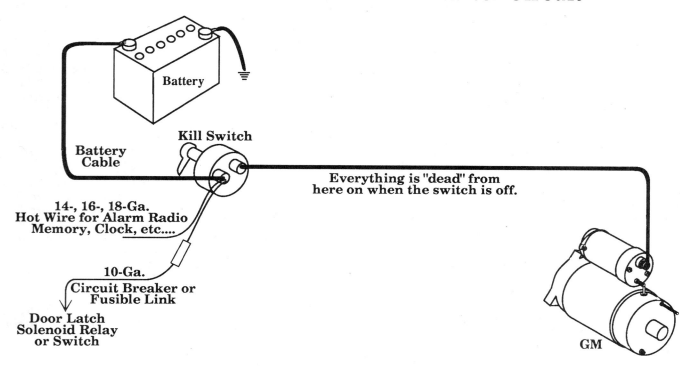

Battery

Kill Switch

Battery Cable

Everything is "dead" from here on when the switch is off.

14-, 16-, 18-Ga.
Hot Wire for Alarm Radio Memory, Clock, etc....

10-Ga.
Circuit Breaker or Fusible Link

Door Latch
Solenoid Relay
or Switch

GM

Kill Switch with Terminal Strip

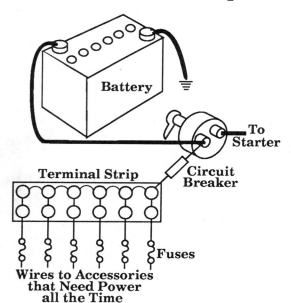

Battery

To Starter

Terminal Strip

Circuit Breaker

Fuses

Wires to Accessories that Need Power all the Time

Kill Switch without Terminal Strip

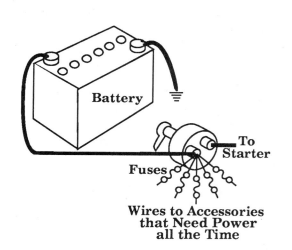

Battery

To Starter

Fuses

Wires to Accessories that Need Power all the Time

GM Headlight Switch

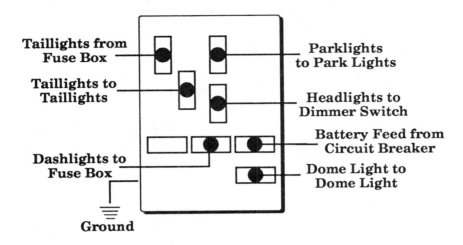

Taillights from Fuse Box

Taillights to Taillights

Dashlights to Fuse Box

Ground

Parklights to Park Lights

Headlights to Dimmer Switch

Battery Feed from Circuit Breaker

Dome Light to Dome Light

GM Headlight Switch Wiring

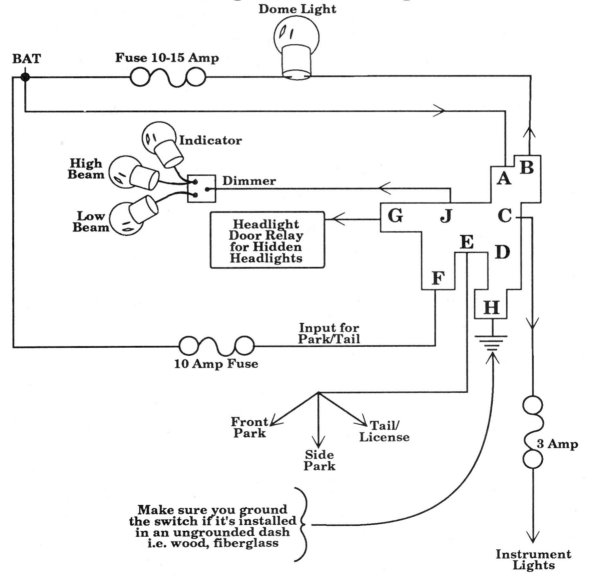

Dome Light

BAT

Fuse 10-15 Amp

Indicator

High Beam

Low Beam

Dimmer

Headlight Door Relay for Hidden Headlights

A B

G J

C

E D

F

H

Input for Park/Tail

10 Amp Fuse

Front Park

Side Park

Tail/License

3 Amp

Make sure you ground the switch if it's installed in an ungrounded dash i.e. wood, fiberglass

Instrument Lights

GM Turn Signal Plug

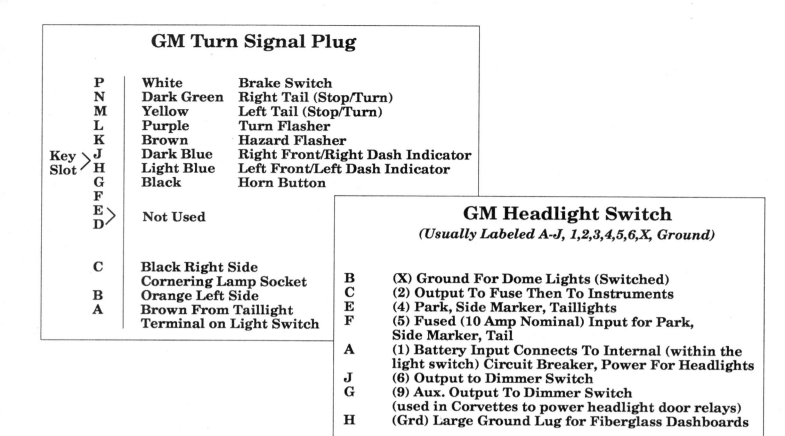

P	White	Brake Switch
N	Dark Green	Right Tail (Stop/Turn)
M	Yellow	Left Tail (Stop/Turn)
L	Purple	Turn Flasher
K	Brown	Hazard Flasher
J	Dark Blue	Right Front/Right Dash Indicator
H	Light Blue	Left Front/Left Dash Indicator
G	Black	Horn Button
F		
E	Not Used	
D		
C	Black Right Side Cornering Lamp Socket	
B	Orange Left Side	
A	Brown From Taillight Terminal on Light Switch	

Key Slot > J, H

GM Headlight Switch
(Usually Labeled A-J, 1,2,3,4,5,6,X, Ground)

B	(X) Ground For Dome Lights (Switched)
C	(2) Output To Fuse Then To Instruments
E	(4) Park, Side Marker, Taillights
F	(5) Fused (10 Amp Nominal) Input for Park, Side Marker, Tail
A	(1) Battery Input Connects To Internal (within the light switch) Circuit Breaker, Power For Headlights
J	(6) Output to Dimmer Switch
G	(9) Aux. Output To Dimmer Switch (used in Corvettes to power headlight door relays)
H	(Grd) Large Ground Lug for Fiberglass Dashboards

GM Air Conditioner Relay

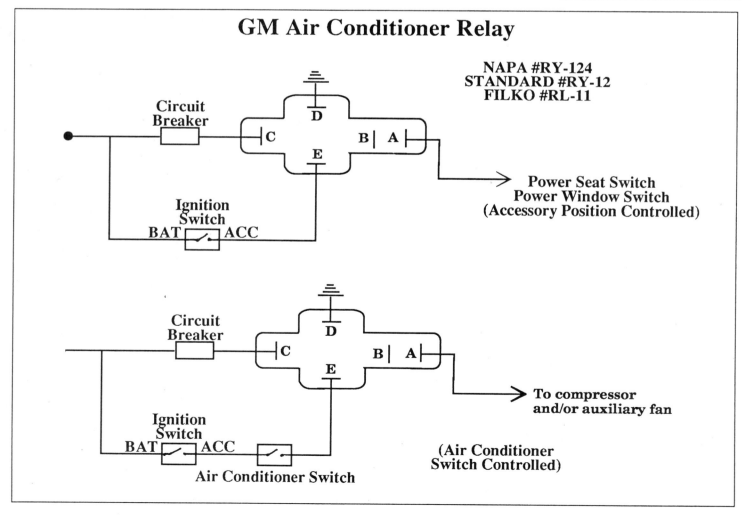

NAPA #RY-124
STANDARD #RY-12
FILKO #RL-11

Power Seat Switch
Power Window Switch
(Accessory Position Controlled)

To compressor
and/or auxiliary fan

(Air Conditioner
Switch Controlled)

GM Single Wire Alternator

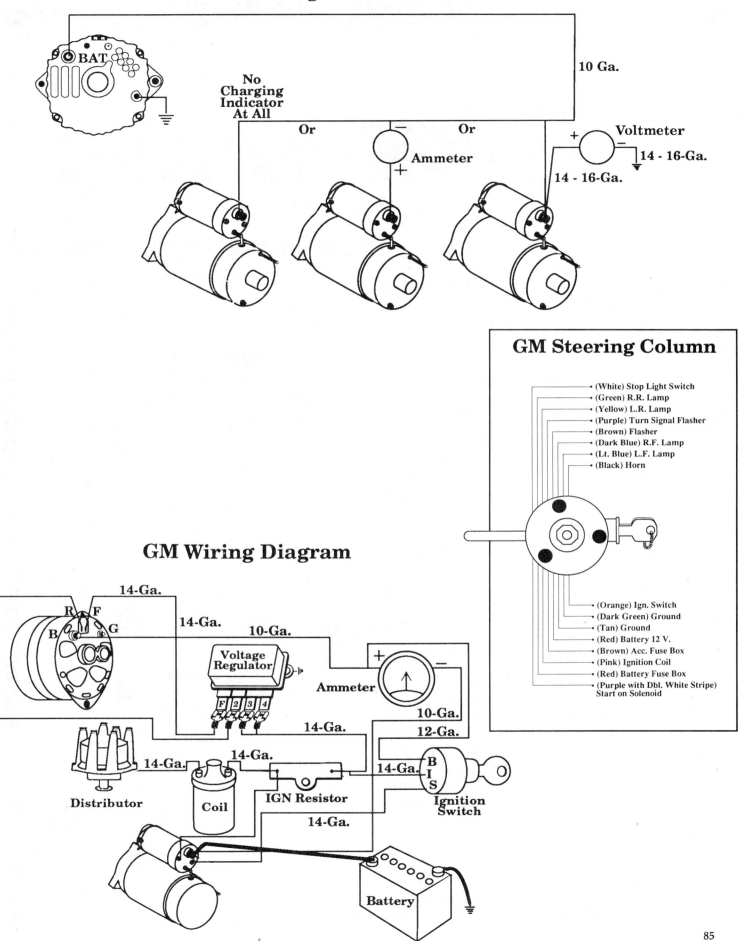

BAT

No Charging Indicator At All

Or

Ammeter − +

Or

+ Voltmeter −

10 Ga.

14 - 16-Ga.

14 - 16-Ga.

GM Steering Column

- (White) Stop Light Switch
- (Green) R.R. Lamp
- (Yellow) L.R. Lamp
- (Purple) Turn Signal Flasher
- (Brown) Flasher
- (Dark Blue) R.F. Lamp
- (Lt. Blue) L.F. Lamp
- (Black) Horn

- (Orange) Ign. Switch
- (Dark Green) Ground
- (Tan) Ground
- (Red) Battery 12 V.
- (Brown) Acc. Fuse Box
- (Pink) Ignition Coil
- (Red) Battery Fuse Box
- (Purple with Dbl. White Stripe) Start on Solenoid

GM Wiring Diagram

14-Ga.

R F
B   G

14-Ga.

14-Ga.

10-Ga.

Voltage Regulator

F 2 3 4

Ammeter

10-Ga.

14-Ga.

12-Ga.

14-Ga.

14-Ga.

Distributor

Coil

IGN Resistor

14-Ga.

B I S

Ignition Switch

14-Ga.

Battery

by Jack Chisenhall

Air Conditioning

Keeping Your Cool

As Pete Chapouris once said, "To be cool, you gotta stay cool." As long as our surroundings are somewhere between 70 and 80 degrees Fahrenheit, most of us feel comfortable (that's cool). Below 70 degrees most of us feel cold, above 80 degrees most of us feel hot (and that's not cool). Air conditioning is one way to keep our immediate surroundings within man's comfort zone.

In order to properly select air conditioning system components, it is helpful to understand a few of the basics of how the system works. We aren't going to discuss air conditioner theory in-depth here, but the following three basic laws of nature are used in an automotive air conditioning system to make it all work. 1. Heat Transfer, 2. Vaporization, and 3. Pressure's effect on vaporization. We'll define each one individually.

1. Heat transfer - Differing temperatures always try to equalize. Heat always travels to cold. The greater the difference in the temperatures, the faster it travels.

2. Vaporization - Heat is released by condensation, and heat is absorbed by evaporation.

3. Pressure's effect on vaporization - Increasing pressure on a liquid raises the boiling point.

These three laws of physics work together in an air conditioning system to remove heat from the passenger compartment and transfer it to the outside. The liquid refrigerant (R-12) is contained in a closed system that has two different pressure areas in it. By moving the refrigerant from the high-pressure side of the system to the low-pressure side, its state is changed from a liquid to a gas. When it changes its state, it absorbs and gives off great amounts of heat, and the various system components transfer the heat to the outside of the vehicle.

Some important safety precautions must be followed when working around R-12 refrigerant. Because R-12 boils at minus 21.7 degrees Fahrenheit, it is cold enough to cause severe frostbite. Always wear goggles to protect the eyes and gloves to protect the hands. Also, be sure to never expose a can of R-12 to direct sunlight.

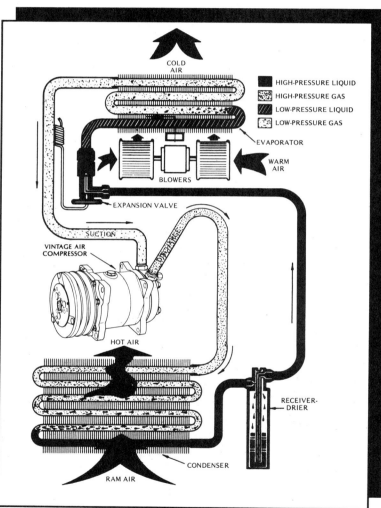

This schematic illustrates how the refrigerant travels through a typical air conditioner system.

Even under the pressures normally found in R-12 containers, if heat is added, the refrigerant will boil. This could raise the pressure inside the can to a dangerous level. One last caution — when R-12 is exposed to an open flame or to hot metal, poisonous gas called phosgene is formed. You don't want any of that stuff around — it was used as nerve gas in World War I.

Air conditioning refrigerant travels through the system of components that consist of the compressor, evaporator, condenser, receiver/drier and the various hoses and fittings. These components provide a system where the R-12 can evaporate and condense to remove heat from the inside of the car and give it off to the outside air stream.

As we discuss the components, keep in mind that all automotive air conditioners work basically the same way. Three distinct types of systems are in common use now. The difference is in the control of the flow of the refrigerant. One type is a cycling clutch expansion valve system (CCEV). The second is a cycling clutch fixed orifice system (CCOT). The third is the pressure regulating expansion valve system.

The first two types (CCEV and CCOT) control the temperature by cycling the compressor to stop refrigerant flow and avoid freezing of the evaporator. The third type controls the pressure with the evaporator, thus controlling its temperature and avoiding freeze-up.

Aftermarket manufacturers use the CCEV system with rare exceptions, primarily because it remains the most efficient in operation and works well with the type of evaporator coils that are popularly used.

The CCOT system is rapidly becoming the most common original equipment (Ford and GM) type system. It is inexpensive to produce, its fixed-orifice metering device is molded plastic with no moving parts, compared to the expansion valve's relatively costly construction. The CCOT system floods the evaporator with refrigerant because it does not meter according to evaporator demands. This flooded condition requires an accumulator to prevent unused liquid refrigerant from returning to the compressor, and uses increased horsepower to drive the system. Head pressure is higher as a result of this flooded evaporator condition.

The CCEV system is the most common in hot rods and will likely remain so for a while.

CONDENSER

The condenser is the most misunderstood, mismatched and misplaced component in street rod air conditioning. Space, air-flow and air temperature will affect condenser selection. As a general rule of thumb regarding two-row 5/16" or 3/8" copper tube and aluminum fin condensers, surface area should be a minimum of 210 square inches. These condensers are

normally 1.25" thick, giving about 262 cubic inches of mass. This basic minimum assumes a few other variables.

1. Ten or twelve fins per inch is ideal for street rods, letting enough air-flow through the condenser.

2. Air-flow should be good at low driving speeds (approximately 1500 to 2000 cfm).

3. The evaporator is about 210 cubic inches of mass. The condenser should be about 20 percent greater in mass than the evaporator. Again, this is a rule of thumb with many variables.

4. The condenser should be mounted so that the tubes run horizontally. If not, the oil that flows with the

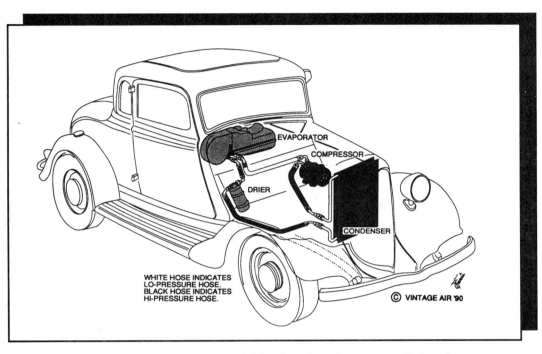

In most cases, the components look like this when they are installed in the car.

refrigerant will settle in the loops at the bottom of the coil. This restriction will cause a corresponding rise in system pressure and refrigerant temperature, reducing the ability of the condenser to dissipate heat.

5. Compressor size is approximately nine cubic inches per revolution. This has proven more than adequate for any single-evaporator hot rod. I would always lean toward a smaller compressor than a larger one. In the average street rod, if you have a special or larger-than-typical application and want to increase the refrigerant capacity, increase condenser size not compressor size.

The temperature of the air flowing across the condenser should be 100 degrees Fahrenheit or less. The greater the difference between the air and refrigerant temperatures, the greater the heat transfer. That the air temperature is below 100 degrees Fahrenheit is more critical to your condenser than your engine radiator because refrigerant boils at a much lower temperature than water (coolant), and begins expanding and creating pressure at a very rapid rate above 100 degrees F.

The condenser should always be mounted in front of the radiator. Here it uses less plumbing, takes advantage of the engine fan, and is in the best place for the highway air stream which is the coolest air available. If you use two condensers to do the job, the last one in the series should be in the coolest air stream. Leave 1/8" to 1/2" distance between the radiator and the condenser. That's enough to prevent metal-to-metal heat transfer, but close enough to ensure air-flow. Condensers can be mounted anywhere, but ignoring the basics will leave you with a system you cannot use.

Condenser construction falls into two basic types.

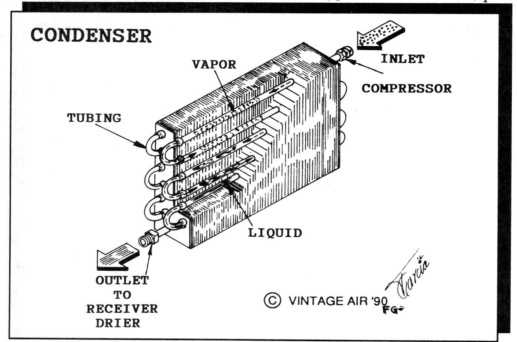

Vaporous refrigerant condenses as it is cooled by the air passing over the condenser. The condensing refrigerant gives off heat that was absorbed when the refrigerant evaporated inside the passenger compartment evaporator.

They are either serpentine — a continuous flat tube with multiple passages that run back and forth with fin material between the tubes to form a flat slab (serpentine condensers are generally extruded aluminum with fittings welded on each end of the tube); or they are "tube and fin" type — round tubes (usually copper) running back and forth through flat fins (often aluminum) to form a flat slab. I generally prefer copper-tube-and-aluminum-fin condensers for street rods because they are easily modified with a torch and silver solder.

A larger condenser is almost always better. We are trying to remove heat. Heat and pressure within the A/C system are directly related. The more heat we remove, the lower the pressure within the high side of the air conditioner, and the better we've done the job. This lower pressure/temperature also requires less horsepower to turn the compressor and causes less vibration, which is the most common cause of compressor mounting bracket breakage.

COMPRESSOR

The compressor must be sized right for the system, and it is important that it looks good under the hood of a street rod. We have found that in a typical rod (with at least a basic minimum condenser and a typical evaporator of about 220 cubic inch mass) an 8.5- to 9-cubic inch per revolution compressor capacity is ideal. If you are short on condenser and cannot simply increase its size, you might opt for less compressor capacity. Generally speaking, if the compressor is oversized in relation to the condenser, it will create excess pressure and heat, placing extra load on the engine and leading to premature compressor and mount failure. Lack of compressor capacity will normally result in reduced performance, but you would probably only notice it at a stoplight or in traffic. This might be a blessing, however, as you would also be adding less heat to the radiator. So, if it sounds like I'm saying to downsize the compressor, maybe I am.

The York/Techumseh-style compressor was once the most common, but the Sanden (previously Sankyo) has closed the gap with its more contemporary radial design. The Sanden/Sankyo compressor is about five inches around with a length of 8-1/2 inches for the 508 model and 6-3/4 inches on the 505 model. Model 708 is a seven-cylinder unit totaling eight cubic inches per revolution, and it weighs 18 percent less than its predecessor 508 (which has five cylinders and eight cubic inches per revolution). More cylinders means greater smoothness while increasing volumetric efficiency by seven to ten percent at 800 RPM. Many other radial designs are available including Frigidaire, Nippondenso, and Diesel Kieki (licensed by York in the U.S.). Let's take a look at each.

Frigidaire — The time-honored A-6 is a real dinosaur. Steer clear unless you are building a limousine with room for a dinosaur under the hood. Its 12+ cubic inches per revolution is more compressor than you would normally need or want! The R-4 is the short, fat compressor found on the later '70s and early '80s GM cars. It has 10 cubic inch per revolution displacement via four cylinders radiating from its crankshaft. Smaller and lighter than the A-6, it is still larger than I like in capacity for a street rod.

Diesel Kieki — This is a clone of the Sanden/Sankyo and will mount with commonly available brackets. However, I have found that they are not nearly as durable as the slightly more expensive Sanden.

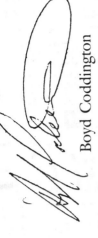

Nippondenso — This compressor is original equipment on the new Ford and Chrysler cars. Many versions exist and most are sized at just over nine cubic inches per revolution. The fittings connect in the middle of the compressor, making it difficult to fit a pleasing hose arrangement. Although these compressors have a little more capacity than I would want on most '28-'32 street rods, they may be well suited for later cars with larger condenser area and cabs. Brackets, however, are limited to original equipment. York/ Techumseh — Radial compressors should be, in my opinion, the only style compressor you consider. The old style York/ Techumseh reciprocating two-cylinder compressor is simply outdated and no bargain at any cost. It can be identified by its square shape, closely resembling a lawn mower engine. Its displacement is on a plate riveted to the front of the compressor in a space marked "Pt" or "Part" and it will say something like R-209. The 209 tells us it is a two-cylinder compressor with nine cubic inches of displacement per revolution. The three compressors in this line are the 210 (10.3 cubic inches), 209 (8.7 cubic inches), and the 206 (6.11 cubic inches).

The major drawback of a reciprocating compressor is that, because it has only two cylinders, the peak torque loads are very high on each stroke, causing excessive vibration. This makes for lots of noise, broken parts and drivebelt flop.

Another consideration for compressor selection is the way it fits into the available space and how it mounts to the engine.

COMPRESSOR BRACKETS

Brackets that will fit most street rods are available for both the York and Sanden type compressors. The radial compressors are easiest to mount because of their alternator-style construction. They do not shake as much, so they require less bracketry as well. Generally, building brackets for air conditioning compressors follows the same principles as any other steel bracket design and fabrication — the simpler the better. A few things,

however, are peculiar to this type of bracket.

You must have a way to adjust the tension of the driving belt. Sliding the compressor, or using an idler pulley mounted on an adjacent eccentric are the simplest methods. I don't like to use idler pulleys because they wear out rapidly and are excess hardware. If you do elect to use an idler pulley, however, (and sometimes you must), try to put it on the slack run of the driving belt. A driving belt always has a tight side and a slack side. By doing this, you increase the bearing life of the idler by putting less load on it, and reduce belt flop which is always greatest on the slack side. You should also make sure you have enough belt contacting all driving or driven pulleys. This area of contact should be no less than 33 percent of the pulley's circumference.

Brackets are commercially available for most common applications like small-block Chevy, Ford and Chrysler engines. If you need special brackets, universal mounting plates are available for building your own for both York/ Techumseh and Sanden compressors.

HOSE AND FITTINGS

Hose and fittings are most commonly used to plumb an air conditioning system. Because of the exacting duties that mobile fluid lines and fittings have to perform, a few industrial groups have set some standards. The three that apply here are Society of Automotive Engineers (SAE), Joint Industrial Council (JIC), and International Mobile Air Conditioning Assn., Inc. (IMACA). Automotive tubing and fittings are built to SAE specifications. Within the aircraft industry, manufacturers adhere to JIC specs. The aircraft parts would not apply to us except that someone decided a long time ago that it was neat to use airplane parts on a hot rod. Many of us do just that, so a little knowledge of these parts can't hurt, especially if you might be trying to mix JIC parts with SAE components. The IMACA standards that apply are the test standards that the parts should meet.

The condenser is usually placed in front of the radiator because this is the area with the greatest amount of cool air flow. Mounting the condenser on most hot rods requires locating mounting surfaces, drilling and attaching the condenser. Brackets are usually furnished when you buy the condenser.

SAE/IMACA Hose and Fittings — Automotive fitting manufacturers make an incredible number of different fittings for almost any situation. Knowing where to find that fitting is the trick. The simplest way to plumb your street rod air conditioner is to use these fittings, available at auto air conditioning supply outlets.

Vintage Air {10305 IH 35 N, San Antonio, Texas 78233; (512) 654-7171} has come up with a line system of stainless steel tubing and SAE/neoprene O-ring fittings that will complement the best-detailed car. A small amount of flexible refrigerant line isolates the engine's movement.

AN/JIC stainless braided line and fittings — This type of hose and fittings has found fairly widespread use on street rods. It is visually appealing, however these fittings can be a real pain when it comes to making them work. JIC flare fittings have 37-degree seats, while automotive air conditioning components are designed with 45-degree SAE seats on their fittings. When you place a 37-degree flare fitting on a 45-degree seat, it cuts a ridge in it. This may seal well once, or even a few times, but eventually the seat will be rendered defective. But that isn't the real problem. The problem is really in the hose and its connection to the fitting. This hose is designed for hydraulics, not refrigerant-12. The manufacturers' engineers flatly state that the Teflon or neoprene hose liners will not contain R-12. Further, the connection between the hose and the fitting is not suitable for containing R-12. Nonetheless, street rodders continue to use it. Just be aware of what goes with the territory.

DO'S AND DON'TS OF A/C PLUMBING

DO push the hose all the way on the barb of a fitting.

DO use rubber hose inside the cab on the suction line, or wrap any metal line or fittings inside the cab of your street rod with insulating tape.

DO try to tie the suction line (cold line from the evaporator to the compressor) to the liquid line (from the condenser to the drier then evaporator) so that heat transfer takes place from the hot liquid line to the cold suction line. This helps further remove BTUs from the liquid refrigerant and further vaporize the refrigerant going back to the compressor. Compressors are designed to pump vapors only; liquid droplets are hard on the delicate reed valves that separate the high side and the low side.

DO NOT allow the hose to rub against sharp points.

· DO NOT allow the discharge line (from the compressor into the condenser) to contact the liquid line (from the condenser to the drier and then evaporator).

DRIER

Moisture must be removed effectively from your street rod air conditioner. This is the greatest problem in any refrigeration system. Moisture combines with the metals in the system to produce oxides, primarily iron hydroxide and aluminum hydroxide. It also combines with R-12 to produce acids, notable carbonic acid, hydrochloric acid and hydrofluoric acid. These acids attack the base metals within the system, producing a substance like a combination of dust and sand.

The drying function of the receiver/drier is a simple process. The drying agent (desiccant) is held inside a felt bag placed within the receiver tank. When the refrigerant flows across and through the desiccant, moisture is captured.

The drier also acts as a surge tank to take the sudden surges when the engine accelerates quickly. This keeps the pressures throughout the system fairly constant.

The sight glass is a window to the refrigerant leaving the drier. Pure liquid refrigerant is clear. When there is

The Sanden compressor is compact, smooth and attractive. The compactness of a Sanden unit makes it easy to install in a cramped engine compartment. The small 505 unit is available for very crowded compartments.

no liquid seal in the bottom of the receiver tank, the refrigerant will draw gas bubbles into it. These will make the refrigerant foamy. Discoloration means a contaminated system. This is a guide only. If you are not sure, ask a qualified A/C technician.

DO mount the drier according to the manufacturer's specifications to ensure a liquid seal.

DO mount the drier in the coolest spot you can — in

the air stream if possible.

DO install the drier where you can see the sight glass.

DO replace the filter/drier any time the receiver is exposed to the atmosphere for any period of time, or whenever you perform any maintenance on the system.

DON'T neglect drier maintenance.

DON'T allow excessive heat around the drier.

DON'T lay a vertical-style drier on its side.

EVAPORATOR

From the drier, the refrigerant travels to the coolest component in the system — the evaporator. This is the part that draws air in the cabin, circulates it through the evaporator coil to remove heat and moisture, then returns it to the cab as cool, dry air. A typical evaporator has a coil, an expansion valve, a housing, a blower and air outlets.

When selecting an evaporator, the two considerations have to be: 1. Will it fit in the car, and 2. Will it cool the car adequately? Choosing the appearance you want, there are two basic choices: under-dash and in-dash units.

Under-dash units work well in some applications. The contemporary under-dash unit is the slim-line type. Its stylized design has a long, thin front bezel containing multiple air outlets. The direct air delivery of this type unit is very effective and it does not interfere with glove box, radio or other in-dash accessories.

With an in-dash unit, the big questions are, 1. Will it fit in the dash, and 2. What will you have to give up to get it there? In-dash units with molded ducts from the evaporator coil are found in the higher-performance applications such as vans and better-quality aftermarket manufacturers. This allows direct, large volume air delivery from a concealed unit.

Selecting an evaporator involves consideration of the size you are trying to cool. If you have a coupe, you can obviously use a smaller unit, a sedan would require more capacity, and so on.

Fitting the unit to your car can be very critical if you are ordering by mail or fitting a non-standard vehicle. The best way is to start by looking at the space behind the dash and trying to make a rough sketch of the area between the firewall and the dash and then over to the kickpanel. Note radios, instruments and other difficult-to-remove items. When talking with the supplier, specify the type of car you have and its body style. If the car has been altered in the firewall or dash area, say so. If he isn't familiar with the space available, get any descriptive literature he may have. Measurements would make it simple. If you can tell him the dimensions behind the dash from your drawings, chances are he can recommend a unit that will fit and cool the car. Plan ahead, it takes a lot of the work out of it. Rewiring a car

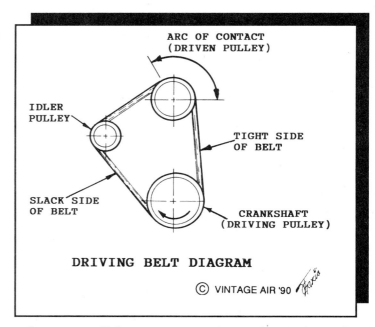

DRIVING BELT DIAGRAM

© VINTAGE AIR '90

When you install the compressor, make sure that the drive belt makes contact on at least 33% of all driving pulleys. The drive belt has a tight side and a slack side. If you want to use an idler pulley to adjust belt tension, put it near the center of the slack side of the belt.

or moving a radio can be tough and might make you settle for less than you want.

Selecting a unit that is capable of cooling your car can be tricky. Capacity ratings are a lot like EPA gas mileage ratings, except they can be even more deceptive. You must be sure the manufacturer is actually rating the output of the unit, not just giving a theoretical coil output. Ask local street parts dealers or builders. They are pros and usually have experience with street rod components.

A few of the factors that contribute to evaporator performance are air delivery, coil capacity, blower assembly, and case design. The under-dash unit is effective because of its direct air delivery from the coil. When a unit is concealed behind the dash, the air has to find its way out. The simplest and most common way is to run flexible duct hose to dash-mounted vents. Unfortunately, flexible ducting limits the air delivery of any unit because the convoluted wall in the flexhose surface creates turbulence within the hose. Molded ducts are always more effective and produce much quieter air delivery. The difference shows up when you move back from the vent. Flexhose displays a rapid drop-off of air flow, whereas smooth molded duct will produce greater velocity for an extended distance from the vents.

Coil capacity is determined by a number of factors, including coil mass, fins per inch, circuit design, the number of circuit passes. Most in-dash evaporator coils are between 190 and 240 cubic inches and contain between 20 and 60 circuits. Rated capacity of an automotive evaporator coil is based on IMACA Standard 20 and is much more complicated than any one or two factors.

The last major component affecting evaporator capacity is the blower motor and wheel. There is no way for you to check the capacity of the blower assembly, but a few generalities can be stated.

1. The larger, single-blower-wheel assemblies are by far the most advanced today.

2. The larger wheels operate with lower blade tip speeds, making them quieter.

3. The old-style, double-shaft motor and blowers should be avoided. They were not designed for in-dash air conditioners and are very ineffective in conditions when air is being ducted to vents.

OUTSIDE FACTORS

The evaporator removes heat from the interior of the car, but it's just as important to keep additional heat out. A number of things can be done to keep heat from getting inside the car in the first place. Seal all holes in the car. Make sure the floorboards and covers are screwed down tight. Seal all cracks in the car with silicone sealant. Insulate the car thoroughly. Finally, tint the windows (check your local laws regarding the darkness of tint allowed).

When outside air comes into the car, it brings moisture with it, which takes a great amount of energy to remove through the air conditioner. Not only does it make it harder to cool the car, the moisture accumulates on anything cold, creating water problems.

Generally speaking, street rods are not yet up to speed when it comes to sealing and insulating. Many builders are using the wrong kinds of insulation and most street rods aren't sealed adequately at the floorboards and doors.

Two other groups of accessories deserve mention before we wrap this chapter up. They are pressure and safety switches. A high- head-pressure safety switch cuts the compressor off when the internal pressure is excessive. When the pressure drops to an acceptable level, the switch engages the compressor. The high-pressure fan switch turns an electric fan on when the head pressure rises, and turns it off when the fan removes enough heat to lower the pressure to the minimum pressure level. Finally, the low-pressure safety switch is a safety switch that protects the compressor if R-12 loss occurs.

Cool you should be if you have gotten this far. We have covered all the major components of a hot rod air conditioner system, and you should be able to select and install each in an intelligent way.

This drier is installed properly on the firewall. It is best to install the drier in the coolest spot possible.

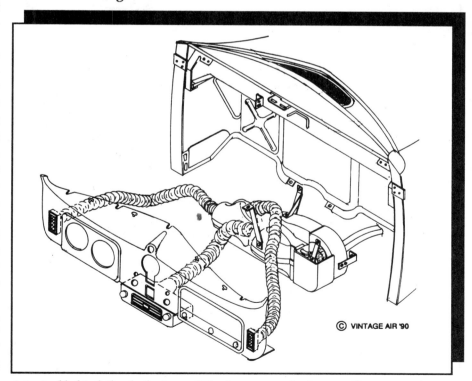

A typical behind-the-dash air conditioning evaporator has a coil, an expansion valve, and a blower housing or case. The evaporator unit fits behind the dash something like this. This under-dash unit is made to fit in a wide variety of cars with a minimum of effort.

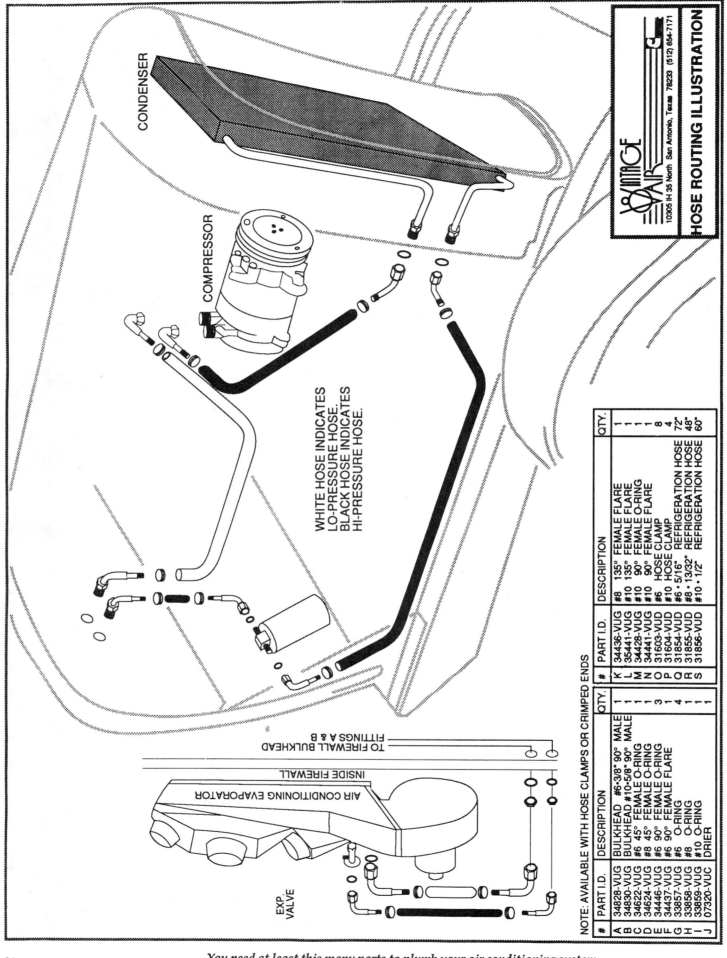

HOSE ROUTING ILLUSTRATION

10305 IH 35 North San Antonio, Texas 78233 (512) 654-7171

CONDENSER

COMPRESSOR

WHITE HOSE INDICATES LO-PREASURE HOSE. BLACK HOSE INDICATES HI-PRESSURE HOSE.

EXP. VALVE

AIR CONDITIONING EVAPORATOR

INSIDE FIREWALL

TO FIREWALL BULKHEAD FITTINGS A & B

NOTE: AVAILABLE WITH HOSE CLAMPS OR CRIMPED ENDS

*	PART I.D.	DESCRIPTION	QTY.
A	34828-VUG	BULKHEAD #6-3/8" 90° MALE	1
B	34830-VUG	BULKHEAD #10-5/8" 90° MALE	1
C	34622-VUG	#6 45° FEMALE O-RING	1
D	34624-VUG	#8 45° FEMALE O-RING	1
E	34446-VUG	#6 90° FEMALE O-RING	3
F	34437-VUG	#6 90° FEMALE FLARE	1
G	33857-VUG	#6 O-RING	4
H	33858-VUG	#8 O-RING	1
J	33859-VUG	#10 O-RING	1
J	07320-VUC	DRIER	1

*	PART I.D.	DESCRIPTION	QTY.
K	34436-VUG	#8 135° FEMALE FLARE	1
L	35441-VUG	#10 135° FEMALE FLARE	1
M	34428-VUG	#10 90° FEMALE O-RING	1
N	34441-VUG	#10 90° FEMALE FLARE	1
O	31603-VUD	#6 HOSE CLAMP	8
P	31604-VUD	#10 HOSE CLAMP	4
Q	31854-VUD	#6 - 5/16" REFRIGERATION HOSE	72"
R	31855-VUD	#8 - 13/32" REFRIGERATION HOSE	48"
S	31856-VUD	#10 - 1/2" REFRIGERATION HOSE	60"

You need at least this many parts to plumb your air conditioning system.

by Jules Glogovcsan

Small Block

Some said, back in 1955 when Chevrolet first introduced the 265 cid V8 OHV engine, that it was 20 years ahead of its time. Perhaps they were right. Today we still see advancements taking place with the now famous small block Chevy engine. From hot rod enthusiasts and racers to aftermarket parts suppliers and GM itself, we see wrenches and cutting tools working over this engine series for continued advancements.

First offered as a 265 cid the small block Chevy grew to a 400 cid for regular production use. There have been a few others but the more familiar sizes that the small block came in are the 265, 283, 302, 305, 307, 327, 350, and 400. All sizes have the same external dimensions and only vary in torque and horsepower relative to internal parts and modifications.

Racing versions of small blocks have been built to produce over 500 hp, and with the correct factory parts, knowledge and engine building skills (or just lots of bucks) displacements of 480+ cubes can be cranked in.

Hot rod Chevy builders get the best of both worlds; a lightweight proven design, and, a variety of parts from an extensive offering. Whether aftermarket or Chevrolet-produced, there are hundreds of choice hot rod items available such as cams, headers, carbs, pistons, intakes, heads, and ignitions to turn a stocker into a hot rod engine.

Armed with the proper tools, knowledge and basic engine building techniques it is easy to bolt on nearly 100 extra horsepower on an 8.5:1 engine and never even pull the heads or remove the engine from the car for that matter.

For this engine builder's section we will look at the 350 cid Chevy small block V8. The engine will be unleaded gasoline compatible and will run in the 325 to 350+ hp range. While normally aspirated and focused on cheap torque, a look at other contemporary induction systems will show what else can be done for both torque and horsepower on the street.

The 5.7-liter Chevy small block with its 350 cid will makes a nice pump-gas-compatible street engine. First introduced in 1967, and still available today from Chevrolet, this engine is available in abundance. It has seen power output levels ranging from 175 to 370 hp from the factory and a lot more from various engine builders and racing engine machine shops.

The bore size is 4.00" and stroke is 3.48". All stock 350 cid small blocks use a 5.7" connecting rod. Another reason we will consider the 350 is that it lends itself to further torque output increases with the use of a 400 cid crankshaft due to increased stroke length.

When selecting any engine as a candidate for hopping up, preference should be given to one that is in good running condition. This gives you a good base from which to start, and you very likely will have the various brackets and pulleys that you need to use for the engine's accessories. Good runners will cost more and a core engine (as in rebuild REQUIRED!) may be had for several hundred dollars...complete. Best bet with the salvage yards is to shop them all and compare prices. Also remember to research your local Chevy dealer. Here you will find many of the correct parts for building a genuine bow-tie hot rod Chevy engine with GM parts. Many may have to be special orders but you can still get the parts.

You may be able to purchase a complete long block, 350 cid type LT-l, for about $2,500. This 11:1 engine uses a high performance mechanical cam and is rated at 370 hp from the factory. It is a four-bolt main block with pink forged rods and crank. Pistons are forged. It is a beautiful engine by any stretch of the imagination, and it's a runner.

You can consider the LT-l for pump gas use by lowering its compression ratio. There are a number of Chevy small block heads available. Best is a set of heads with the 76 cc combustion chamber. Ideally, a set of the 462 series heads as they have the 76 cc combustion chamber and they have the 2.02" intake valves with the 1.6" exhaust valves. Most smogger heads have the 76 cc combustion chamber but will most likely have the 1.94 intakes and the 1.5 exhaust valves. Using the 76 cc head delivers a 9.5:1 compression ratio with an otherwise stock LT-l short block. These heads can be bolted on an assembled LT-l short block and the engine will run on premium unleaded pump gas.

If you walk into an automotive/racing engine machine shop cold-turkey for a high performance rebuild on your Monte Carlo's 350, you may drop an easy $2-$3K. Whereas if you plan the project and look at the cost of what you plan to build you may be able to justify a new LT-l.

Besides the stock 8.5:1 smogger or the famous LT-l factory hot rod Chevy mill, another powerplant worth considering is the late model Corvette engine. The L-82 is a nice 9:1 engine and has a crisp cam. The current generation 5.7-liter 'Vettes also offer a nice engine for consideration, which come with fuel injection electronics worth considering. Expect to pay $1750 and up for the latter.

The key to building a small block is to know your octane requirements and then design the engine to maximize the potential of the parts combination, taking into account the fuel you have to use. But before I get off the subject, you will do well to look into the feasibility of using the LT-l at its stock performance level or slightly de-tuned. It's a very strong short-block. Building up or down, two bolt or four bolt mains, with 5.7 rods go 11:1 (piston part #3989048 STD, 3989051 +.030), use press fit wrist pins and the 64 cc or 76 cc combustion chamber heads and an appropriate sized cam for your purpose. Either version with a mild cam and a 600 cfm carb will easily pull 6000 rpm.

Once selected, the engine assembly should be pre-

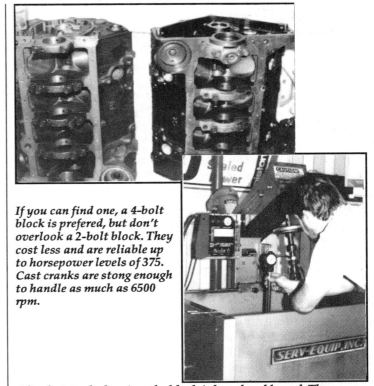

If you can find one, a 4-bolt block is prefered, but don't overlook a 2-bolt block. They cost less and are reliable up to horsepower levels of 375. Cast cranks are stong enough to handle as much as 6500 rpm.

After hot-tank cleaning, the block is bored and honed. Then a bore micrometer is used to control final honing. This will establish the cross-hatch ring pattern and bore to piston clearance.

pared for a trip to the machine shop. A good runner may not need any machine work, if you only plan to clean it up and change a cam or an intake. Used blocks are preferred for performance rebuilds. New blocks are called "green blocks" and until they have been heated up the thousands of times a daily driver gets they are subject to some movement relative to the machined surfaces. If you are assembling an engine from acquired parts, look for the four-bolt block. But for power levels up to 350 hp, a cast iron crank two-bolt engine will serve you well.

Take it apart and look for wear areas, if it is to be a rebuild. If you are taking apart a complete running engine, put all nuts and bolts in separate bags and label. For example, put all brackets, bolts and lock washers for the power steering in one bag. Engine accessory parts use many 3/8" x 16 bolts. They all go back together quicker and easier if they are organized.

Most factory blocks are not square to the crankshaft centerline, so that should be checked. They can be out by as much as .007"-.018". Generally, the mains will be OK, but they should be checked to be sure. All small block Chevys have a well designed casting. Loose main caps in the block are things to look for, and the bearing's roundness and the main's diameters. Decking the block adds to the sweetness of a small block Chevy as things get closer to blueprint. The block should be hot tanked and all plugs removed for a thorough cleaning.

Cast pistons are OK in many cases, but require different piston/bore clearances than do forged pistons.

Piston type should be considered when deciding on a cam, as you don't want any valve to piston contact. You will be safe with cams in the area of .500-.525 lift with flat top pistons, or the .100 pop-up. But always check piston to valve clearance. Clay is an accepted method of measuring the clearance.

The block is bored to fit the new pistons and then honed. Final honing stone grit will depend on the rings chosen. The top ring should be a moly ring for high performance street use. After the block is squared up, you should check the deck. Prior to this is a good time to determine actual compression ratio. If you are hunting for power and have an 8.4:1 ratio when you really want a 9.0:1 ratio, you are loosing power and torque.

If running a steel shim head gasket, the deck will be different than if running a composition gasket such as Fel-Pro offers. In any event small block Chevys with steel rods like about a .035-.040" quench and the deck, along with the piston pin location, will determine what the quench will be.

Unless the engine project is only a simple overhaul, the rods should be rebuilt. If high performance rod bolts are used, it will be necessary to rebuild the rod. General rule is to put in the good rod bolts. Know your parts, as small block Chevys are offered in 5.7 lengths with 3/8" and 7/16" rod bolts. Pre 1967 use 11/32" rod bolts. When rebuilding the rods, they should be straightened, and the big ends made round again. High rpm usage will suggest polished rod beams to eliminate cracks from getting started. Make grinding marks the length of the rod's beam, not crosswise. Then polish smooth. (Pink rod part # 14095071).

Let's talk about the popular 383 cid option. Here we come up with a cubic inch displacement of 383 cid from a 350 block. The key to torque, all else held constant, is more cubic inches. The 350 block, when using the longer stroke crank from a 400 cid small block, yields 383 cubes. The 400 cid crank has a .270" longer stroke. With the 350 block, use the stock 5.7" 350 rods. The

mains on the 400 cid crank are machined down to the main bearing size of the 350 cid block, which is 2.449". It is necessary to clearance the block web near the pan rail to make room for the 350 rod bolts to clear, because they are longer than the 400 bolts at the head. Also, machine the rod bolts for camshaft clearance as is required.

Whether the engine is stroked or one with a stock stroke, give the crank a regrind if the rod and main journals are in need of resurfacing. Cranks are very durable items and they can be reground as much as .050" without any loss in reliability. Just watch the rolled radius at the journal/stroke arm and have the crank radiused and polished.

Cam selection should be given some careful considerations. Be conservative here. If budget will allow, consider the roller type cam for increased torque. Its design allows a steeper cam profile in that the roller tip ends of the lifters follow easier. Thus it is possible to run a quicker acting cam. There are also very good flat tappet cams in both hydraulic and mechanical grinds.

Generally, when building a street engine, select a cam for a stock block 350 cid type engine in the .440" to .460" lift range with a duration of about 215-220 degrees at .050" lifter lift. Stock cams typically have lift ranges in the .390" to .404" range. Cam lifts up to .500" in a small block Chevy generally will give no valve to piston clearance problems. Of course, always check it. These cams are designed to produce a higher pressure in the cylinder as the piston comes up on the compression stroke. Durations are short and performance is very good.

Chevrolet offers some nice cam profiles as do many of the aftermarket cam suppliers. The LT-1 mechanical cam has lifts of .435" on the intake and .455" on the exhaust with a lot of duration. The 242 degrees on the intake combined with a 254 degree duration on the exhaust at .050 give the LT-1 strong mid to upper rpm power (part # 3972178). The L-82 cam profile offers

Nearly every engine will benefit from having the block squared and decked.

Polish the rod beams for high-rpm application. This adds to the rod's life by eliminating cracks from starting at areas of sharp angle.

more lift than the LT-1 but it has less duration. L-82 lift is .450" for the intake and .460" lift for the exhaust with duration of 222 degrees at .050". Soft bottom ends on the street are the result of too much duration. Go for more lift and be conservative in duration specs.

An old hot rod trick is to increase the stock rocker arm ratio from the 1.5:1 to a 1.6:1. This increases lift and keeps duration about the same. Most cam companies offer the 1.6 series ratio in half sets. The stock Chevy exhaust port will out-flow the stock intake port (all else being equal), so you would want to put the 1.6:1 rockers on the intake valves. You can do both and in any event be sure to check valvetrain geometry. The 1.6:1 rockers should not roll off the valve stem tip and should not bottom out on the rocker arm stud. Lash caps can be used to correct the geometry and to spread the load evenly across the valve stem tip. The 1.6:1 rocker on the intake valve will increase the rate of the valve lift and this will help improve bottom end torque by allowing better cylinder filling.

The cylinder head for the small block Chevy destined for improved performance is one place to spend some time. The cylinder head can be used to increase compression by milling it. Increasing valve size can improve cylinder filling. Generally, increased valve size will improve bottom end torque as well as the rest of the power curve. Cleaning and polishing the intake and exhaust ports improve power by aiding engine breathing.

When building a high performance small block Chevy engine, plan on doing some head work. At least match the the gasket to the intake ports of the head and the intake manifold. And work the mill marks out of the bowl area. Here's why.

As the piston moves down on the intake stroke, it creates a lower pressure inside the cylinder than outside in the surrounding atmosphere. The atmosphere's higher pressure forces air in, which draws fuel, into the cylinder through the open intake valve. All of this happens very quickly. Each time the air, now laden with fuel, has to negotiate an obstacle it takes time. But the piston is still moving downward. If the there are obstructions in the air/fuel mixture path, they must first be negotiated before the mixture can continue into the cylinder. Typical is the 1/16" to 1/8" mismatch at the head/intake transition point.

We also find this situation in the bowl area under the valve where there are mill ridges on stock castings left over from the factory's cuts for the valve seats. By grinding the bowl areas smooth and matching the ports to the gasket the path the air/fuel must travel is smoothed. With the restrictions and ridges removed, the cylinder fills sooner relative to the piston's downward movement, and that spells torque.

Street Econ-O-Port jobs go a bit farther and clean up the runners also. Installing larger valves such as the 2.02" in the place of the 1.94" allows the short turn radius to be increased and this also smooths flow and improves cylinder filling.

When selecting valve springs, do not mix and match. Use springs designed for the cam selected. Use only spring pressures recommended by the cam manufacturer. Many of the good Chevy cams require seat pressures of only 85-115 lbs. Too much spring pressure is an effective way to increase the chance of cam lobe failure. Street engines should use the dual-plane intake manifolds such as are available from the Edelbrock Corporation. By reducing the effective size of the plenum area, it is possible to feed the cylinder runners quicker. This is effective in increasing torque, and the Performer Series dual-plane aluminum intake by Edelbrock increases both horsepower and torque and does so earlier in the engine's lower rpm range. Single-plane intake manifolds allow the engine to rev higher than the dual-

High-performance LT-1 harmonic balancer makes a nice addition to a warmed-over Chevy mill (part #6272224). 400 cid engines use an external balance ~ part #6272225).

Hot rod Chevy engines should be balanced. Here bob weights are placed on the crank to add weight equal to the rod and piston combination. The engine balancer uses electronic sensing devices, and a vertical drill is employed to remove metal at locations indicated by the balancer scope.

plane but will require lower gears or a higher stall torque converter.

The small block Chevy responds well to a variety of carburetion set-ups. Carter or Edelbrock AFBs work fine as do the various Holley carbs. For general street use with a semblance of highway gears, use a vacuum-secondary carb. Don't overlook the benefits of the Quadrajet carb, which was original equipment on many 350 cid small blocks. These carbs offer both economy and performance. The folks at The Carb Shop in Ontario, CA (714) 947-7744 offer a variety of Q-jet modifications ranging from low-buck overhauls to full performance rebuilds. All of their work is aimed at improving both throttle response and wide open throttle performance. For street use, unless the car has a low set of gears or a high stall torque converter, stay away from double pumper carbs because they are for the strip. But with low gears they are quite nice just out of the box.

An engine performs best with a free flowing exhaust system and this will be an aide to bottom end torque. Nick Tauber at Flowmaster in Santa Rosa, CA (707) 544-4761 tells us how the exhaust system affects torque. "Once the headers are on and you have plumbed the exhaust system, take a spray can of enamel black paint and spray a line from the headers down the side of the exhaust pipe about two feet long. Don't used lacquer, use enamel paint. Take the car out and run it good and hard through the gears. Look underneath the car at the painted line. Up near the header end you will see where it burned off and transitions back to a painted line. At this point, install a balance tube in the exhaust system. Installed at this point it will improve bottom end and driveability. Make the balance tube out of tubing about 1/2" smaller in diameter than the overall exhaust system."

Engines built along the above lines of recommendation should produce 325-390 horsepower, depending on just what you do and how you do it. Along with the increase in horsepower you will get an increase in torque.

Should you want more power than that, you can consider either a supercharger or a nitrous oxide injection system, or both. Supercharging is a reliable way of getting a big performance increase from an engine. Superchargers are driven by a belt connected to the crankshaft. Inside the supercharger are rotors which capture air as they rotate and move it into the induction system's plenum at rates above what the engine can use. In effect the supercharger packs the air/fuel mixture into the plenum. Typical boost levels that work well on stock engines are around the 5-6 psi boost level for compression ratios in the 8.5:1 area. By lowering the compression ratio, additional boost can be employed. Superchargers increase the horsepower output of a stock engine by 35-40%. What they also do is increase the engine's ability to breath at low valve lift, low rpm levels. This results in increased filling of the cylinders with air/fuel and low rpm torque increases.

Serious torque increases can be had with the use of nitrous oxide injection. When used in an internal combustion engine, nitrous allows the use of additional gasoline by virtue of the fact that the nitrous releases extra oxygen molecules. Additionally, the change from a cold temperature (nitrous remains at minus 128 F under pressure) to a warmer one, as is found inside an intake manifold, makes the air/fuel mixture more dense. This allows for a larger charge of air/fuel to enter the cylinder, and the net result is a serious increase in both torque and horsepower. As long as the correct air and fuel ratio is maintained, long-term use can be successfully achieved. When using nitrous on the street, it is best to be conservative and use low levels. As experience is gained, power levels can be increased.

Rick Lucero, production manager at Nitrous Oxide Systems in Cypress, CA (714) 821-0580 tells us how to maintain a safety factor. "Once you decide upon the

Good street heads include a precision 3-angle valve seat grind, and should have the mill marks and ridges ground out from beneath the valves. This promotes early cylinder filling, better high-rpm air flow and improved performance.

Both the intake manifold and cylinder head ports should be matched to the gasket. Grind back 3/4" to 1-1/4" in the intake ports on both the intake manifold and cylinder head.

system you will use, the best bet is to install safety pressure switches. Use them on the fuel side of the system. By using these switches, anytime you do not have enough fuel pressure the nitrous system will shut off. This will eliminate the possibility of running low on fuel pressure and a lean situation. Nitrous makes the engine run much faster and things happen much quicker. If you are not on top of your system's management you can burn up a piston. When you start to use nitrous, be conservative in the jet size you select. Follow all instructions and make all electrical connections with solder."

Hot rod Chevy builders can also take a good look at electronically controlled fuel injection systems. TPI (Tuned Port Injection) systems as found in a salvage yard from a late model 'Vette or IROC Camaro can work well for the street. These systems are designed to provide good torque at the bottom end and ideal fuel mixtures through the rpm range. Also, aftermarket suppliers are offering improved performance with TPI systems using custom runners. Systems are available

today that will make 375 hp on unleaded gas. These systems typically have on-board management systems to electronically control the ignition timing to avoid detonation problems.

The future for the small block Chevy engine looks as bright as ever. Advancements made by Chevrolet lend themselves well to the world of the hot rod Chevy mill. New head designs are available from various suppliers. Besides the factory, there are numerous suppliers of low rpm high torque engines that you can buy direct. Several large warehouse parts houses offer high torque engine kits that are ready for assembly. Some even offer the new electronic fuel injection kits.

Nothing quite sounds like a built small block Chevy. Interest in them is still keen and they have changed little in over thirty years. Chances are they will still remain the number one choice in hot rod engines. Building and owning a hot rod Chevy small block will not only give you serious power potential, it also lets you own and operate a piece of hot rod history.

SMALL BLOCK ENGINE TORQUE SPECIFICATIONS

Main Bearing	2 bolt: 80 ft.lbs.
	4 bolt: 70 to 75 ft.lbs. (inner), 65 ft. lbs. (outer)
Connecting Rods	3/8": (265 to 350 V8) 35 to 40 ft. lbs.
	(302 to 400 V8) 45 ft. lbs.
	7/16": 60 to 65 ft. lbs.
Cylinder Head Bolts	65 ft. lbs. (short)
	70 ft. lbs. (long)
Rocker Arm Stud	50 ft. lbs.
Camshaft Sprocket	20 ft. lbs.
Intake Manifold	30 ft. lbs.
Flywheel	60 ft. lbs.
Spark Plug / gasket	25 ft. lbs.
Spark Plug / tapered	15 ft. lbs.
Crankshaft Balancer	50 to 60 ft. lbs.
Oil Pan	165 in. lbs.
Timing Cover	75 in. lbs.
Rocker Cover	25 in. lbs.

CLEARANCES

Piston To Bore	.005" to .0055"
Piston Ring	.020" to .022" (top) .014" to .016" (2nd)
Rod Bearing	.002" to .0025"
Main Bearing	.002" to .003"
Crank End Play	.005" to .007"
Deck Height	.035" to .038"
Valve To Piston	.100" minimum
Side Clearance	.015" to .025"

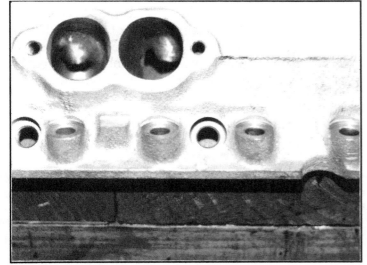

Cleaning up the exhaust ports will improve exhaust flow. Grind mill marks from under the valve and round the edges on the guide.

Using 1.6:1 rocker ratio on the intake will improve the small block's ability to breathe. It's like adding a bigger cam, but much easier to do.

by Jules Glogovcsan

Big Block

With huge 4-inch bores and better than 3-3/4 inch stroke, the big block Chevrolet Mark IV engine (396 cid to 454 cid) is the perfect solution for almost any Chevy hot rodder looking for both maximum torque and horsepower. Affectionately called Rat motor, Semi-hemi and Porcupine, these engines represent some of the best factory hot rod engines ever produced by Chevrolet. Best, that is, for brute strength, horsepower and the ability to produce torque. More than twenty years after initial introduction to production vehicles, a big block under the hood is still a sight to see. Unique valve covers clearly spell out what motivates this Chevy hot rod.

Numbers like 396 cid, 427 cid and 454 cid all say big block. All three engine sizes were available in versions ranging from low to high performance. The 396 cid big block sports minimum advertised horsepower levels of 325 hp in most applications. 427 cid big blocks can easily run upwards of 400 horsepower with sane compression ratios, and the LS-6 can be had at 9.0:1, 10.25:1 or 11.0:1. Full-floating LS-7 versions can be had at 12.5:1 and are conservatively rated at 465 hp.

A big block need not be an expensive engine building project. They can be had in salvage yards for $500 and up in serviceable condition. LS-6 short blocks go for $500 and up. With a pair of $250 open-chamber oval-port heads, you'd have (depending upon exact piston dome height) a 9.0:1 or 10.0:1 compression ratio.

There are many ways to build an engine, and if your target is for street use with pump gas, here's the correct way to put together a performance blueprinted 454 aimed at producing in the 450 to 485 hp range on pump gas.

The best way to start is to acquire a complete running engine, because you get all the brackets, pulleys, and things that cost extra if you piece it out. The engine used in our example was supposed to be an LS-5 454. It had been transplanted into a '67 El Camino. It was a nice runner, although it had a slight knock that sounded like a loose rod bearing, but it turned out to be piston slap. It had 8.5:1 pistons and the 118 cc combustion chamber with the correct LS-5 hydraulic cam. So who knows for sure, since it's nearly 20 years old. But it is a 454 cid, and we'll call it an LS-5 that we are going to build to LS-6 specs, with a target of 500+ ft. lbs. of torque.

After removal of the engine from the donor El Camino, the engine was immediately set into its recipient vehicle, a 1976 Chevy Nova. This was done since the engine/chassis combo we'd end up with was not ever offered by Chevrolet and we planned to run factory air conditioning on it. With cast iron exhaust manifolds, this is a 100% bolt-in operation. We opted for 2" tube headers and had to rework them a bit. All the stock factory air conditioning components on the firewall clear, and you can remove valve covers with no problem.

Satisfied with the fit, the engine went on to the engine stand. During disassembly, note areas of wear and relay this information to the machine shop. We found considerable carbon build-up on the underside of the intake valves, suggesting worn guides. We noticed the scuffed cylinder and piston that was knocking. The mains and rods were worn through the babbitt and the bronze colored layer was showing, but not everywhere, suggesting loose main caps or an out of true crank. When tested, the crank proved to be on the money, but there were two loose caps on the mains.

With the oval port heads at 118-120 cc it was decided to use a compression ratio of 9.1:1. Here's a tip when building an engine for the street: keep compression ratio at about 9.0:1. Spend a few dollars and have the stock compression ratio measured. We did this one for $71.00. It entailed cc'ing the head's combustion chamber and measuring the bore and deck etc. As it turned out the engine had a true ratio of 7.8:1. Knowing this allows us to consider what needs to come off the deck and piston crown to achieve the desired ratio.

When having head work done, have a stock port flowed. Then reflow it afterwards to determine the amount of improvement. Our heads got a complete port and polish job, including the combustion chambers.

With the engine's oil plugs and freeze plugs removed, give it a good soaking in the hot tank along with the crank, heads and other parts. Be sure the harmonic balancer does not end up soaking overnight, or it will be damaged. If a new heavy-duty harmonic balancer is needed, the part number is 3936530 for a 8" counter-weighted dampner.

Since our block had loose mains, it was align-honed after the caps had been trued. When the crank was later reassembled, it turned almost effortlessly and the entire short block took only 28 ft. lbs. of torque to turn the rotating assembly.

Bores were slightly out of round with a bit of a ridge at the deck. We bored it .030" for a standard oversize. It's OK to use cast pistons after a re-bore if plans are for street performance. They are plenty strong, but be sure to have cast pistons balanced. Forged pistons tend to be right on the money, but they should be checked. The piston selected for our build-up was the 9.0:1. It is available from Chevrolet (part #6262977) and also from others such as TRW or Sealed Power (Sealed Power part #7060P). It has about a .100" pop-up dome and fits nicely in the 120 cc oval port head. The only reason we

When doing a professional engine rebuild, torque the main caps down and check them. If they are out of round or not on a common centerline, fix them. The crankshaft must rotate true.

Sunnen alignment honing machine brings all mains to common centerline for crankshaft by cutting the caps a few thousandths. This makes for a nice bottom end.

If the cylinder bores are worn and out of round, they can be restored by an overbore. Usually no more than .030" overbore is necessary to restore cylinders.

Use a tap to clean all bolt holes. Bolts are the key to proper torque force when installing such things as cylinder heads on the block. Dirty threads prevent proper stretch and torque specifications.

A honing stone is great for cleaning engine block deck surfaces. This works on any gasket surface. Keep the stone flat and parallel.

A deck plate is used for pre-loading the block when boring and honing. It ensures a nice round bore for maximum ring sealing and helps bottom end torque.

opted to use the more expensive piston is for strength as our engine will run a direct port nitrous injection system. Rings are moly top Speed-Pro. The engine shop can gap the rings in about an hour for a minimal charge. Each ring should be marked by ring land number and hole. Then chamfer the ring gap edges and check the gap. Hint: get a $4 ring expander when installing rings to prevent bending the rings.

To go a step farther, balance the engine and square the decks. Match the ports to the gaskets in the intake manifold and heads. Clean up the valve bowls. Select a mild cam, something between stock and hot. These few bits of extra work will be beneficial.

All bolt holes should be tapped and chased to clean them up. This is essential in the head bolt holes if the plan is to use a deck plate for honing the bores. The deck dowel pins are removed and the deck is cleaned up. A honing stone will clean the deck up if you plan to leave it alone. We used a B-H-J big block deck plate to load the deck as it will be with the head bolted on. Head bolts distort the bore a bit when torqued and using a deck plate corrects to a round bore. This helps with combustion sealing, and that's power.

The block should be deflashed in the entire valley area to aid oil return. In our case, it was determined that to run a .0385" quench deck we would use a .000" deck and let the FEL-PRO performance O-ringed head gasket maintain the deck. Street driven big blocks with steel rods work well with a .038 - .045 quench. Remember to radius the quench line, to help accelerate the squish and turn it slightly up into the compressed mixture.

After the compression ratio was measured our block was decked, and about .030" was removed. Remember, in our engine the stock 8.5:1 actually measured to be 7.8:1. It was then set up for further mock-up in the piston to valve area and to fit the intake manifold. On most engines the deck at the cylinder bore edge protrudes a bit into the path of the intake and the exhaust gasses. The L-88 427 and the LS-6 and LS-7 have reliefs at the edges of the deck. With the cylinder head mounted to the deck, reach up into the bore and scribe a line where they meet. Then grind that area, being careful not to get into area where the top ring will be at TDC. This will aid cylinder filling especially at lower rpm, delivering more torque.

Polishing the crank and chamfering the oil holes are other inexpensive procedures that are worth doing. The chamfer delivers more oil to the bearing surface of the rods and mains.

There are several styles of big block Chevy oval port open chamber heads. The 120 cc heads with oval ports are preferable to the smaller round-type ports that came on some truck engines. We selected Manley 2.19" SS Street Flow valves for the intakes to replace the stock 2.06" valve. The stock 1.72" exhaust valve was replaced with the Manley 1.88" SS Street Flow valve. Manley valves are fairly inexpensive as far as valves go and are rated for severe duty. With the larger valves the valve seat and bowl area can be opened up. This provides the opportunity for some port reshaping (slight) and a reworking of the short side radius. Low rpm flow is increased and thus we further increase torque in the driving ranges. In this case, the heads were fully ported and polished from intake to exhaust. Both the backside of valve and the front edge in the combustion chamber were radiused to promote early flow at low rpm, which creates more torque. A three angle valve job was done, keeping the seats as wide as possible for unleaded fuel use and cooling of the valve. The only way the exhaust valve cools itself is during the time it is on its seat.

To compliment the custom cylinder head work, an Edelbrock Performer dual-plane intake manifold was opened up to the gasket. The manifold has a small opening to promote high port velocities, but running a 4.56:1 gear will make it flow just fine. So we opened them up all the way.

To help the bottom end, a Competition Cams 280H Magnum flat tappet hydraulic grind was selected. Also we opted for their complete valvetrain kit which included the roller tip rockers and heavy-duty pushrods and valve springs. The 280H Magnum specs out at .526" lift and 230 degrees of duration at .050" tappet lift. We could have used the 290H or the 305H, but this is to be a daily driver, so we wanted a flat power curve with lots of torque. Redline will be 6500 rpm. Chevrolet offers some nice factory cams, too. With the duration at 230 she'll sound real nice. Valve to piston clearance is ample, so with flat top cast piston there'll be no problem. Rule of thumb is to check it anyway.

The heads also got new guide plates and studs, and for the cam a new Manley roller timing chain. Cam will be installed heads-up, which with this cam is a 4 degree advance. The engine was balanced and required some heavy metal to bring it in as a result of the overbore. But not much. Remember ours is a 454 cid big block and they are externally balanced.

A dial indicator is used to locate TDC for measuring the deck. Deck is then cut to arrive at desired quench height and compression ratio. We chose 9.1:1 for unleaded gas use.

Serious rebuild will include rebuilt rods and racing rod bolts. Most engines that lose a rod do so because the rod bolt breaks, not because the rod breaks through the beam.

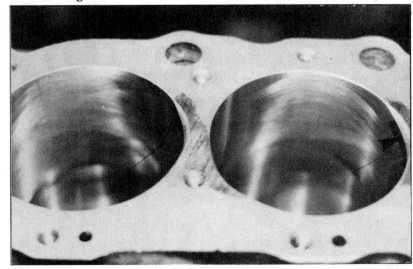

Relieve the deck at the cylinder bore edge to improve bottom end torque on big blocks.

Not all oval port heads are open chamber. You want open chamber heads (118 to 120 cc) for an unleaded, low-compression engine. Hardened valve seats are not required.

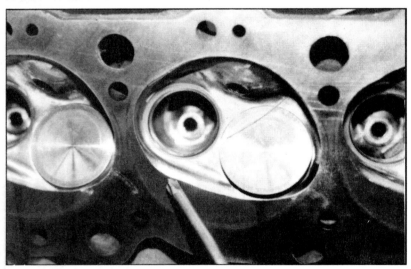

Help the big block breathe by rolling back the quench line. Use a 3/32" radius. This will help bottom end torque and flame propagation.

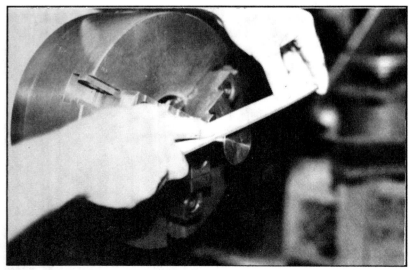

Back cut valves 20 degrees on back side and roll the combustion chamber edge with a chamfer to help low valve lift, low rpm port flow both into and out of the engine.

Heads required new guides, and after the valve heights were set and the springs checked, the heads were assembled. We bought a new GM heavy-duty nodular 454 flywheel (part #3993827) with 14" diameter, 168-tooth starter ring, which uses an 11" clutch disk. This improves throttle response off-idle.

During assembly, the empty block, all spic-n-span, was turned mains up. The Vandervall main bearings were washed in lacquer thinner as were all small parts, and air blown clean. Bearings were coated with a thin coating of white grease as were the undersides of the crank main journals, and the crank was carefully installed in the block. Look at the back side of the bearings to be sure they are the correct undersize to match the crank's regrind.

Main caps were washed in lacquer thinner and the bearing shells installed and coated with assembly grease. The main bearing caps should fit snug and be torqued to 100 ft. lbs. Proper fastener lubrication is important to get correct torque. Clean the bolt in lacquer thinner, air blow dry, and put a drop or two of 30 weight oil in the thread hole. Put oil on the threads and under the bolt head and a drop or two where the underside of the bolt turns on the cap. This insures a well-lubed mating of the threads. The crank should turn absolutely effortlessly at this point, but do not turn the crank until all mains are torqued properly, because the centerlines won't be perfectly true until it is all torqued down.

Rings must be installed the correct way. For most rings, the proper position is with the dot up and stagger the gaps. Keep gaps out of the notches in the block. Clean piston and rod, unassembled rod cap (wrist pins already pressed in) with lacquer thinner and air blow dry. Do not wash lacquer thinner into the wrist pin area as it is lubed. Shoot some oil there anyway and move piston back and forth to work it in on pin and piston pin bore. I prefer to assemble each piston on clean paper one at a time. Before installing the rings, run a hone over the edges of the gap to remove burrs that may be left over from machining. Install rings, being careful to follow instructions with rings and ring expansion tool.

Install upper rod bearing and place other half in cap. Place the assembled piston and rings into a pan filled with a quart of engine oil. Get oil into all areas of rings, pin and on skirts. On the ring compressor, keep band closest to edge at bottom of piston skirt so it will stabilize the compressor as the rings pass through it and into the block. Put rod bolt protectors on, oil bore and install piston, ring and rod assembly. Set crank throw at TDC. Take special care to prevent scratching or nicking the crank journal as the rod mates with the crank. Install rod cap correctly with tangs together. All rod caps should be numbered and correspond to the hole you are working in. Go slowly, carefully and one hole at a time. If any doubt remove piston and check...but do it correctly the first time. PS: you can't use too much oil here!

Carefully install the cam using cam assembly lube on the lobes and oil on the bearing journals. Install cam gear and timing chain. Check rod side play and crank end play. Be sure to remember the intermediate oil pump/distributor shaft. No fun with oil pan on and you realize it's not in the block. We used the LS-7 oil pan assembly (part #14091356). It is a five quart unit with trap doors and accepts the LS-7 windage tray. You can use this windage tray (part #3967854) with your stock pan, but you have to remove the pan baffle. And, you'll need four mounting studs (part #3902885). Install oil pan loosely.

If you are going to check cam specs do it now. Engine should rotate with a torque wrench at 25-30 ft. lbs. max, to be properly set up. Install oil pan and timing cover. Be very careful with silicone type RTV sealers, as excess can enter oil pan area, and will end up in the oil pump pick-up and could starve a bearing.

In this case we used a Fel-Pro performance line gasket set. When tightening head bolts, lube with sealant. Some head bolts go through the deck into the water jacket, and you don't want to have water migrate up the treads to the deck and into the bore.

Install the lifters, pushrods and rockers. Set valves by taking up the lash on hydraulics so there is no rocker movement, but the pushrod still turns. Then go about 1/8 to 1/4 turn to establish pre-load setting.

Install the intake manifold and distributor with piston at TDC, compression stroke on # 1 cylinder. With a motor like this, more torque in the lower rpm range can be had with Edelbrock's Performer series dual-plane intake manifold. By dividing the plenum below the carb you allow four cylinders to feed off of one plenum vs. having to draw from a turbulent air/fuel mixture. This strengthens the signal to the carb, producing more power. An engine like this will also run fine with the Edelbrock Torker. It is a single-plane manifold and will flow more at higher rpm, but moves the torque range up the rpm scale. A higher stall or lower gear may be required for best throttle response and driveability.

Deflash the lifter valley to aid oil return to the pan. Use a valley shield to keep hot oil off the bottom of the intake manifold.

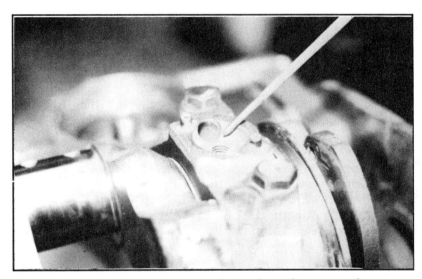
Chamfer the rear main cap to remove sharp edge and improve oil movement from the pump to the block.

Be sure that the camshaft timing gear and the crankshaft gear are in perfect alignment, or you may wear out the timing chain prematurely and cause erratic timing.

We opted for The Brass Work's FLOW-KOOLER big block water pump with anti-cavitation disk installed. These pumps are available in both cast iron and aluminum versions, ready to install. You can also acquire just the FLOW-KOOLER cavitation disk. Cost for disk is about $10. It is easy to install and will help to lower engine operating temperature. We installed a heavy-duty three-core radiator from a Chevelle that had been recored. Big blocks make more heat, so a good cooling system is important.

To further control engine heat, we selected Hedman Hedders. Ours use a 2" tube into a 3" collector. By getting rid of the hot exhaust gas efficiently, we scavenge each cylinder by itself and keep it cooler under the hood. We also limit any reversion potential as a result of the cast iron exhaust manifold feeding a log-type with all four cylinders dumping into it. Hedman Hedders are precision made units that fit well and are made of single mandrel bent tubes. We sent our headers to High Performance Coatings in Oklahoma, to be coated to keep the outside surface of the tube a bit cooler. By also coating the inside we prevent deterioration of the inner tubes which will detract from performance as the tube rusts. HPC also provides TBC (Thermal Barrier Coatings), which they say helps control the transfer combustion chamber heat into the piston dome. The manufacturer claims that TBC slows heat transfer into the dome while still allowing proper heat transfer to the head where it is carried out of the engine through the cooling system. This is supposed to help control the amount of heat passed to the air fuel mixture and help limit pre-ignition.

We have incorporated these ideas into our big block Chevy because it is a hot rod engine. We want no detonation or pinging characteristics at all. This is one reason we opted for the full port and polish job. Cool intake charge is what we want and these products, in our opinion, will aid us in this quest.

For carburetion we decided to use a rebuilt 780 cfm Rochester Q-jet, which had been worked over by The Carb Shop in California; (714) 947-7744. The Q-jet has small primaries to increase the signal to the carb at low rpm. Both good mileage (if a big block can have good mileage) and crisp throttle response result. While the Q-Jet is a great economy carb, longer duration cams want different mixtures as the rpm increases. Idle tubes were replaced with high-performance units .040" in diameter. Off-idle air/fuel mixture was enriched for better throttle response and driveability. An APT kit was installed to allow adjustment for richer or leaner setting. For open throttle operation, a secondary jet kit was installed, which provided significant power gains. The secondary well was modified for more fuel at wide open throttle. It was increased from .040" to .043". Jets were installed below the air doors — size was .059" to replace the original .052" size. 5/32" pickup tubes replaced the 1/8" units. The primary jets were increased to number 73 with the primary rods 44B. The secondary rod is the DH size, which has a .0567" power tip. Additionally, the stock 15cc accelerator pump was replaced with a high-performance silicon cup, 30cc unit. Then, we topped the carb with a K&N Filtercharger air cleaner.

With oil in the pan, the radiator hooked up, the engine primed and properly timed, it's time to fire it up. Bring it up to about 2,000 rpm and run it for about 20-30 minutes. This will break in the new cam and lifters and insure their long life. Watch gauges for temperatures and pressures. Look for leaks. After this time, shut the engine down, drain oil and change the filters. The new Chevrolet PF-35L heavy-duty oil filter is recommended (part #25013454).

From a general tune-up to a blueprinted high-performance big block engine rebuild, the Mark IV will serve you well. Don't abuse the engine while it is cold and don't over-rev it. You own a piece of Chevrolet history.

BIG BLOCK ENGINE TORQUE SPECIFICATIONS

Main Bearing	396 V8 2 bolt: 95 ft. lbs.
	4 bolt: 110 ft. lbs.
	427 to 454 V8: 2 bolt: 100 ft. lbs. 4 bolt: 110 ft. lbs
Connecting Rods	3/8": 50 ft. lbs.
	7/16": 70 ft. lbs.
Cylinder Head Bolts	2 bolt: 80 ft. lbs.
	4 bolt: 75 ft. lbs. (long), 55 ft. lbs. (short)
Rocker Arm Stud	50 ft. lbs.
Camshaft Sprocket	20 ft. lbs.
Intake Manifold	25 ft. lbs.
Flywheel	60 to 65 ft. lbs.
Spark Plug	25 ft. lbs.
Crankshaft Balancer	85 ft. lbs.
Oil Pan	165 in. lbs.
Timing Cover	75 in. lbs.
Rocker Cover	25 in. lbs.

CLEARANCES

Piston To Bore	.0065" to .0075" (iron engines)
Piston Ring	.022" (top), .016" (2nd)
Rod Bearing	.002" to .003"
Main Bearing	.002" to .003"
Crank End Play	.005" to .007"
Deck Height	.040" for steel rod
Piston To Valve Clearance	.100" minimum
Side Clearance	.015" to .025"

Inline Six

Like their big brother V8s, the Chevy six-cylinder is a four-cycle internal combustion engine that burns a mixture of gasoline and air in about a 13:1 ratio. But unlike the V8s that have a short distance from the carb to the cylinder, the six has a long distance to make its air/fuel mixture travel before it hits home in the cylinder. This is detrimental to performance. You just might say the old stovebolt, in stock form, has trouble breathing much over light-duty.

However, fill the cylinder well and improve the engine's ability to breathe and you can pull well over 300 horsepower from the Chevy six. While the six has been hot rodded for many years, today's technology brings major improvements to the high performance output potential of the engine. Today, turbochargers, superchargers, nitrous oxide injection, and electronic fuel injection are all available for the Chevy inline six — both early and late models. These bring major increases in the engine's volumetric efficiency and power output levels.

Well known inliner engine builder Kay Sissell in California has been nostalgic drag racing of late in the NDRA classes. His Chevy six-powered T roadster cuts low to mid nine second quarter mile ETs, and turns in excess of 8,000 rpm with a stock crank! With the average T roadster weighing in at 2,000 lbs or a bit less, cutting mid-nines in the quarter mile suggests horsepower levels of 450 to 475 hp. In fact, in conversations with Mr. Sissell, he states that his inline six Chevy with the Sissell "lump-port" head is running about 500 hp!

The fact that sixes can be made to run has been a career commitment of Jack Clifford of Clifford Per-

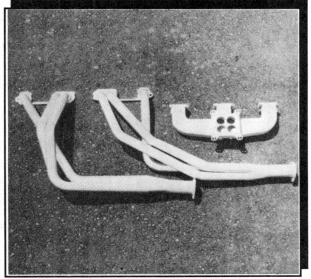

Four-barrel intake manifolds, proper cam selection and a set of headers will wake up the inline six Chevy mill. (Photo by Clifford Performance)

formance in Corona, CA (714) 734-3310. With performance cams, tuned headers and special inductions, Jack's company has coined the phrase that 6=8. Both the 235 Chevy six series and the 194/292 Chevy six series engines can run many of the clutch and transmission combos that any Chevy hot rod V8 can.

The first American made sports car was and is still the Corvette. The powerplant was the famous Blue Flame six. It was a factory hot rodded Chevy 235 inline six. We can get our feet wet fast by investigating what the factory did to make a high performance engine out of the economy minded stovebolt.

The stock passenger car engine for 1953 had a one barrel carburetor and a single exhaust. It had a stock compression ratio of 7.5 to 1 and delivered a little over 110 horsepower at 3500 rpm. Torque was about 200 ft. lbs. Inline Chevy sixes were always known for lots of torque relative to their cubes and horsepower ratings. Corvette engineers raised the compression ratio from the stock passenger car level of 7.5:1 to 8.0:1 The single carb was replaced with tri-power — three Carter side mount carbs (to clear the hood) mounted to an aluminum intake manifold especially designed to provide smooth power through the entire rpm range. The exhaust system was improved to handle the increased exhaust flow with a dual outlet exhaust manifold. Timing was improved and the Blue Flame engine ran the automobile industry's hottest stock production camshaft for a while. It sported lift on the intake at over .400" lift and the exhaust valve lift was nearly .415". Cam timing was improved and each valve used dual valve springs.

The result of this factory hot rodding of the 235 Chevy six was a respectable sports car high-performance engine that could produce nearly 160 horsepower and about 225 ft. lbs. of torque. The engine required Premium gasoline.

When building the Chevy six today, many inline enthusiasts opt for the truck version with its 261 cubic inches. About a 25% increase in power can be had by enabling the engine to breathe. Specialty inline six intake manifolds and headers will help to improve the volumetric efficiency of the engine. Both two barrel and four barrel carbs are available. Headers (Clifford Performance part number 52-0640, for example) are designed to help the cylinders scavenge the exhaust out and allow more of the intake charge to enter the cylinders, producing more power. These engines with their point-type distributors can be run on 8-volt Group One batteries and can use hotter coils such as the Voltmaster by Mallory. Conversion to a 12-volt system will allow the use of the Mallory Hy-Fire electronic system for a much hotter spark that burns longer in the plug's gap. Chevy 235s respond well to a hot ignition system. The 390 cfm vacuum secondary carb by Holley is a nice addition, also. Clifford Performance now offers its new Street Rod Header for the 235 series Chevy six for ease of exhaust system/chassis combo management. These headers have collectors that are located near the pan rail. If your chassis/engine combo is real unique, Clifford offers easy to assemble U-bend-U-Do-it-UR-self header kits—welding skill required. Hedman Hedders also offers U-Bends for custom exhaust. Patrick Dykes of Patrick's Antique Cars & Trucks offers Fenton headers that are cast iron and so very popular in hot rodding the Chevy six. To further perk up this performance combo for your sweet running 235, you might want to consider the Clifford 256H street performance grind cam. Lift figures are near the Blue Flame lift specs (.408" lift) and the advertised duration is 256 degrees. This will add about 10% more power to an otherwise stock engine.

An early Chevy six built along these specs and in good running condition will easily cruise all day and will get you up to freeway speeds in a hurry.

For producing higher performance in the early Chevy six, we only need to increase the volumetric efficiency of the engine. You say you want to keep your '54 Chevy 2-dr with the 235 but you want it to beat 5.0 Mustangs from the stop light? Well, here's how to do it.

This build-up requires an engine tear down. Give the

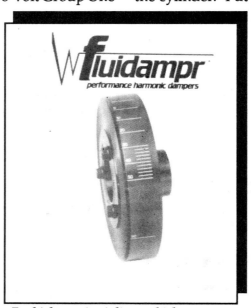

For high-revving inlines, a high-performance harmonic balancer is a must. The Fluidampr balancer lets the inline six see 7000 rpm, and controls crankshaft harmonics.

block a complete going over with a new bore, bearings, rings etc. Clean up the crank journals. Use the insert type with full pressure oiling system to the rods and mains. Square up the deck and balance the reciprocating parts. Set the rods and mains at .0025" to .003". Select forged pistons and dial in a compression ratio of about 9.0:1.

Clean up the head and mill it as required to get a true surface. Milling up to .125" can be done for a boost in compression. Clean up the ports and grind out all mill marks under both the intake and exhaust bowls. If you mill the head over .060" you will have to reset the valve in the pocket. Polish the inside of the bowls and back-cut the intake and exhaust valves to improve low rpm low lift flow characteristics. Cut the bores for O-rings and chamfer the deck ridge where the intake flows into the cylinder. Put the head on the block and reach up inside and scribe any area that hangs out in the port's way. Then grind down about 1/4" like you see on the big block Chevys. Don't get too near the ring's top position relative to the piston lands.

Use the single four barrel intake from Clifford (part number 42-4500 and base plate 08-1014). Either the 390 cfm Holley or the 600 cfm Holley will fit. Both are vacuum secondary carbs.

Select a high performance street/strip cam in the range of .450" to .490" lift with a duration of about 270 to 280 degrees. With a bit more compression, headers, hot ignition and cam you should get a conservative 135 hp to 140 hp. With a supercharger giving an additional 40% more power (see chapter about Blowing The Stovebolt) we can have about 190 to 195 horsepower. The Mustang has 220 hp in the 5.0 version.

More scat can be had by plumbing in either a nitrous oxide plate or a direct port injection NOS Fogger nozzle kit, adding perhaps 50 to 75 hp for a conservative 250 hp total. If you use the NOS Fogger system, run the fuel enrichment system at about 5-6 psi of fuel pressure and start off with NOS jet sizes of 18 for the nitrous and 23 for the gasoline. Conservative nitrous kits will work fine on any six cylinder engine. Today's kits are well engineered and reliable. Horsepower increases up to 100 hp should be fine as long as the engine is in good condition. Any nitrous engine should run an EGT gauge and the engine builder should understand the requirements for safe use of the product. Reasonable usage will suggest rpm limits in the 4750 to 5250 rpm range.

This will produce a strong running engine that will

be able to put out the torque and power to pull hard from the line. But we can help it some more.

There are kits available in the aftermarket to adapt a late model bellhousing to the back of your 235 block (see chapter about Transmission Adapters). This will allow use of a torque converter in the 2200 to 2500 rpm stall range with the TH350. You can also run a late model four-speed or even a Doug Nash five-speed. Select an appropriate open driveshaft posi rearend and you are in business.

Even though the 235 Chevy six only has four main bearings, it is built like an oak tree and will hold up well under these levels of power augmentation. You may want to consider studs in the engine for the deck and mains. With only four head bolts per cylinder, additional clamping forces can be achieved with 1/2" studs.

Watch for signs of detonation, and start off with your ignition retarded about 4 degrees. Run a hot ignition such as described earlier. The automatic with the higher stall torque converter will let the torque load be absorbed gently.

HIGH PERFORMANCE LATE-MODEL SIX

The late model Chevy six engine made its grand appearance in the very early 60s. First introduced as a 194 cid engine, with bore and stroke changes it grew to be as big as a 292 cid version. The engine in Novas, Camaros and Chevelles was a basic economy version. Economical transportation was part of the marketing presentation from Chevrolet. But the Chevy six-in-a-row had made a lot of friends over the years and as soon as the new engine was out it became a focus of inline enthusiast hot rodders. Some early 194 cid engines even had forged cranks.

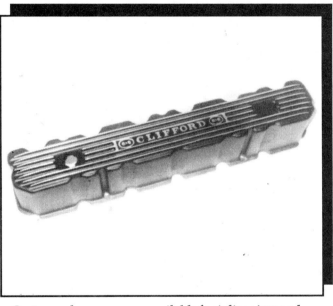
Custom valve covers are available for inline sizes and help dress up the engine compartment.

One of the popular sizes of the 194/292 series is the Chevy six 250 cid engine. With its seven main cap crankshaft it is well suited to high performance use. The 194 cid engine has a 3.56" bore and a 3.25" stroke. The 230 cid engine has a 3.875" bore and a 3.25" stroke. The 250 has a 3.875" bore and a 3.53" stroke. It just so happens that the 307 cid Chevy V8 also has a bore of 3.875" and a stroke of 3.25". Are you seeing the picture?

With the extra strength on the bottom end we might want to raise compression and go for extra breathing and rpm for an increase in power from the 250 series Chevy six. What works out real nicely is that we get a factory stroker crank of better than 1/4" more than the 230 cid, and we can use the flat top pistons from the 307

cid V8. Best of all it is a proven parts change-over.

The picture gets better, too. We not only eliminate the stock reversed deflection pistons in the 250, but raise compression with the flat top pistons. And the connecting rod wrist pin location is approximately .020" lower in the piston skirt, which effectively raises the compression even more. So, one of the first considerations in building a late-model hot rod Chevy six, using the 250 block, is to install Chevy 307 pistons.

A lot of compression building can take place in this manner. By eliminating the reverse deflection pistons and replacing them with flat top pistons, we effectively move the piston about .075" up the bore. Add to that the .020" increase due to wrist pin relocation and we are already pushing nearly a point or so of compression. The stock piston is down in the hole about .028" to .033" below the deck for a quench when you add the gasket thickness of .060 +/-. So we can cut the deck to give us a zero or slightly minus deck and get the quench from the compressed composition head gasket of about .040". Since flat top pistons are being used, the mountains are kept out of the flame propagation path and the burn is enhanced, which provides an aid to limiting detonation problems. Further compression considerations can be realized by milling the head as much as .060". The 307 cid pistons are available in both cast and forged versions.

High dome pistons can also be employed, and manufacturers such as Venolia Piston Company can cut any special piston you may need. Custom pistons are also available from Clifford Performance.

Select a compression ratio in the 9.0:1 area. Ratios as high as 11:1 can be obtained by using these procedures, but that requires good gas or an octane booster to control detonation. Many six-cylinder vehicles use two-core radiators, so a three-core may be needed for proper cooling.

There are other machine shop operations to consider for a high performance six. The engine should be balanced, including the harmonic balancer, flywheel and pressure plate if you run a clutch and manual transmission. The 250 cid connecting rods have the same rod bolt diameter as a Chevy 327 cid V8 so use these. Installing the high performance rod bolts requires rebuilding the rods. The crankshaft should be polished and chamfered. O-ring the deck for copper wire.

For street driving, select a camshaft in the .450" to

.460" lift area. Keep duration at about 220-225 degrees when measured with a lifter height of .050". For the street, if you go for more lift be sure to keep the duration down. Cams with 225-230 degrees of duration or more at .050" require lower gears. These cams have a lot of overlap, so while things sound great through headers they deliver a soggy bottom end. Low gears will be needed to crispen it up.

When installing a high lift cam, be aware of any changes you may have made to the valve train geometry. As you go up in lift, the rocker arm may hit the rocker arm stud. Do a mock-up and rotate the cam and valve train. Look at the front of the rocker arm slot relative to the rocker arm stud. With the valve at its maximum lift, the minimum clearance around the stud must be .050". Failure to insure these clearances may result in broken and/or bent parts, perhaps even camshaft failure. If there is not adequate clearance, install a small diameter grinding stone in a die grinder and enlarge the slot. Be careful not to grind or nick the ball and rocker arm surfaces. Lash caps can be used to help correct the geometry. They also spread the load of the rocker tip over the valve stem instead of on the valve stem tip alone.

Chevy sixes use four head bolts around each cylinder. Extra clamping force can be added to the deck by using studs. These work nicely on the mains as well. Head studs allow higher clamping forces without having to twist the threads into the block.

Crankshaft scrapers and windage screens can be a big help in controlling the crank's oil throw-off and oil pan windage velocities. Start with the crank in the block, on the engine stand, and make a paper template that fits the pan bolts and clears the crank counter-weights and rod throws. Transfer this to cardboard. Trial fit and then transfer the pattern to balsa wood. Shape the balsa wood template until it fits, then transfer the shape to .050"-.060" thick aluminum. Put two studs in the pan rail to locate the aluminum strip. Fit and trim. Keep clearance about .050" to .075" from the rotating parts. This will strip the accumulated mass of oil from the crank as it rotates. A windage screen can be acquired from Moroso and is specially made diamond mesh screen for oil pan use. The crank's spinning rotation produces a high pressure area above the windage screen. This forces the spun off oil into the screen and through it, into the low pressure area of the pan. Oil returning to the sump is controlled in this manner.

Head gaskets should be matched to the ports. Go inside and under the valve and grind out the mill marks and ridges in the bowl. Blend in the casting roughness. Head bolt bosses in the intake ports can be removed (see sidebar). Service life of the pressed in rocker arm stud can be improved by drilling it and putting in small roll-pins. Oil caps can be welded to the push rod side of the rocker arm, which stops the oil from the pushrod from shooting out and hitting the valve cover. Instead, it hits the oil cap, then it fills the rocker arm with an oil bath and further lubricates and cools the rocker arm ball and socket. Since this is a high-load area, this is very helpful to component longevity. Make the caps from mild steel about .060" thick. Weld to rocker tip, then grind and shape as required. Heat up the rocker almost cherry red and quench in a pan of oil. Do this outside, as the hot part can cause the oil to flash. Valves can be back-cut on the underside to improve low rpm, low valve lift air flow.

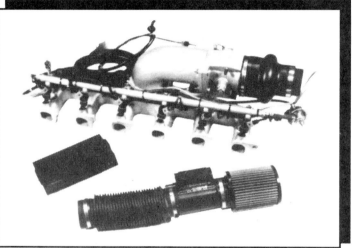

Multi-port electronic fuel injection is available for the Chevy six. The system used state of the art electronic components such as digital ECU computer and mass air sensor. Throttle body injection is also avilable.

Headers help the Chevy sixes a lot. Headers for most six cylinder Chevy engines and chassis combinations are available from Clifford Performance. Some of the late-model six header kits have exits on both sides of the engine which allow for easy dual exhaust system hook ups.

For ignition there are a number of good units on the market. Mallory offers dual-point distributors for the Chevy sixes. Or, you may want to look into a late-model HEI unit. While the V8 HEI distributor has the coil integral to the cap, sixes have remote coils. This means a Hy-Fire electronic module can be installed. These items combined with the six HEI make an excellent high performance system. You may want to recalibrate the advance rate to bring it all in by 2,000-2,250 rpm for a mild streeter, or by 1750 rpm for hot street use. HEI is good for jaunts up to 6,500 rpm.

While the hot rod Chevy six of the '50s may have run dual two barrels, today we see four-barrel carbs being selected. Even dual quads are available. You can select superchargers, nitrous oxide injection or multi-point electronic fuel injection such as Clifford Performance offers. Side-draft Webers are also available. With these induction systems, correct cam selection, headers and some cylinder head work, it is easy to pull one horsepower per cube from a Chevy six.

REMOVING THE CHEVY SIX HEAD BOLT BOSS

This relatively easy procedure will help wake up a Chevy six. The bolt boss in its stock configuration is directly in the path of the air/fuel mixture entering the head's port. With these bolt bosses removed, the engine can breath much better at both the bottom end and at the top end.

Set the head (clean and bare of its valve parts) up on a mill table. Drill and tap a 3/4" hole through the head at the head bolt boss. This gives access to the work area from the top for keeping the machine work perpendicular to the the head bolt hole. A 59/64" drill is the correct drill size to use, but you can use a 15/16" drill and the 3/4" pipe tap will be a bit easier to start.

Bring the cutter down onto the bolt boss shoulder and mill down to the port floor. Cut the top of the hole inside the head for a beveled-head Allen bolt, the same size as the head bolt (1/2").

With the head on the block, trial fit all of the head bolts and the Allen head bolt. Make sure the Allen bolt seats properly. Trial fit the 3/4" pipe plug. Smooth out any parts with a die grinder, as required.

Install head reassembled with valve parts. Torque head to block using the same specifications for the Allen bolt as the head bolt. Install a 3/4" pipe plug in the hole in the head. Use a proper non-hardening sealant such as Permatex or a silicone sealant.

This high-volume oil pump is a Clifford Performance item which improves oil flow to the bearings.

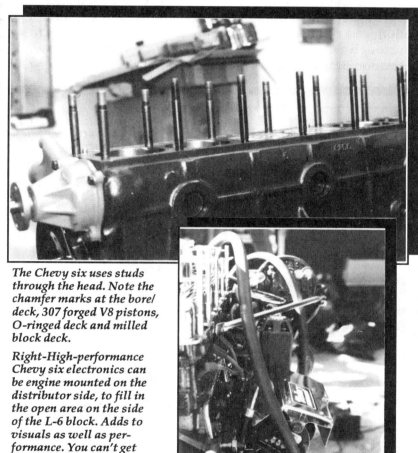

The Chevy six uses studs through the head. Note the chamfer marks at the bore/ deck, 307 forged V8 pistons, O-ringed deck and milled block deck.

Right-High-performance Chevy six electronics can be engine mounted on the distributor side, to fill in the open area on the side of the L-6 block. Adds to visuals as well as performance. You can't get too hot an ignition system.

PATRICK'S STUFF

If you happen to be hopping up an early Chevy or GMC six, and are searching for speed equipment to do the job, here's a source for just about everything that you could possibly need. Contact Patrick's Antique Cars & Trucks, P.O. Box 648, Casa Grande, Arizona 85222; (602) 836-1117. Patrick Dykes is the owner.

Included in Patrick's inventory are items such as can be seen in these photographs — essentially all the trick goodies to hang on the outside. But, the stuff you can't see is also available. All the zoomies for the inside, like cams, cranks, pistons, whatever. It's kind of a one-stop shopping mall for everything to do with the Chevy and GMC sixes.

by Rich Johnson

Blowing
The Stovebolt Six

Everyone is familiar with blown Chevy V8 hot rod engines, but many folks are not aware that the Chevy six can be made into a dynamite hot rod engine by installation of a supercharger.

One of the manufacturers of Chevy six supercharger equipment is Stovebolt Engine Company, P.O. Box 166, Corbett, Oregon 97019; (503) 695-2571. When we contacted company owner Dick Larrowe, he reported that some people question the durability of the six cylinder engines, with comments such as, "That blower will blow the bottom end right out of that wimpy six." According to Larrowe, that isn't the case, and he cites examples of just how tough a Chevy six is. "Our '40 Chevrolet convertible with a destroked GMC 302 (292) that we use for demonstration drag racing has endured missed shifts with over-revving, and defective automatic transmissions that don't shift into high gear and then try to pull the car down from 75 mph. Just take a look at normal truck use. Holding a heavy truck back on compression is harder on an engine than anything you can do in a street rod."

So, the Chevy inline six is a hardy powerplant, ripe for a bit of hot rod massaging. And in this case, we're talking about supercharging. Stovebolt Engine Company manufactures the manifolds necessary to install a blower on not only the Chevy sixes but other brands as well. The manifold shown in these photographs will not allow the hood to close on a late-model Chevy (unless the hood is modified), but it will fit under the hood of older models. The GMC 302 engine in the '40 Chevy has a height of 11 inches from the top of the cylinder head to the top of the B&M air filter. The supercharged engine shown in these photos has a top of head to top of air filter distance of 14 inches. By substituting a lower profile air filter, the hood can be closed on older model cars without cutting a hole in the hood for the blower to poke through.

Stovebolt Engine Company has an economy kit for customers who want to drill and tap their own holes, and do some finishing metal

Stovebolt Engine Company supercharger equipment is seen here from all sides, topped with a B&M blower. Note the routing of the blower belt around the crankshaft and camshaft pulleys, and then past the adjustable tensioning idler and over the snout of the supercharger. From the rear, the polished intake manifold and the header pipes are visible.

work. Next most expensive is the unpolished but assembled manifold, and the top of the line is the polished and assembled manifold.

Using the proper type of puller, remove the stock harmonic balancer.

Here's a basic stock Chevy 235 inline six with generator, long water pump, one-barrel carb and single exhaust. This is the kind of engine that is so very adaptable to supercharging.

Another source of supercharger equipment for the Chevy six is Hunter Performance, 9302 Livernois, Houston, Texas 77080; (713) 461-BLWN. Jules Glogovcsan is owner, and offers a supercharger kit based on the B&M 112 cid blower. The kit fits with either Clifford headers or the stock OEM exhaust manifold. Installation is fairly quick and easy, as the following photographs illustrate. However, if you are planning a trip to Texas and want to contact the company in advance, they will do the installation free of charge, including hooking up the exhaust system.

The first step is to remove the intake system. Also remove the stock exhaust system if the plan is to use headers.

Drill and tap the stock crankshaft snout. Use a 25/64" drill. Be sure to drill on the crankshaft's centerline. Then use a 7/16" x 20 tap to thread the hole.

Next, install the remachined harmonic balancer and special drive system components. Hunter Performance will do all the harmonic balancer machining, if desired.

Install the headers at this time. Shown are the Clifford 235 Chevy six headers.

Now it's time to install the supercharger intake manifold. The Hunter Performance unit uses stock OEM-type O-rings for the intake port alignment. Install studs, blower gasket and then install the supercharger. The idler arm system and 6-rib poly V belt can be installed at this point, then set the drive belt tension. Carburetor and fan go on next, followed by the air filter.

117

Stovebolt
Shuffle

Almost everyone is well versed in the practicalities of swappin' different shapes and sizes of bowtie bent eights into later model Chevy engine bays. If a straight six occupied the space between the front fenders, anything from a 265 inch mouse motor to a 500+ inch fat block will drop right in. Or at least that's how the story goes.

Unfortunately, the simple "drop 'n swap" routine isn't always that easy, even with Chevys in general and early Camaros in particular. While the basic engine compartment found on vintage '67 through '69 Camaros as well as '68 to '72 Novas (along with the myriad of Nova clones such as the Ventura, Skylark and Omega) is certainly massive, there are a number of obstacles that might thwart your progress should you decide to play engine swapper. As an example, a series of different frame mounts were used for the respective

Chevrolet powerplants. Alternator locations varied with engines and model years. Different transmission crossmembers were offered for the myriad of applications. Varied *motor* mounts were included in the package. A number of clutch linkage setups were utilized...and the list goes on!

Because of this plethora of variables, swaps are not always simple and in many cases, it can become more of a "twist, shove and cut" operation rather than a common bolt-in. Of course, the following information also applies to '67-'69 Firebirds and the previously mentioned '68-72 "X" bodies as well... all Camaro "sisters" under the skin.

BOWTIE ENGINE DIMENSIONS

In terms of overall size, the assorted Chevy powerplants are relatively compact. V8, L6 and V6-90 starter

1	ENGINE	HEIGHT @ AIR CLEAN.	OVERALL LENGTH	OVERALL LENGTH TO DIST.	OVERALL WIDTH @ VALVE COVERS	OVERALL WIDTH @ EXH. MAN.	HEIGHT @ VALVE COVERS	HEIGHT @ CARB.
	L-6	28	32.5	N/A	16	23.5	24	25.5
	V6-90	27	22.38	22.1	19	26	20.5	25
	V8-SB	27	26.78	26.5	19	26	20.5	25
	V8-BB	33	29.4	29.4	22	27	23.5	29.5

2	ENGINE	STARTER LOCATION	OIL SUMP LOCATION	DISTRIBUTOR LOCATION	APPROXIMATE WEIGHT-ALL IRON
	L-6	Right	Rear	Right	410
	V6-90	Right	Rear	Rear	N/A
	V8-SB	Right	Rear	Rear	550
	V8-BB	Right	Rear	Rear	625

NOTE: - Dimensions are approximates.
• All figures are for powerplants with pre-'69 or Corvette "short" water pump/pulley arrangement.
• Aluminum cylinder heads and/or blocks available for V6-90, small block and big block

location is identical as are the oil pan sumps. Block motor mount bosses are in very similar locations and all feature the conventional Chevrolet three bolt pattern. Each and every engine listed in chart #1 will easily slide into the engine bay of your vintage GM "F" or "X" body.

FRAME MOUNTS:

Due to the varied dimensions of the available production powerplants during the halcyon days of the Camaro, three different frame mounts were utilized; the six cylinder mount, the small block mount and the big block mount. All of these mounts will effectively accept any of the powerplants, however the actual location of the engine in the compartment will be affected. As an example, a set of factory big block frame mounts feature a distinct difference in height between left and right hand versions. In addition, the OE mounts place the powerplant further forward in the respective engine compartment.

This is not to say that you cannot fit (for example) a fat block onto small block frame mounts. It is entirely possible, however the engine will sit further to the rear of the compartment and the driver's side of the engine will sit slightly lower than "normal." This creates some header fit problems and makes for tight clearances between the engine and the firewall. Savy racers of the sixties picked up on this point immediately! By using small block frame mounts, the powerplant could then easily be slid *rearward* in the compartment, effectively placing more weight on the rear axle. By the same

token, a set of six cylinder frame mounts can be used with a V8 for slightly more setback, but in this case, the firewall will have to be "tickled" for distributor clearance. Additionally, the respective bellhousing bolts become almost impossible to access.

What about the V6-90? While no factory-fitted bent-six powerplants were available for the early "F" and "X" bodies, the engines can easily be mated to conventional small block V8 frame mounts. Part numbers for the respective frame mounts (Chevy officially calls 'em "Bracket Assembly, Engine Mounting") are as follows:
• Chevrolet Group Number 0.029 applies to all examples in chart #3.

MOTOR MOUNTS

It's no big secret that Chevy had a bit of a motor mount problem in the late sixties. A couple of fixes were in order, but in general, the rubber/steel composition mounts had a bad habit of tearing apart. Espe-

3	Application	Engine	Location	Part Number
	•67-69 Camaro & Firebird &	L6	Left	3892731
	68-72 Nova, Ventura, etc.	L6	Right	3892732
	•67-68 Camaro & Firebird &	V8-SB	Left	3955183
	70-71 Nova, Ventura, etc.	V8-SB	Right	3980938
	•69 Camaro & Firebird &	V8-SB	Left	3945507
	69 & 72 Nova, Ventura, etc.	V8-SB	Right	3945508
	• 67-68 Camaro & Firebird &	V8-BB	Left	3912597
	68 Nova, Ventura, etc.	V8-BB	Right	3912598
	•69 Camaro & Firebird &	V8-BB	Left	3980941
	69-72 Nova, Ventura, etc.	V8-BB	Right	3980942

NOTE: The above part numbers were taken from a 1983 edition of the Chevrolet parts catalog. While many of the numbers may (and probably will) change up, use them as a basis and check with your dealer or restoration parts company for availability.

cially at an inopportune moment. Because of this, there are several "fixes" available, but the ultimate cure is the installation of a set of solid motor mounts. Much has been said about these steel beauties, with the most derogatory statements advising that they transmit a bunch of noise to the cockpit. From this writer's perspective, it is preferable to have a bit of noise and vibration rather than taking the risk of ripping apart a motor mount (even an upgraded version with built-in locks). These

The 1967 through 1969 Camaro (along with its sisterships) makes use of a conventional three point mount system. This vehicle features aftermarket steel motor mounts - a set of components that stop engine flex and torn mounts cold in its tracks.

4	Dimensions:		
Mount	Dimension "A"	Dimension "B"	Thickness
#1	1-11/16"	2-1/2"	.250"
#2	2-1/8"	2-3/8"	.187"
#3	1-3/4"	2-5/8"	.187"

5		Applications:

(Note: All are body style/engine combinations for use with previously described frame or chassis mounts)

Mount	Engine	Vehicle
#1	283	1958-68 Chevrolet
		1964-67 Chevelle, Chevy II
	307	1968-72 Chevelle, Nova, Monte Carlo
		1969-71 Camaro
		1968 Chevrolet
	327	1969 - all models
		1967-69 Camaro, Chevy II
		1964-68 Chevelle
		1965-67 Chevy II
		1958-69 Chevrolet
	348	1958-61 - all models
	350	1970-72 Chevrolet - two barrel
		1971 Camaro
		1970-71 Nova- except special high performance
		1970 Camaro - except special high performance
#2	302	1969 Camaro
	327	1967-68 Chevrolet
		1968 Chevelle
	350	1972 Nova
		1969-72 Chevelle, Monte Carlo
		1970-71 Chevrolet
		1970 Camaro with special high performance
		1969 - all models
	396	1967 Chevrolet
		1968-70 Chevelle
		1969-70 Camaro, Nova
	402	1970-72 - all models
	427	1968-69 Chevrolet
	454	1970-72 Chevrolet, Chevelle, Monte Carlo
#3	302	1967-68 Camaro
	305	1980 California-only Corvette
	307	1968-69 Chevrolet Police Package
	327	1963-68 Corvette
	350	1966-68 Corvette
		1967-68 Camaro, Chevy II
		1965 Corvette
	409	1961-65 - all models
	427	1966-69 Corvette
	454	1966-67 - all models
	454	1970-74 Corvette

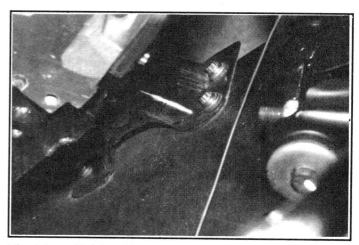

The right and left hand frame mounts used on big block examples differ. The right hand mount is taller, allowing the engine to sit slightly higher in the chassis. The use of the right frame mount for the engine installation makes for better header fit and clearance around clutch linkage and the like.

Chevrolet used two different systems of mounting the alternator between '67 and '69. With the advent of the 1969 model year, the alternator was moved to the passenger side of the engine. Coupled with the move was a longer water pump and a different pulley system.

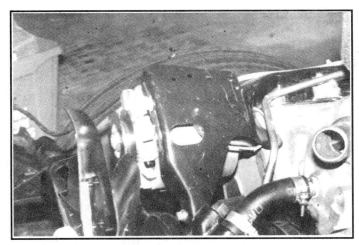

The topside of the alternator shows the mount position in front of the passenger side cylinder head. This later model design provided for a more compact engine (overall) since the alternator did not "hang out in the breeze." Replacement upper mounts such as these are still available from Chevrolet.

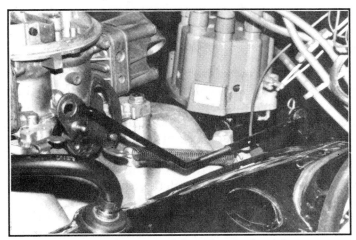

Vintage Camaro and Nova models make use of a rather conventional lever/rod throttle arrangement. In most cases, a setup designed for use with a Holley carburetor will work on either big or small block applications. The setup depicted here is from a Z/28 - - adapted to work with a big block.

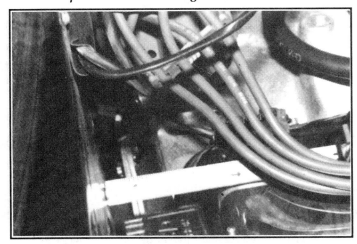

When big block frame mounts are used with a big block powerplant, the firewall clearance is tight but acceptable. Substituting small block or six cylinder mounts moves the engine rearward eliminating this clearance factor. While great for all-out drag racing, it makes accessing the bellhousing bolts almost impossible, not to mention the distributor clearance problem.

6	Part Numbers:	

Steel motor mount part numbers from both B&B and Moroso are as follows: Dimensions and applications are in charts #4 and #5.

Mount #	B&B Performance	Moroso
1	6650	62500
2	6651	62510
3	6653	62530

In general, mount #1 replaces Chevrolet P/N 3990914, 3988989, 377409 and 3989488. Mount #2 replaces Chevrolet P/N 3990918 and 3990920 while mount #3 replaces Chevrolet P/N 3990916.

all-steel examples stop engine flex cold in its tracks and make life a whole bunch easier on the clutch and carburetor linkage. In addition, the need for troublesome torque straps or chains to stop engine movement is eliminated. Companies such as Moroso and B&B Performance offer a full range of mounts for the early "Chebbies."

TRANSMISSION CROSSMEMBERS & MOUNTS:

The nature of the vintage "F" and "X" bodies as "everyman's car" proved to be more than influential in the transmission department. Because the basic vehicles were seen as anything from pedestrian econo-sedans to all-out boy racers, the availability of transmissions was prolific to say the least. Everything from the much maligned Powerglide to race-inspired "rock crusher" Muncies occupied the space under the floor-

7	Transmission	Crossmember #
	•Three-speed manual, Four-speed manual, Turbo Hydramatic 350, Powerglide - all except HD and Big Block	3899006
	•Turbo Hydramatic 400 - all except Big Block	3912573
	•Turbo Hydramatic 400 - Big Block	3912570
	•Four-speed manual, HD three-speed manual - Big Block	3912570

NOTE: The above part numbers were taken from a 1972 vintage Chevrolet parts manual. While availability from Chevrolet may be scarce on the special big block crossmembers, the others are readily available. Part numbers may change up, however they will still fit.

What makes the fat block crossmembers different? In general, the rat motored examples featured sturdier construction and that's it. In a pinch, a small block crossmember will easily work. Just be sure to use the right crossmember for the appropriate transmission.

In addition, the basic transmission mount (affectionately referred to as the "mounting" in bow tie parts catalogs) is similar for all examples. Aftermarket solid versions are available, but it has been our experience that these pieces are best left to the drag race only crowd. Coupled with solid motor mounts, these parts have a tendency to bind the entire powertrain together *too-tightly* . The result is often broken mount ears on four-speed cases or completely fractured case assemblies on autoboxes. Stick with the OE style rubber stuff. Your transmission will be much happier! OE Chevy part numbers (circa '72) are listed in chart #8.

Chevrolet offers a myriad of rubber transmission mounts such as this example. While aftermarket versions are available we generally stay away from them - simply because they create too harsh an environment for a street-strip automobile.

Two basic types of HD starters are available from Chevrolet - one for use with 153 tooth flywheels and one for use with 168 tooth flywheels. This version is for a large diameter 168 tooth setup. How can you tell? Large diameter flywheel starters have an offset or staggered bolt pattern.

This rather scrungy piece is a small block stick-shift/powerglide/turbo350 transmission crossmember. Big block versions are slightly beefier and feature a different hole on the bottom. Fortunately, a big block can use a small block crossmember if required. In addition, this crossmember can be used to slide a Powerglide behind a fat block. It should be noted that Hydramatic crossmembers are different breeds again.

8	Application	Part Number
	• Three speed, four speed manual, TH 350, Powerglide	3913498
	• Turbo Hydramatic 400	3895831
	• HD Mounting - 302 & 396 Special High Performance	3895830

boards. And due to this fact, swappin' gearboxes in an early "F" platform is an easy task.

Many non-stock combinations are possible. Examples include Powerglides behind fat blocks, Muncies behind straight sixes, Turbo-hydro-backed V6's and a host of others. It was almost like Chevrolet engineers envisioned the whole swapping scheme. They included a number of different crossmembers and a series of holes drilled into the front subframe just for this purpose.

The basic crossmembers can be broken down into three groups; the 'Hydramatic 400 examples, the non-hydramatic examples and the big block versions. Chart #7 dipicts what fits and what doesn't.

FLYWHEELS, FLEXPLATES

Just when you think you have the entire engine swapping routine down to a science, Chevy throws a curve at you - in the direction of flywheel (and flexplate) size and balance. To make a long story short, two different systems of balance were used on Chevy V8's - internal balance and external balance. 400 cubic inch *small blocks* and 454 cubic inch *big blocks* made use of externally balanced (or "counter-weighted") flywheels and harmonic dampers. The proper flywheel/flexplate must be used for these engines. Otherwise, you can expect premature engine failure coupled with a not-so-pleasing vibration problem.

Of course, there is one more fly in the ointment. Chevrolet offered

9	*Flywheels & Flexplates:*	
Description		Part Number
Flywheels -		
• 12-3/4" nodular iron, 10.4" clutch, neutral balance		14085720
• 12-3/4" nodular iron, 10.4" clutch, counterweighted for 454		3963537
• 14" iron, 11" clutch, counterweighted for 400		3986394
• 14" iron, 11" clutch, counterweighted for 454		3993827
• 14" iron, 10.4 & 11" clutch, neutral balance		3991469
Flexplates -		
• Flexplate - 14", neutral balance - 168 tooth - SB		471598
• Flexplate - 14", neutral balance - 168 tooth - BB		471597
• Flexplate - 14", counterweighted for 400 - 168 tooth		471578
• Flexplate - 14", counterweighted for 454 - 168 tooth		14001992
• Flexplate - 12-3/4", neutral balance - 153 tooth - SB		471529

10	Description	Part Number
	• HD starter, 12-3/4" flywheel or flexplate	1108789
	• HD starter, 14" flywheel or flexplate	1108400

In the event that you already have a Chevy starter for a particular application and wish to convert to a different flywheel diameter, the following nose pieces are offered by Chevrolet. Additionally, we have included the part number for Chevy's HD starter brace - a sure fire cure for a balky starter caused by excess movement on the block (See chart #11).

11	Description	Part Number
	• Starter nose piece - for use with 12-3/4" flywheels	1968122
	• Starter nose piece - for use with 14" flywheels	1984098
	• Starter brace - HD	354353

flywheels in two different sizes - 14 inch and 12-3/4 inch. The large diameter flywheels are characterized by a 168-tooth ring gear count while the 12-3/4 inch versions feature 153 teeth on the ring gear. With the dawn of the 1986 model year, Chevrolet changed the rear main seal design (and consequently changed the crankshaft bolt circle). The '86 and newer versions feature a smaller 3.00 inch crank flange bolt circle while earlier examples have a 3.58 inch pattern. Chart #9 depicts several of the various configurations of early OE Chevrolet flywheels and flexplates that you might come across.

STARTERS

As indicated previously, two different types of flywheels and flexplates were (and are) used on bow tie powerplants - 153 tooth and 168 tooth. Fourteen inch versions make use of the 168 tooth pattern while 12-3/4 inch examples use the smaller 153 tooth pattern. Due to this difference in tooth count, a pair of distinct starters (or more accurately, starter nose pieces) are required. Large diameter versions require a starter with offset bolt holes in the nose piece while small diameter versions use a starter with bolt holes that are parallel. The majority of Chevrolet blocks are drilled for both types of starters. Chart #10 depicts Chevy's heavy duty starter offerings.

CLUTCH LINKAGE:

Autobox freaks will love this section - they can skip it entirely! Unfortunately, followers of the stick shift faith have a minor (or major - depending upon your perspective) stumbling block in the way when it comes to slippin' a fat block where a mouse motor once grew. And that stumbling block is the clutch cross shaft or "Z-bar."

It seems that the Chevy engineers threw us another curve with this piece. You see, a small block cross shaft just doesn't work with a big block. The additional

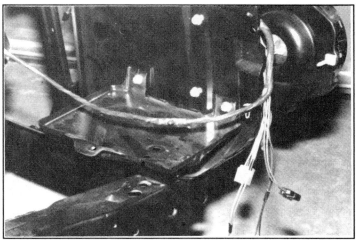

Chevy engines have their starters on the passenger side. As a result, the battery tray is mounted on the passenger side of the radiator support. If you are swappin' a Chevy into a Firebird (or "X" body with non-Chevy power), it is a good idea to move the battery to this side of the vehicle. A common Camaro tray will work on most Firebirds and "X" bodies.

A lone radiator support was used on all applications. Larger radiators simply bolt up with the factory installed holes. See the next photo:

On the driver's side of the radiator support will be an extra set of holes. This support already has the outer holes fitted with OE rad mount insulators. The matching set of inner holes are for use with a small block or six banger radiator.

width of the rat motor creates a small dilemma with the mouse motor shaft - it doesn't fit. And to make matters worse, the gennie part number (3912602 and its myriad of changeups) has long since been discontinued.

On a brighter note, Steve Pardini of Steve's Camaros (1197 San Mateo Avenue, Sand Bruno, CA 94066, PH# 415-873-1890) has tooled up with a neat reproduction that both fits and works. Steve's Camaros has the parts in stock and take our word for it - it looks just like the original. What about the other bits and pieces? For the most part, the remaining components are generally available. Heavy duty accessory hardware is available from Mr. Gasket (as well as its Lakewood subsidiary).

Small block and bent-six pieces are readily available in the aftermarket. Many speciality Camaro shops handle complete kits that included everything from the pedal pads to the clutch return spring. And best of all, these parts are also applicable to Chevy-powered Novas, Firebirds, Venturas and a host of other "X" bodies.

ALTERNATORS, WATER PUMPS & PULLEYS:

While bow tie alternators are all similar in their external size, you should be forewarned that '67 and '68 examples featured alternators mounted on the driver's side of the engine while later units featured alternators mounted on the passenger side. This happened to coincide with the introduction of the later "long" style water pumps. The newer pumps are a bit over one inch longer and as a result, there is no interchange between the various pieces.

In a nutshell, if you are swapping engines from model year to model year, just be certain that the water pump/pulley/alternator mount arrangement is compatible with the powerplant. Obviously, it's better to use the proper late model "long" arrangement for '69 and later model years only because the various wiring components on the harness will already be in place.

Due to the myriad of part numbers available for swapping alternators, we would almost require an entire volume just for documenting that purpose. If you decide to change over to a late system, try using a '73 and later pickup truck as a donor. These vehicles are plentiful in wrecking...err...recycling yards and since it is a truck, you won't get gouged on the price. Just don't mention that your swap is for a big block Camaro...the price will go up tenfold!

Before leaving the topic of alternator mounting, keep in mind that Chevrolet did not convert the Corvette over to the long water pump design in 1969 - it remained as a "shorty" setup for many years. This could also be a source for complete bits and pieces, especially if you are changing over to a "short" configuration.

COOLING:

Obviously, a six popper is going to be a lot less of a hot head than a full tilt fat block and because of this, you

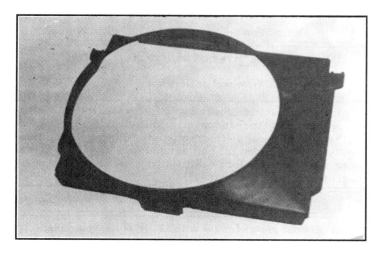

Different fan shrouds were used with different engines/radiators. This slim unit is a full circle affair that is designed for use with the big block radiator. Reproductions are readily available in the aftermarket.

Griffin Racing Radiators offers this COPO "gooseneck" radiator reproduction. Identical to a factory Harrison setup, it provides for great cooling - even with a full tilt big block. Note the repro radiator hoses. They fit and actually provide for safer cooling than some "fits-all" jobber components ...but that's another story!

The differences between small block and big block hi-po pulleys are evident in this photo. While the small block pulley will physically bolt on to a big block, it is shallower - the result being misaligned pulleys. In addition, pulleys designed for '68 and older engines cannot interchange on '69 and newer examples.

Small block heater shroud covers featured outlets that appear next to the cylinder block (visible as small semi-circles at the side of the cover opposite the blower). When a big block is installed in the engine compartment, the heater inlet/outlet hoses will interfere with the passenger side cylinder head. Big block heater cores featured a reversed core - placing the hoses in the center of the shroud.

The "long" water pump design introduced in 1969 is significantly longer than the early version. As you probably have guessed, pulleys and alternator mounts are different with this system.

Due to the heavier weight of the big block (versus a small block or six cylinder), the springs should be changed. Keep in mind that the weight of a small block with aluminum heads is very close to a six cylinder, while an aluminum head rat motor approaches a small block in "dressed" weight. Springs are generally available from both Chevrolet and the aftermarket.

should consider your cooling options. Generally speaking, Chevrolet offered a wide range of Harrison radiators for the varying applications. In other words, one rad for the stick shift six cylinder cars, one rad for similar autoboxes and so on. Adding air conditioning or specifying HD cooling on the order blank changed the rad dimensions.

Fortunately, the vintage "X" and "F" bodies used similar radiator supports. As an example, a six cylinder Camaro support is identical to a fat block support. The mounting holes for heavy duty radiators are included in the package. You just have to line up the holes and bolt the HD unit into place.

On the down side, the passing of time has contributed to the disappearance of many HD radiators from the Harrison stockpiles. As an example, the HD air conditioning radiator for a '69 396 Nova has long since been discontinued. Luckily, the good folks from Griffin Racing Radiators (Rt. 1, Box 66, Townville, SC 29689 PH # 803-287-4898) has noticed this disappearing act and have geared up to create replacement radiators for the various applications. Griffin offers rads for virtually all hi-po and HD vintage Camaro/Nova applications, including the four core COPO 427 "goose neck" units. Also, the Griffin price is substantially better than the gennie Chevy figures. Give 'em a call - you'll be glad you did!

Last but not least, give some consideration to using the proper shroud for the application. Fat block models used their own shroud as did small block cars and six cylinder applications. The shrouds are currently being reproduced by several manufacturers and are readily available from Camaro parts vendors.

ODDS 'N ENDS:

Before we leave, we should say that some other bits 'n pieces require attention when swapping powerplants in vintage Camaros (and their sisterships). Items like the throttle linkage, front springs, headers (or exhaust manifolds) and so on are varied. Beginning with the header system:

Headers:

In general, headers designed for a small block Camaro will fit a small block Nova or other "X" body, provided that you don't breach the model year differences. The rule is rather simple: Headers for a Camaro from 1967 through '69 fit a '68 through '72 Nova (or other "X" body with a Chevy V8). On the other hand some headers designed for '70 and newer Camaros will not fit. Just remember to keep the engine families and body style restrictions in place.

Batteries:

Certain GM "X" bodies not powered by Chevrolet as well as Firebirds will have the battery tray on the wrong side of the engine compartment (mounted on the driver's side). Due to this fact, you will require a massive length of cable to reach the passenger-side starter. Another solution to this problem is moving the battery tray to the Chevy location or relocating it completely to the trunk. Take your pick, but we would opt for the Chevy location.

Front Springs:

As you can determine from the engine dimension chart shown in the beginning of this article, different engines have different weights. While an aluminum-head equipped rat motor will approach the weight of a standard small block, an all-iron rat motor will not. A plethora of springs are available from both Chevrolet and the aftermarket. Just be sure to use the right spring for the application.

Throttle Linkage:

Early "F" and "X" cars used a mechanical throttle linkage. In other words, no cable setups - instead, a simple lever and rod arrangement. While most of the Holley pieces for a big block and a small block will interchange (even though they feature different bends and have different part numbers), the other parts will not. The simple solution is to procure the right parts the first time out rather than trying to cobble up a linkage from scratch. In the event that Chevy doesn't have the appropriate parts in stock, contact your local Camaro parts dealer. Reproductions are readily available.

Fuel Pickup:

Even in its formative years, the Camaro had a different fuel tank sender/pickup for the hi-po 396/427/302 powerplants. A larger line size was utilized and even if you decide to upgrade with aftermarket goodies, keep the volume requirements in mind. A larger engine requires more fuel volume.

Heater:

When the first fat blocks were shoe-horned into the '67 Camaro engine bays, one of the first changes was the relocation of the heater hoses. In essence, a new heater core was designed - one with reversed inlet/outlet fittings. Rather than exiting near the cylinder head, the fittings were placed near the inner fender. Reproduction heater cores are readily available and by simply cutting new holes in the heater core cover, you can reposition your heater hoses. Incidentally, the same pieces work on all vintage "F" and "X" bodies covered in this article.

That wraps up our look at swapping various powerplants into early Camaro models. By taking your time and sorting out the variables, your personal swap will look like it grew there instead of being a butchered and dangerous hack job. Welding isn't necessary, but care in component selection is. Take the time and do it right - you'll enjoy the results. We know that we do!!!

ENDANGERED SPECIES LIST

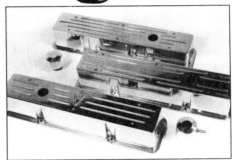
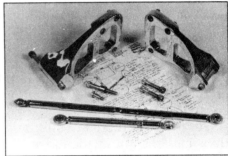

by Wayne Scraba

Transmissions
Bowtie Gearboxes

A few years back, transmission choice was simple. You were either a stick-shift artist or a follower of the autobox faith. Most hot rodders picked one of three types of Chevy gearboxes to slip between the bowtie frame rails. The transmissions of choice? Either a Muncie four-gear, a Hydramatic or a venerable Powerglide. While there's absolutely nothing wrong with any of these trannys, today's marketplace has evolved considerably.

In essence, there are still only two basic types of transmissions, automatic and manual. Some are stronger than others, and certain examples may prove easier to install in hot rods than their counterparts. There is a tremendous amount of interchange in regard to Chevrolet transmissions, and from our perspective there has never been a better selection of gearboxes for the bowtie set.

MANUAL TRANSMISSIONS

There have been far more manual transmissions than automatics available for Chevys over the years. The list of available 4-speeds is staggering — the vintage Borg Warner T-10, the myriad of Muncie 4-speeds, the Saginaw 4-speeds and more recently the Nash (Borg Warner, now Richmond Gear) 4-speed. Add in the variety of different 3-speeds — the overdrive Corvette 4+3, the recent ZF 6-speed gearbox and the Borg Warner T5 and it is obvious that stick shift transmission options are plentiful for your Chevy hot rod.

Muncie 4-Speeds

By 1963, the torque output of Chevrolet engines had taxed the original Borg Warner T-10 to the max. The solution was the introduction of the Muncie transmission (named after the city in which it was produced — Muncie, Indiana). The first versions of the Muncie (produced from 1963 to 1965 inclusive) made use of a 7/8-inch diameter countershaft and brass configuration synchronizer rings sans shoulders. Muncies were produced with two different gear ratios during the era, close-ratio and wide-ratio. The close-ratio box featured gear ratios of 2.20:1, 1.64:1, 1.28:1 and 1.00:1 for first through fourth gears respectively. The wide-ratio trans-

mission had ratios of 2.56:1, 1.91:1, 1.48:1 and 1.00:1 (first through fourth).

In 1966, a revised Muncie 4-speed was introduced. Changes included a 1.00-inch diameter countershaft and a combination of wider brass synchro hubs and wider synchronizer rings. The close-ratio gearbox ratios remained unchanged, but the wide-ratio transmission now featured ratios (from first through fourth) of 2.52:1, 1.88:1, 1.46:1 and 1.00:1.

A special Muncie gearbox, designed for high output applications, was introduced during the 1965 season. Dubbed the M-22 or "rock crusher," this transmission was produced until the end of the 1974 season. This transmission featured 9310 nickle alloy gears with a relatively low helical cut of 21 degrees. Because of this helix angle, the M-22 generated a considerable amount of noise when operated in first through third gears. A 1-inch diameter countershaft was used in the "rock crusher" and, contrary to popular belief, the input shaft was either a 26-spline or a conventional 10-spline unit. Overall gear ratio selection for the M-22 model was limited to the familiar 2.20:1 close-ratio set up.

Yet another incarnation of the Muncie gearbox made its debut during the 1971 model year. Dubbed the "third design" or "heavy duty" gearbox, this transmission was not as strong as the "rock crusher" but the overall construction was beefier than past conventional transmissions. The output shaft of these transmissions received 32 splines (as opposed to the previous 27 splines), while the input shaft was standardized at 26 splines. Gear ratios were identical to the 1966 and newer Muncie transmissions.

One other Muncie gearbox that bears mentioning is the special long-tailshaft model. Produced from 1964 to 1968, this transmission carried all of the features of the previously described versions (per the specific model years), but featured a six-inch longer overall length for use in full size Pontiac and Oldsmobile passenger cars.

Borg Warner / Nash / Richmond Gear 4-Speeds

Perhaps the original charter member of the Chevrolet 4-speed family tree is the 1957 vintage Borg Warner T-10. Introduced as a high-performance option for the

Corvette, the T-10 featured relatively low overall weight, a close-ratio gearset and aluminum construction. The close-ratio version of this transmission carried a 2.20:1 first gear while the wide-ratio original T-10 made use of a 2.54:1 first. By 1961, there was a changeover in regard to mainshaft diameter and during the 1962 season, the cluster gear was revised.

By 1972, the Super T-10 again required revision. The latest versions featured another increase in the second gear thrust flange (which required a rework of the actual second speed gear). Further experimentation and development at Borg Warner saw the inclusion of several drag race type gear ratios. With the decade half over, B-W released a sixth design Super T-10 (sometimes called the Super T-10; 2nd design). This transmission family featured an enlarged cluster gear countershaft (up to 1 inch in diameter) as well as an enlarged output shaft complete with 32 splines (similar to the last Muncie gearboxes and identical to the HD Turbo Hydramatic 400). The gears were cut with a coarser pitch and were manufactured from nickel chrome moly alloy (SAE 8620). The main case was cast in iron while the tailshaft was an aluminum casting. Input shaft splines were standardized at 26 and several shifting improvements were made. Available gear ratios for this family of transmissions were as follows:

vette ante with a German designed ZF 6-speed gearbox. The OEM need for a 4-speed manual transmission was minimized and Nash sold the Super T-10 tooling to the Richmond Gear Division of the Regal-Beloit Corporation. Combining the production of the Super T-10 with the new Nash (or more correctly, now the Richmond) 5-speed, several changes were incorporated. The ultra-low 3.44:1 first gear ratio transmissions were discontinued. A familiar face, the 2.43:1 gear ratio transmission ("S") was reborn while the remaining "X" ratio, "W" ratio and "Y" (now dubbed the "CC") ratio gearboxes continued. The basic transmission case was now cast aluminum, however the overall configuration remained as previously produced. Ratios for the "S" transmission are as follows: 1st - 2.43:1; 2nd - 1.61:1; 3rd - 1.23:1, 4th - 1.00:1.

Internally, the latest Richmond T-10 features construction identical to past second design Super T-10 transmissions. In other words, a 26-spline input shaft, a 1-inch diameter mainshaft, wide cut coarse pitch gears complete with nickel chrome moly construction and a 1-inch diameter cluster countershaft (1/8-inch larger than previous designs). The oil ring grooves on the cam selectors have been eliminated for added strength and first gear has been sleeved to improve oiling and to protect the mainshaft.

TRANSMISSION		1ST GEAR	2ND GEAR	3RD GEAR	4TH GEAR
Special close	(X)	2.64:1	1.61:1	1.23:1	1.00:1
Special wide	(W)	2.64:1	1.75:1	1.33:1	1.00:1
Extra low	(Y)	2.88:1	1.74:1	1.33:1	1.00:1
Ultra	(U)	3.44:1	2.28:1	1.46:1	1.00:1

With the redesign of the T-10 came several significant shifting improvements. The gear cones feature a much finer surface finish. This results in increased synchro ring life

Although the "Y" and "U" transmissions are obviously different, what was the reason for the pair of 2.64:1 transmissions? The "X" series transmission has a larger percentage drop from first to second gear, but the percentage drops from second, third and fourth are much smaller. In a drag race application, this substantially reduces the rpm loss on the 3 to 4 gear shift. With a restricted rear tire size, the large drop from first to second on the "X" transmission can reduce or at least minimize tire spin.

By the early 1980's, a number of changes had taken place at Borg Warner. Transmission technology for production cars mandated the use of smaller, lighter overdriven 5-speed gearboxes. Front wheel drive vehicle production had increased and the market for a beefy 4-speed was beginning to shrink. At the very same moment, Doug Nash Engineering was developing a heavy-duty overdrive unit to mount on the Super T-10 for use on the new 1983 Corvette. Because of this transition, Nash purchased all of the Super T-10 tooling and began production of various OEM-style gearboxes.

With the decade closing, Chevrolet upped its Cor-

under the most severe conditions. The synchro assemblies utilize hubs without grooves for sleeves to catch on and feature lightweight strut keys for smoother shifts. Similarly, the synchro rings are thicker and have a slight mismatch to the gear cone. This provides for much more positive and quicker gear changes. The synchro sleeves are manufactured from S.A.E. 4027 steel with a special heat treat and an enlarged area around the fork grooves to prevent breakage under severe use. In the shift fork department, the forks were revised so that the alignment and contact with the sleeve would be better, resulting in faster shifts. Finally, the synchro teeth feature a sharp angle which provides a much cleaner, faster shift. The revisions contributed to a transmission that is butter smooth in the shifting department, but more importantly, is durable enough to withstand the punishment handed out by a hi-po street-strip bowtie!

The overall dimensions for the Richmond T-10 4-speed are very similar to a Muncie gear box. In fact, with very little work, a late design T-10 will easily slip into the spot normally occupied by a vintage Muncie.

Saginaw 4-Speed

The Saginaw 4-speed manual transmission was introduced in the latter half of the '60s. Designed as a light- to medium-duty transmission, it saw service in everything from low horsepower small block Camaros to Vega 4-cylinder applications. Identification of this gearbox is simple. It features a driver's-side side-cover, but unlike the tougher Muncie or B-W transmissions, the Saginaw has its reverse lever mounted on the side cover, instead of being mounted to the extension housing. In terms of mount location and basic size, the Saginaw also parallels the dimensions provided for the Richmond T-10 4-speed.

In typical V8 applications, the ratios were as follows:

1st Gear	2nd Gear	3rd Gear	4th Gear
2.54:1	1.80:1	1.44:1	1.00:1

Four-banger Vega models featured much different ratios (obviously due to the anemic powerplant jammed between the fenders). The following chart depicts the gear spreads:

1st Gear	2nd Gear	3rd Gear	4th Gear
3.11:1	2.20:1	1.47:1	1.00:1

3-Speeds

During the early and middle '60s, GM released several fully synchronized 3-speed manual transmissions for use on the entire product line. The bare bones 6-cylinder and small block versions were supplied by the Saginaw Division while fat block examples came equipped with Muncie 3-speed gearboxes. It should be pointed out that the Muncie was also available as a heavy-duty 3-speed while the 6-cylinder Saginaw also saw service behind many base 307 powerplants. The Saginaw featured three different gear ratio combinations, while the heavier-duty Muncie had one common ratio package. Gear ratio charts for the respective transmissions are as follows:

Transmission	1st Gear	2nd Gear	3rd Gear
V8 Saginaw	2.54:1	1.50:1	1.00:1
6-cylinder Saginaw	2.85:1	1.68:1	1.00:1
4-cylinder Saginaw	3.11:1	1.84:1	1.00:1
Muncie	2.42:1	1.58:1	1.00:1

Borg Warner T-5

With the advent of the '80s, engine torque levels dropped dramatically. At the same time, the gas crunch, and federal gas miser regulations, were in full swing. Because of these factors, a new breed of internal shift rail 5-speed transmissions were developed by Borg Warner. All feature overdriven fifth gear ratios but torque capacity is very restricted. As a result, a common T-5 cannot be used behind a late model 350 in vehicles such as the Camaro or Firebird. Tuned port injection 305 powerplants are at the top of the heap as far as torque capacity is concerned. Due to this fact, we certainly would recommend that you give the torque factors serious consideration before swapping one of these transmissions into your hot rod. If you have a warmed over 292 inline six, it might have too much torque for the transmission.

Still, the T-5 does have a purpose, and if you have a mild powertrain combination, it just might be your ticket to overdriven bliss. The following chart depicts gear ratio selection on two commonly available T-5 gearboxes. We should point out that there have been a variety of available ratios for both Chevrolet and FoMoCo applications. The chart depicts common late model Chevy figures.

Transmission	1st Gear	2nd Gear	3rd Gear	4th Gear	5th Gear
MB-1 V6	4.03:1	2.37:1	1.50:1	1.00:1	0.76:1
M39 V8	2.95:1	1.94:1	1.34:1	1.00:1	0.63:1

Nash / Richmond Gear Street 5-Speed

The Richmond 5-speed gearbox is a direct descendant of the Nash 4+1 race transmission. In reality, this is a true high-performance 5-speed that has more than enough beef to handle almost any healthy Chevy powerplant. The overall size is marginally larger than the conventional Richmond 4-speed and can easily be swapped into a bowtie project car.

This particular transmission features very wide and strong gears, a roller-bearing-supported cluster along with conventional synchro rings and sliders. The first 4 gears are lower than those found in many 4-speeds while fifth gear is direct at 1.00:1. Because of this gear ratio spread, the transmission can be installed in a vehicle with a mild low-three series rear axle ratio and still provide the same performance as a close ratio Muncie coupled with a 4.56:1 rear axle ratio! The following chart depicts the gear ratios found on the Richmond 5-speed manual transmission:

1st Gear	2nd Gear	3rd Gear	4th Gear	5th Gear
3.27:1	2.13:1	1.57:1	1.23:1	1.00:1

Some specialized equipment is required for the installation. You will need a shifter, and several different models are available from Hurst. The front of the gearcase is drilled to bolt directly to a conventional Chevy bellhousing. If you obtain the correct GM -spec transmission assembly (Richmond part number 70-21710), it will be supplied with a conventional 1-1/8 inch x 26 spline Chevrolet input shaft. The tailshaft housing is sized to accept standard yoke assemblies. Richmond offers several different types of output shafts with splines to match the more popular Chevrolet yokes (ie: the HD Turbo 400 examples).

AUTOMATIC TRANSMISSIONS

Automatic transmissions found in Chevrolets aren't quite as prolific as their stick shift counterparts, but don't despair! There's plenty of choice, ranging from 2-speeds to 4-speeds complete with overdrive. In between, there are a couple of traditional heavyweights in the popularity department, and one of these is probably tough enough to handle anything in the horsepower and torque department that you can throw at it! Check out our overview of the more common Chevy autoboxes:

Powerglide

The basic Powerglide 2-speed automatic was introduced eons ago, but the version you should concern yourself with is the aluminum-case unit introduced in 1962. Earlier cast iron versions are becoming scarce (read "resto-collector's items"). Bits and pieces are getting tough to find and, from a performance perspective, the lightweight later model is the way to go. While production of the Powerglide ended in 1973, the 2-speed automatic was (and is) an extremely popular and diverse transmission. Used in everything from 400 HP tri-power 'Vettes to 4-cylinder Vegas, the 'glide has seen a tremendous amount of service in drag race competition. Because of this racing background, there are a massive amount of parts available for it.

In stock form, two different planetary arrangements were included in the design. Engines of 327 cubic inches and larger made use of a 1.76:1 first gear while smaller displacement powerplants were backed with 1.82:1 planetary sets. The aftermarket has stepped up the gear ratio ante, offering 1.90:1, 1.98:1, 2.08:1 and other ratios.

Overall dimensions of the Powerglide are compact. Check out the following chart:

Front of Case to Back of Case	Front of Extension Housing to Tailshaft	Front of Extension Housing to Center of Mount Pad
16-1/4"	9"example and 12" example	4-1/2"

Turbo Hydramatic 350

The turbo 350 is without question the most popular hot rod transmission. Fitted to a myriad of applications, GM used the TH350 with almost all engines displacing less than 400 cubic inches (some hi-po small block Chevys received the stronger TH400). There are three relatively common turbo 350s — the Chevy example, the Buick-Olds-Pontiac examples and the universal

example. In a nutshell, the major difference is the bellhousing bolt pattern and shape. B-O-P versions cannot bolt up to a Chevy block without an adapter, while the other two types can be snugged right up to the bowtie powerplant.

In Chevy applications, the turbo 350 was commonly used behind 350 cubic inch and smaller powerplants. This transmission featured a design which was similar to the TH400 HD transmission, however there was quite a bit of internal down-sizing, simply because the transmission was designed for use behind lower horsepower and lower torque engines. Common gear ratios for the TH350 are as follows:

1st Gear	2nd Gear	3rd Gear
2.52:1	1.52:1	1.00:1

As far as hi-po parts are concerned, the turbo 350 is well blessed. A variety of valve bodies, shift-improver kits, torque converters, input shafts and other bits and pieces are currently available. While not as popular among the drag race set as the Powerglide, the turbo 350 is beginning to gather a large following. In terms of size, the TH350 dimensions are as follows:

Front of Case to Back of Case	21-11/16"
Front of Extension Housing to Tailshaft	6" - standard 9" - passenger car 12" - station wagons 12" - LWB pickup trucks
Front of Extension Housing to Center of Mount Pad	N/A

Turbo Hydramatic 400

The Turbo 400 is the transmission to get if you have a heavy breathing, brute force fat block under the hood. It first saw duty in other GM marques, but was introduced to the Chevy in 1965. There are a number of different versions of TH400 transmissions along with several different gear ratio planetaries. Pontiacs, Buicks and Oldsmobiles received one gear ratio pack while Chevrolet and Cadillac models received another. Additionally, the aftermarket has stepped up with a number of specialty ratios designed specifically for the big Hydramatic. Stock gear ratios are as follows:

Vehicle Line	1st Gear	2nd Gear	3rd Gear
Buick-Olds-Pontiac	2.97:1	1.56:1	1.00:1
Chevrolet-Cadillac	2.48:1	1.48:1	1.00:1

As expected, there are also several different available bellhousing patterns — the standard Chevy model, the B-O-P version and a unique AMC version! Additionally, the turbo 400 has also seen service under Rolls Royce motorcars, but that's another story entirely. In terms of parts availability for the TH400, the sky is the limit. You name it and you can probably get it. This transmission is the darling of the aftermarket transmission manufacturers and as a result, there are countless hop-up and service components available.

The following chart depicts the various TH400 dimensions:

Front of Case to Back of Case	Front of Extension Housing to Tailshaft	Front of Extension Housing to Center of Mount Pad
23-3/8"	7-1/4"	N/A

Front of Case to Back of Case	Front of Extension Housing to Tailshaft	Front of Extension Housing to Center of Mount Pad
24-1/4"	Chevrolet - 4" Cadillac - 13-1/2" B-O-P - 9-1/2"	2-1/2" 3-5/16" 3-1/2"

Turbo Hydramatic 700R4

Fuel economy mandates, along with the move to downsized vehicles, have affected transmission technology. Hydramatic Division's contribution to the fuel mileage wars was a special 4-speed overdrive automatic. In addition to the overdriven fourth gear, these transmissions feature a lockup torque converter, with the lockup controlled by the onboard ECM (computer). This transmission has had its share of teething problems. You might even say it was tested and developed in the field via the General's warranty program. At this point in time, the transmission is relatively reliable, but don't plant the unit behind a blown big block (or a healthy mouse motor for that matter) and expect it to live.

Many aftermarket transmission companies have flogged the 700R4 (now called the 4L60 by Hydramatic Division) with the results being better life, the elimination of the computer converter lockup and other refinements. Two different input shaft splines were used with the 700R4. From 1982 until 15 April 1984, the transmission had a 27-spline input. After 15 April 1984, the transmission featured a 30-spline input shaft. The respective gear ratios for this transmission are as follows:

1st Gear	2nd Gear	3rd Gear	4th Gear
3.059:1	1.625:1	1.00:1	0.696:1

In terms of overall dimensions, the four speed 700R4 is a rather compact assembly. Front bellhousing flange dimensions are identical to all previous Chevy automatics while the balance of the dimensions are as follows:

Turbo Hydramatic 200, 200-4R

The turbo 200 and the turbo 200-4R are very light duty transmissions. While readily available, they should not really be considered for high performance use. If an overdrive feature is required, you should consider the much superior late model 700R4 automatic. Very little is available in terms of aftermarket hop up equipment and for the most part, these light-weight automatics are best replaced with any of the previously discussed Chevy autoboxes.

"LOOK'S LIKE OL' NICK'S BEEN OUT FISHING AGAIN."

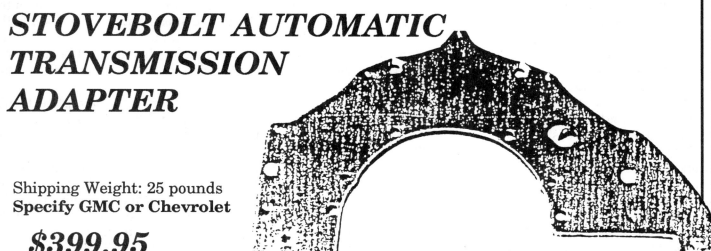
133

by Rich Johnson

Transmissions
Installing TH350 or TH400 on Stovebolt Engines

Automatic transmissions were available for the Chevy 216, 235, 261 and the GMC 248, 270, 302 inline six-cylinder engines, but they didn't exactly perform up to modern standards. Fortunately, it is now possible to transplant a late-model GM automatic onto the backside of the GM six engines and take advantage of recent technology.

Stovebolt Engine Company has developed all of the necessary adapter hardware required to make the swap. In the infant stages of development, company owner Dick Larrowe discovered how to make the adapter plate by placing a 1950 Chevy Powerglide factory bell housing adapter face to face with a 1955 Chevy 265 V8 Powerglide bell housing adapter and bolting them together with a plywood board in between. He marked the holes and drilled them. The resulting adapter could be compared with the stone wheel B.C. rides in the funny papers. Now, the company sells adapters that are the result of intensive research and development involving many different Chevy engines. During development, Dick discovered that no two engines and bell housings are exactly alike concerning the pin location at the rear of the block relative to the center of the crankshaft. Even the factory-matched GMC Hydramatic set was off-center .020". But the Stovebolt Engine Company adapter is as close as .003" and is a precision product made to bolt together quickly and easily.

Dick related the installation process to us. "We use brand new Chevy 350 V8 162-tooth flywheels. Chevrolet calls this piece a flywheel, Borg Warner calls it a flexplate. In the case of Chevy, we use a spacer ring between the flange of the crank and the flywheel. The flywheel is drilled for the 216, 235, 261 pattern, including the three stock pins. The GMC does not require the spacer ring. The flywheels for the GMC are drilled for the GMC 248, 270, 302 six-bolt pattern. So far, we haven't made any flywheels for the early Chevy and GMC 4-bolt flange pattern, but we could if the demand existed. We use a late-model Chevrolet six-cyl-

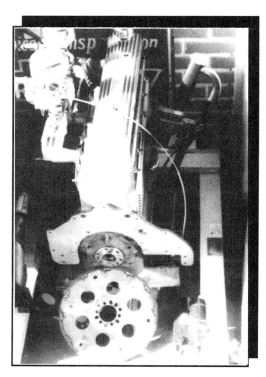

Adapter positioned at the rear of the venerable Chevy six makes it possible to install a modern automatic transmission. Note also the new flywheel (flexplate) and starter in the photo, part of the Stovebolt Engine Company conversion kit.

inder starter (250 - 292) that mounts to the bottom of the adapter with 2 bolts. We attach a support bracket to the front of the starter bolt and attach the other end of the bracket to the oil pan flange. This may not be necessary because our adapter plate is 5/8" thick and the starter will not flex.

"There is a provision on our adapter plate to use several types of Chevrolet and GMC anti-rocking mounts that attach with two 7/16" bolts in the stock bell housing position. We sell rear crossmembers made by Chassis Engineering that fit under the transmission rear mount and attach to the frame of the car or truck. We make our own kit for installing late-model open driveline rearends in old Chevy chassis. These are the proper width for the stock springs and locate the axle in the stock wheelbase position.

"Here's how we installed the 350 Hydramatic in a 1947 Chevy coupe. Before removing anything, place a protractor on the face of the flat rear side of the transmission where the torque tube retainer bolts up, and check the angle. When installing the new transmission, make sure the rear (where the driveshaft slips in) is the same angle — usually 3 degrees.

"Remove the stock rearend assembly by unbolting rear spring shackles, U-bolts, shocks, parking brake cables, and brake line. Disconnect it from the transmission and slide it out from under the car as a unit — torque tube and rearend. Support the engine by jacking up under the rear of the oil pan, or suspend the engine from above. Remove the front seat cushion, front floor board, and disconnect the battery. Unbolt the transmission, clutch, flywheel, starter and bell housing and remove. Take off the brake master cylinder and pedals. Remove the hydraulic brake line. Remove the stock front exhaust pipe. Remove the stock crossmember (this can be done by drilling out the rivets or with a torch, if you are very careful). Save the stock crossmember. Clean off the back of the engine.

"Install the 5/8" thick adapter plate, using the bolts in the kit. Use the 7/16" hex head bolts and lock washers (4 each) and the two 7/16" countersunk flathead Allen bolts. Torque it down to 85 ft. lbs. Install the flywheel and spacer ring (Chevrolet). The ring fits only one way, so rotate it until it fits over the dowel pins. Do the same with the flywheel and bolt it on with the six fine-thread Allen bolts provided. Use LocTite on the threads. Install the starter (Chevy 250 six-cylinder) with the two bolts in the kit. Do not use stock knurled 250 bolts. Manually work the solenoid and see if there are any meshing problems.

"Install the torque converter to the flywheel. Make sure it slides all the way into the end of the crankshaft. If not, some filing of the torque converter hub may be required. Bolt torque converter on with bolts provided. When satisfied it is correctly installed, either leave it on and install the transmission to it or remove it and place it on the transmission to be installed together.

"You may have to lower the rear of the engine and use a transmission jack for the installation. Install it the way you would a TH350 on a stock 250 Chevy. Tighten the torque converter bolts and the transmission-to-adapter bolts. Make sure the transmission is not cocked, or the case will break when the bolts are tightened. Install filler tube, cooling lines and cooler as well as the bell housing bottom cover. Install transmission to frame rubber mount, then the rear crossmember and brackets. Clamp brackets in position, remove from car and weld brackets in place.

"Install the rearend. Using a torch, remove all the original mounting brackets in the area of the stock '47 Chevy springs. Grind the area smooth. Reassemble the rearend to the springs using the installation kit for open-drive rearends. Place the spring perch hole over the center bolt of the spring with the long part of the perch to the rear. Set the axle in place, centering it so the same amount of axle extends beyond the spring on both sides. Install the U-bolts and bottom plates, facing the plates in the proper direction to accommodate the

For repositioning the axle, as well as adjusting the pinion angle to match the angle at the rear of the transmission, spring perches, mounting plates, and U-bolts are available.

This is the modified crossmember, employed for making the conversion possible.

shock absorbers. Jack up the axle until it is starting to support the weight of the car. Move the front face of the rearend drive flange so it is the same angle as the rear of the transmission. Tighten bolts. Remove spring shackles from car and remove springs and rear axle as a unit. Weld the spring perches to the axle, taking great care not to overheat and warp the axle housing. Now the axle can be installed and will be properly located.

"Reinstall emergency brake cable and hydraulic brake line, both of which may need to be modified. Some wrecking yard driveshafts may bolt right up (see chapter about Driveshafts), but if you cannot find the correct length, have a driveshaft shop make one for you. The easiest solution to finding a shifter is to use a Gennie Shifter, otherwise use a Kugel Component bracket if you are retaining stock shift linkage. We used a Kugel Component shift bracket and a Wire Works neutral safety switch in conjunction with modified 1950 - '52 Chevrolet Powerglide quadrant and linkage."

Stovebolt Engine Company is also working on a fiberglass floorboard that will fit the original hole and bolts on so it will look like a factory job. Contact them for further information at P.O. Box 166, Corbett, Oregon 97019; (503) 695-2671.

Driveshafts

You need to come up with a driveshaft to fit your hot rod, but before you head for the machine shop, do some measuring. There is a huge selection of driveshaft lengths available, and surprisingly, there is a great deal of universal joint interchangeability. For example, the Volvo universal joint is a standard Chevrolet item.

You know the type of rearend you have, and you know the type of transmission. At the transmission output shaft and at the pinion, there are yokes that secure the U-joints in place. The critical bits of information about these yokes are the measurements across the semi-circular cups that receive the U-joints. They are not all the same. With a steel tape or a set of calipers, measure carefully the distance across the yoke cup right at the edge of the machined face, to find the size of U-joint that will fit. Be aware that the transmission output shaft U-joint yoke may not be the same size as the yoke at the pinion. The ideal situation is if the yoke cups measure the same at the pinion as they do at the transmission output shaft. This way, you only need to carry one extra U-joint in the spare-parts section of your tool box, and it can fit either position.

Some U-joints are designed with all four cups the same size, while others have two different sizes of cups on the same unit. You may have larger cups for the driveshaft attachment and smaller ones for the yoke. The thing to keep in mind here is that the more unusual the U-joint, the more difficult it may be to find a replacement. If possible, design the driveshaft system to use the strongest and most commonly available components.

To determine the overall length of the driveshaft, measure the distance from the machined face of the rear of the transmission output shaft yoke to the machined face at the front of the pinion yoke. These machined faces represent the centerline points of the U-joint cups. This will get you close to the overall shaft length you need. Now shop the junkyards. Pay close attention to the U-joint sizes. If in doubt, ask what universal joint might interchange with the shaft and rearend that you have.

As you're measuring, keep in mind the splined slip joint which allows the driveshaft to lengthen and shorten as the rear suspension works up and down. Although the slip joint has a built-in travel of several inches, it should ride just about in the center of its travel when the driveshaft is installed between the transmission and rearend, and the full weight of the car is resting on the suspension. Take care to avoid inadvertently measuring the driveshaft length with the slip joint either pushed in or pulled out beyond its center of travel, otherwise you may end up with a slip joint that destroys itself when the suspension gets real active. If you are lucky, you'll find a shaft that fits. Sometimes it's a drop-in.

If you must have a shaft made, plan on paying from $60 to $150. Most communities have machine shops that can custom-make driveshafts. They will cut and fit the tube, or install a new tube (using the measurements you supply), with a yoke that will fit the rearend. Have the shaft balanced while you are at it.

Note: You do not cut a driveshaft in two and butt-weld the pieces to the length you need! This might be ok for a dune buggy, but it doesn't cut it on a street-driven vehicle.

If you are building a car with lots of horsepower, be sure to use the larger universal joints and a large diameter driveshaft tube. A good driveshaft shop will be able to advise you regarding the recommended tube diameter and U-joint size as it relates to your engine's horsepower.

Small Block Chevy
Big Block Chevy
Angle Plug Heads
Small Block Ford
Big Block Ford
Ford Cleveland
Ford Y-Block V-8
Flathead Ford
Buick V-6
Chevy 90 V-6
Small Block Dodge
Big Block Dodge
Inside Chassis
Outside Chassis

Only at Sanderson can we please all of the people all of the time

Send $4.00 for our
25th Anniversary Catalog,
illustrated to answer any
questions on header
installation and availability

*Dealer
Inquiries
Welcome*

1990 SUPER PRIZE PROGRAM SPONSOR

202 Ryan Way, South San Francisco, CA 94080 (415) 583-6617
To order headers, call our toll free hot line, 1-800-669-2430

Sanderson - the only name you need to know for all of your exhaust needs.

by Dave McNurlen

A Case In Point

'34 Chevy

I didn't want a Ford. I wanted a Chevy. None of the transverse leaf spring stuff for me, no way!

About 1982, a package deal on three '34 Chevys came up. At that time, I actually had some money, so I bought 'em. In the true "you can't chop up a cream-puff to build a hot rod" spirit, all the worst parts were culled from the three cars to build this one. This was easy, as two of the cars were totally disassembled and the third one may as well have been. (The other two are gone now, so don't bother calling.)

This car hit the road the weekend of the first NSRA regional nats at Tulsa. It drove out of the garage for the first time on Thursday, and with no glass in it except for the windshield, was driven to Tulsa on Friday. This was just supposed to be a test, so I could bring it back, tear it apart and finish it. Naturally, it stayed just like

it was for more than two years because I didn't want to take it out of commission. Finally, I pulled it in the garage and took some parts off so I couldn't just get in and drive it, and then some things got done.

The hood was hand-built because I thought a friend of mine had built the one on his Model A hiboy. Turned out he hadn't. I don't know that I would have tried it if I'd known otherwise. Thanks anyway, Mike.

If forced to pick the toughest thing to do on the car, I'd say paint. I didn't really want a black car originally, but I knew that was the easiest color to spot paint, and I knew I'd be doing a lot of that. Turned out that black was okay, but the paint still has a ways to go. I even tried flaming it once, but went back to black after two months. One thing I noticed while it was flamed was that a lot of people looked at the car when it was driven around town. With flames, everybody noticed it, I don't care who they were. It might sound strange to think of an unflamed hot rod as being anonymous, but that's how it felt after I painted them out.

Beginning with the chassis, the frame was restored and crossmembers added to accommodate the new engine and transmission. Front suspension got de-arched springs with reversed eyes. They were attached to a 6-1/2 inch dropped axle from Butch's Rod Shop. The front axle was moved forward on the springs 2 inches. 1952 Chevy spindles were installed, and '74 Monte Carlo disc brakes and Gene Reese adapters were added. Brakes are controlled by a GM master cylinder and JFZ residual valves. Steering is handled by a Vega box and Pete & Jakes arm. Rear suspension was treated to de-arched springs with reversed eyes. Tube shocks are mounted both front and rear to keep the spring under control. The rear axle is courtesy of a '75 Nova with 2.73:1 ratio.

The top was chopped 3 inches and the inner wood framework was also chopped and restored to functional condition. Headlights are Dietz and taillights are '40 Chevy pieces.

Interior comfort is provided by a set of Datsun 280Z bucket seats

Here was the original 3-car package deal. The frame on the left and the body in the middle were used for this project.

Can you say "basket case?" Three cars worth of wood and steel was piled up for evaluation to see what could be made of all this stuff. There are lots of great parts and pieces.

that had the base cut down to allow more headroom after the top chop. A 220-watt stereo system booms out the tunes, and a unique A/C system keeps the interior cool. In fact, the best addition to the car was the air conditioning system. In 1980, Texas had 100 days in a row with temperatures over 100 degrees. Driving a car around there without A/C is just nuts. A complete add-on A/C system out of a 1980 Dodge Omni was purchased from a friend for $45, and the evaporator case was cut down to fit behind the '34 dash. A mount was fabricated for the Sankyo compressor which came with it, and a condenser was purchased from Air-Tique for $90. So, for $135 total, this car can be driven in summer-time Texas stop-and-go traffic in complete comfort. Man, it's nice!

Under the hood lives a 355 Chevy V8 with a Competition Cams unit pushing the lifters. An Edelbrock Performer intake manifold is topped by a Quadrajet carburetor. GM HEI ignition provides the spark, and Sanderson headers dispose of the exhaust. A Muncie 4-speed with Mr. Gasket Vertical-Gate shifter takes care of gear selection. A custom-built radiator is assisted in its cooling duties by an electric fan that was scavenged from a 1982 Cutlass Ciera. After the louvers were punched in the hood (by Slots of Fun of Irving, Texas) to ventilate the engine compartment, the interior temperature was reduced and in-town coolant temperature dropped by a few degrees.

Now, let's take a closer look at how this '34 Chevy came to life.

The nosebleed special. Completely stock, the Chevy sits pretty high. Something definitely had to be done to get it down closer to the weeds, and reduce the overall height of the car. Of course, this stage is just for fitting up the body to the frame and to measure and make decisions. The final product doesn't resemble this profile very closely.

This shot was taken during the building of the pedals from 1/2" x 1" bar stock. Tops from an early '50s Chevy pickup were later grafted on for pedal pads. The stock X-member was widened for shifter linkage clearance. This master cylinder was later swapped for a newer one. There's plenty of room under there. If there's a bellhousing that weighs more than this Ansen does, we'd hate to have to lift it.

With the Butch's Rod Shop 6-1/2 inch dropped front axle in place, the car is starting to look like a hot rod should. At this point, the headlights and shock mounting positions were also being played with.

Right-The car was driven like this for the first two years, before it came back into the garage for updating and upgrading. In this stage of development, it has all the appearance of a genuine early hot rod of the '40s.

Below-A 355 Chevy V8 was installed on big-block mounts. Sanderson headers get rid of the exhaust. Those are ET KelStar wheels inside BFGoodrich Advantage T/A radials. Little one up front, big ones out back.

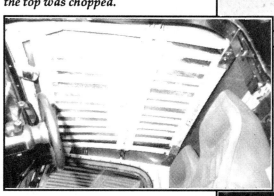

Right-Have a look at that Butch's Rod Shop 6-1/2 inch dropped front axle. Disc brakes are from a '74 Monte Carlo. Note the de-arched front springs with reversed eyes.

Below-A peek at the inside of the roof shows wood framework and the '75 Nova steel cross-piece. High-backed bucket seats came from a Datsun 280Z, but the base of each seat had to be cut down to make a little more headroom after the top was chopped.

Right-A close-up of the right front suspension shows the shock mount that was built from 1/2"x1" bar stock. Brake hoses came with the calipers, and were run through the frame. Butch's Rod Shop supplied the axle, tie rods and arms. With the wheels pointed straight ahead, the tie rods run parallel and handling is great.

Left-Take a peek under the dash and get a glimpse of the air conditioner vents. The evaporator is mounted behind the instrument cluster, with controls in the center of the dash.

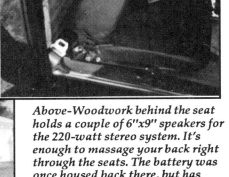

Above-Woodwork behind the seat holds a couple of 6"x9" speakers for the 220-watt stereo system. It's enough to massage your back right through the seats. The battery was once housed back there, but has since been moved to below the front part of the passenger seat.

Left-Flames stayed on the car two months. Amazingly, when the flames were on the car, everyone noticed it. But as soon as the flames were removed, the car became an anonymous hot rod.

Above-The stainless steel gas tank was made up especially for this car by Rock Valley Stainless.

Left-After the louvers were punched in the hood (by Slots of Fun in Irving, Texas), the engine compartment was ventilated enough to bring down the coolant temperature a few degrees as well as keeping some of the heat from coming into the passenger compartment.

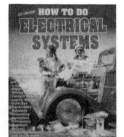

143

by LeRoi Tex Smith

Building A '32
Five-Window Coupe

What is done to this car applies to all 1936 and older Chevys

This is the story of Cedric. It is a story that spans many years, several states, and much of the history of street rodding. It is typical of Chevy hot rods.

I first ran across Cedric on a supermarket bulletin board. Only he wasn't Cedric then, he got that name from my family some months later. The color photograph simply said, "1932 Chevy — $1095.00", with a phone number. I looked at the photo for a week or so, figuring that the car was probably sold. Besides, that was southern California, where everybody builds Fords. But the photo showed a car that seemed in excellent condition, and the price was reasonable, even

This is the original photo, advertising the 1932 Chevy for sale. It remained on a supermarket bulletin board for days. No one bothered to follow up on the car. It was in pristine condition.

for 1973. So, knowing that my teenage son was going to need high school transportation soon, I bought the car. I was the only person who had come to look at it. In southern California, they build Fords.

Cedric was indeed in excellent condition, with the factory black paint in very good shape. Someone had installed a Chevy 265 with Powerglide, a Pontiac rear end, and Pontiac front brakes. A set of Cadillac "fishgill" factory aluminum wheels were in place, and a pair of unknown-brand bucket seats finished it off. Otherwise, the interior was original factory. Here was your basic street hot rod of the Forties and Fifties. Son Scott drove it to high school for two years, part of the time on a 52-mile one-way commute. Cedric did just fine, thank you.

Then, the bug bit. Scott wanted to upgrade the car. More power, better handling, a better office, all the things that hot rodders are prone to do. But, this wasn't something that needed doing over a several-years span. Nope, this was a total rebuild over a summer vacation.

So, the car was disassembled. In the home driveway like so many thousands of hot rod predecessors. Down to a rolling chassis and a bare body. The body paint was removed with hardware store stripper, and a coat of light grey primer applied. In the open air, of course, with a portable air compressor. Since the car had never been in a wreck, no metalwork was needed. However, it was decided that the stock firewall had far too many holes. Metal patches and lead solved the problem. Holes in the stock dash were filled at the same time.

Next, a Nova rearend was located, cleaned, and installed on the stock (but cleaned) '32 rear springs. A square tubing crossmember was designed for tube shocks at the rear, replacing a length of angle iron that had been fashioned earlier. The Nova rearend is just the right width, so that a reasonably wide rear wheel/tire will stay under the fender and still have body clearance. At the front, the springs were removed and each leaf carefully cleaned. Teflon was stripped between each leaf, then the assembled spring was wrapped with

144

black electrical tape. The shackles and shackle bolts/bushings were cleaned up. They were in excellent condition, so no replacement was necessary. While it would have been possible to replace the Buick/Olds/Pontiac front drums with 1949-later Chevy units, we kept what we had. They worked fine, and we really didn't know what other wheels we might use. The Nova rear-end axle flanges could be drilled to the BOP bolt pattern. So, temporarily, we used Chevy rear wheels, Cadillac fronts.

A visit to our friendly wrecking yard yielded a small block Chevy, which we in turn carted off to Dragmaster in Carlsbad, California. Old timers will remember Dragmaster as one of the major forces in quarter-mile racing during the Fifties, Sixties, and early Seventies. We went through the engine, carefully building a high performance runner, and to this added a dummy 350 automatic just to get engine and transmission mounts welded to the frame.

At this point, Scott had wandered off to college, with other transportation, and I had decided to move to central Wisconsin to work on Old Cars Weekly newspaper. Cedric was unceremoniously shipped to friend Herby Gehlken in northern California for a storage rest.

Almost ten years later, the '32 came out of mothballs, little the worse for wear. Light rust was beginning to attack the body via the thin coat of primer, but everything else seemed the same.

Shortly after getting the car to our eastern Idaho home, Mike Conte from the Seattle area called to ask if we might want to change the beam front axle for an independent unit. Conte (Conte Enterprises) makes a variety of independent front end kits, and he wanted to expand into the Chevrolet line. So, we sent the car along for some updating. A short time later, it was back in our garage, but we still hadn't decided what to do with the car. Finally, we put it up for sale. The new owner is Jack Foulk of Pennsylvania. Jack had been building one of Experimetal's '32 Chevy roadsters, and decided that maybe he needed a matched pair. Martz Chassis (508 E. Pitt St., Bedford, PA 15522; (814)623-9501) had completed a contemporary chassis for the roadster, and it was decided to put the coupe body on the new frame. But, first the car went to have the original wood replaced with all new material. Then it went over to Martz where all the final fitting is being done.

So there you have it, the saga of Sir Cedric. Almost 20 years, only a few of which were spent on the road. But all that is about to change, as Jack Foulk brings the old guy back to life in the 1990s.

After serving as high school transportation reliably for several years, the coupe was disassembled for a total rebuild. Original engine was small block Chevy 265 (with Corvette valve covers!). When rebuilding a Chevy, it is often wise to leave the body always bolted to the frame and work around everything, especially if only small portions of body wood framework are to be replaced. This assumes that the frame has not been damaged and misaligned. Wheels shown are Cadillac from the Fifties. From the looks of things, this car was probably first equipped with a V8 in late 1950s.

Chevys through the very late Thirties used semi-elliptic springs up front, except for some versions that used a rather awkward and bulky knee-action front suspension. While the knee-action unit can be rebuilt, it never works well under rods. Dropped axles for these elliptic spring cars can be secured from such places as Butch's Rod Shop, SuperBell, and Mor-Drop. Some are tubing, some are stretched original beams. Frames on the earlier Chevys are built differently than those of the late 1930s and later, but all are very strong.

The stock 1932 steering gearbox was in the car, and used the power steering assist from the stock 265 Chevy V8. It worked, but not really well. Side pitman gearbox could be replaced with a Chevy pickup truck unit from the early Fifties, a Dodge pickup side box, or even a reworked Mustang unit. A cross-steering box works better, either the large Saginaw power unit, or smaller Vega manual box.

Above-Because the early Chevys use a ladder type frame with deep and strong side rails, with plenty of crossmembers, and springs at the four corners, there is no need for an X-member in the center. Even so, some builders make up boxing plates for the side rails and add an X center crossmember. Here, an early Powerglide transmission has gobs of working room in the 1932 frame.

Left-All General Motors front brakes of the Fifties can be adapted to the early Chevy spindle, most bearings are the same but hubs are different (bolt patterns vary). Mix and match bearings/races/seals at local bearing supply.

Above-Fenders, hood, deck lid and other easily removed body parts were taken to a paint stripper, this kind of treatment is really worth the money if you can afford it. But, be sure to thoroughly clean and reclean the parts after they are stripped, then prime them immediately with a new two-part etching primer/sealer. This will ensure maximum resistance to any rust.

Since the body was not to be separated from the frame, a chemical paint stripper was used to remove original factory black paint. Use plenty of water with this job, to neutralize any residual stripper.

It is essential to strip every bit of paint from the car, inside and out. Pay special attention to all the little nooks and crannies.

The pre-37 Chevys have a bunch of wood in the body framework, including an entire floorpan of hardwood. Original intention with this car was to save most of the factory wood, replace things like the trunk floor. Ultimately, the body was completely re-wooded (almost 20 years after this photo was taken).

Early Chevy wood tends to get rot anywhere water has seeped in through the years. Here, the piece of wood in a panel directly below the deck lid was broken.

The broken wood was carefully removed and a replacement made from oak, was shaped to fit with a body grinder.

The panel was held in place with nails and wood screws, by removing the panel, both support wood pieces could be rebuilt.

Right-All the Chevy body wood needs to be carefully inspected. Use a knife blade or ice pick to test wood, especially around all joints, and double especially around lower extremities where water tends to settle. If the wood is soft, it has dry rot. If the wood is basically complete, it can be soaked with Kwik-Poly, and saved. Otherwise, it must be repaired by splicing in new wood, or replacing the entire piece of wood. If Kwik-Poly is used, be sure wood is in exact fit and alignment, since the poly acts as a glue as well as wood pore filler.

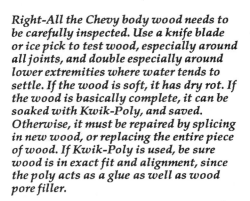

Above right-Wood around the floor area is most susceptible to water and rot damage, but small sections are easy to make and replace at home.

Chevy doors must absolutely be tight at all joints, and all the wood needs to be good.

Here, some damaged wood pieces have been removed and used as a pattern for new hardwood replacement.

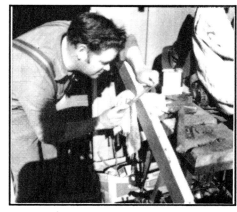

Wood pieces that must be shaped can be worked with hand rasps.

Or they can be shaped with a regular body/fender grinder disc.

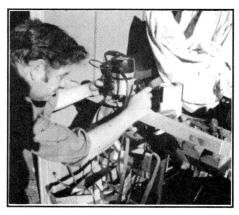

A router is essential when doing Chevy woodwork. Most cuts can be made on an ordinary table saw. Hardwood must always be used, never soft wood such as pine.

This is the rear panel area shown prior, with the two wooden pieces exposed after metal was removed. Old nails/screws didn't hold anything in place.

The piece shown just before was too far gone to be effectively treated with Kwik-Poly. See section on working wood for more info.

Although there was no dry rot in wood frame around rear window and package tray area, wood shrinkage had caused loose joints.

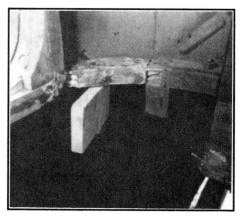

Wire brush in drill motor was used to clean up the wood at all joints. Screws were replaced or tightened, then the wood was given a liberal dose of Kwik-Poly as a form of insurance.

Finally, the exposed joints were covered with a layer of fiberglass cloth saturated with resin. No, this isn't hi-tek, but neither is it expensive. There is one thought that says all joints should be absolutely movement free, others call for some joint freedom. This is discussed in the wood section.

The early Chevy door will be complete wood framework, with a metal skin tacked in place. There are wood kits available for some of the more popular Chevys. You can make most replacement wood if you have enough original wood for a pattern. Otherwise, you're on your own to design as you go along.

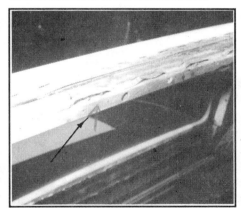

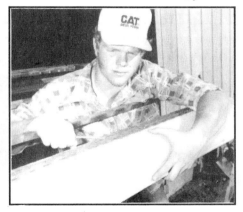

Above-The cloth top insert should be removed and a very careful inspection made of all the wood. Repair any bad pieces of wood. It is almost always necessary to replace the top wood lattice strips. Put in this wood framework, even if the fabric insert is going to be replaced by a welded-on metal top insert. The wood framework gives strength and helps eliminate metal insert oil canning. Arrow points to raised portion of top edge where lattice fits.

Whether fabric or metal top will be used, thoroughly clean all the old gunk and calk from perimeter of insert.

Cross supports for the top lattice will tend to sag over the years. Normally they will have a very slight bow upward. Replace with new wood if there is any doubt about condition.

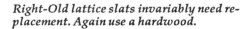

Right-Old lattice slats invariably need replacement. Again use a hardwood.

Far right-Each slat is tucked under the top metal. A screw or nail can be installed at a slight angle to hold this in place. It can also be glued.

Above-A piece of chicken wire is stretched and stapled over the top of the lattice. This is followed by a lightweight material, then cotton or foam, then the outer material. A "hidem" welt is then tacked around the perimeter as the final seal. Juliano's hot rod supply has top insert kits for several products, all fit essentially the same.

Left-Final overall shape of the slats must have a slight crown, which is why the support crosspieces have a slight bow upward.

Above-Firewall was full of holes, including large one where hanging brake pedal assembly has been added. Fiberglass could have been used as a filler, but since the author is skilled in lead use, metal patches and lead were chosen.

Right-It is possible to fill smaller holes without using a metal patch backup. In this case, the hole is slightly countersunk. Lead is used to fill the area, and it is squished on the backside for a double bond. This is not a recommended method, however.

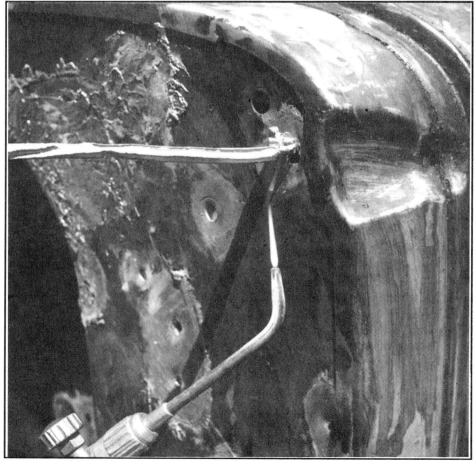

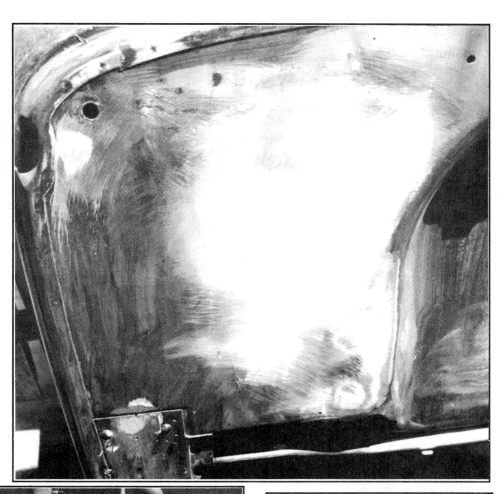

Above-Cut a metal patch from any convenient similar sheet stock of similar gauge. Tack weld this to the backside of any hole being filled. Really small holes can be welded solid with a MIG unit, then finished with lead.

Right-Since this is not an article on how to do leadwork, we only show the finished product. A final coat of plastic filler will make the panel perfect.

Above-The dashboard can be filled the same way as the firewall. Here, a metal piece has been cut. It can be tack welded behind the hole, or can be trimmed to fit into the hole and MIG welded for the best job.

Left-Arrows point to holes backed with patches.

Above-Arrow points to original body seam that was leaded at the factory. Most Chevy bodies will have several areas of lead like this. If the lead has not cracked, it usually does not need to be repaired with more lead, instead a quality plastic filler will cure any imperfections.

Left-Lead is added to the patched holes, it is sometimes possible to use a quality plastic filler if the patches are thoroughly cleaned and tightly tack welded.

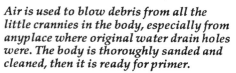

Air is used to blow debris from all the little crannies in the body, especially from anyplace where original water drain holes were. The body is thoroughly sanded and cleaned, then it is ready for primer.

Right-Springs were taken apart and cleaned with a body grinder. If the spring leaves are pitted from rust, they should be replaced. New springs are available through places such as Posies, or your local spring shop can make what you need. Neither way is too expensive.

Far right-To get a slightly better ride, it is possible to remove a couple of spring leaves (usually leaves 3 and 5, counting the main leaf as number 1), but this spring tuning may need to wait until the car has been driven several hundred miles. Teflon strips placed between the leaves will improve spring action.

Here the older type of primer was sprayed outside on the driveway. With the great new two-part etching primers available, it is advised to use them. However, be aware that they are toxic, so adequate clothing and breathing protection should be used, even when spraying outdoors.

Award winning rod builder Herby Gehlken looks over the project just before a Mor-Drop axle is installed. The new axle was from a Fifties era Chevy pickup, and fit the early springs fine.

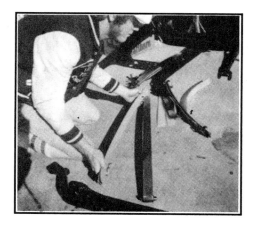

Above-After the spring has Teflon inserted, it can be wrapped with plastic electrical tape. The shackle caps must be thoroughly cleaned, since they are cups for insulating grease.

Right-If the spring main leaf bushings need to be replaced, do so before doing any of the clean-up on the spring. Parts suppliers of old Chevy parts will probably have these bronze bushings, otherwise get something close from the parts house, and hone inside diameter to fit.

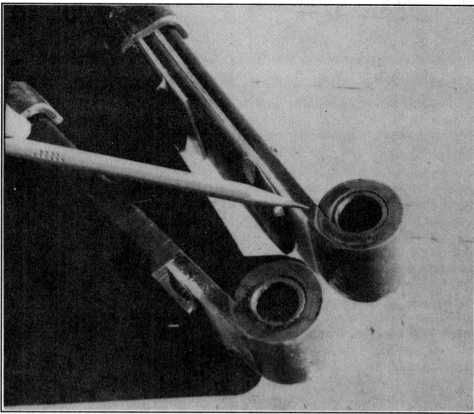

Here is an assembled spring with the Teflon sliders installed, and a spring wrapped with electrical tape. Function of the tape is to keep road grime from between spring leaves, it usually needs rewrapping every year or so. Plastic or leather lace-on boots can be made for the same purpose.

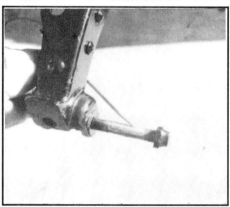

Spring shackle bolts must be in good condition. If not, they need to be replaced. Pointer shows where the spring eye bushing is likely to cause wear.

In the case of Chevy, a grease zerk fits into the end of the shackle bolt.

Far Left-Here, the frame has been cleaned and painted (with the body in place), then the reworked front spring hung in place.

Left-Attention is turned to the axle, whether dropped or stock. A variety of Chevy spindles interchange, mostly it is a trial and error thing, but the stock spindle works fine. Clean the spindle, and install new kingpin/bushing kits. Some parts houses keep them in stock, and often parts from Fifties era Chevy pickups interchange. Whatever, install the bushings with a bearing lock chemical for extra assurance. Usually the Chevy kingpin kits are right on the money and no pin-to-bushing honing is necessary for fit. This is a snug palm-push fit. No slop is tolerable.

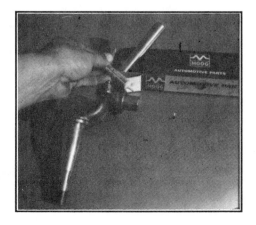

Above-When installing the kingpin, make sure the bearing goes between the bottom of the axle boss and the spindle.

The front axle can be ground smooth prior to fitting the new spindles. Do not drill it full of "lightening" holes.

For really good results on all chassis parts, paint with two-part etching primer and finish with the desired color, doctored with the flexitive agent used on modern car bumpers.

Now attention can be turned to the rearend. Here a Nova rearend has been selected to replace the bigger GM unit. The replacement is thoroughly cleaned, then all bearings are checked and replaced if necessary. Replace the pinion seal at this time if it shows signs of leaking. Do a good brake job as well. Cut Nova spring mounts off.

The stock rear springs do an excellent job, especially if they are removed and cleaned, given the Teflon treatment, and the shackles and pivot bolts cleaned up and lubed. If the rearend needs to be lowered, a spring leaf or two can be removed. In addition, lowering blocks are available through Butch's Rod Shop.

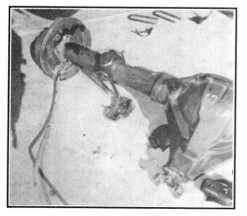

The stock '32 rearend spring clamps fit the late Nova housing fine. Touch the mounts with an arc tack weld when final alignment is made, if there is any doubt about the axle rotating inside the spring clamps. Just a tack, do not weld enough to cause

axle housing distortion. When the engine/trans are in place, and the frame is at driving stance, use a level protractor at rear face of transmission. Duplicate this angle at the pinion yoke of the rearend to insure that driveshaft U-joints are in angular phase.

Above-Since the price for two good junkyard small block Chevy engines was so good, a pair made it home. They were cleaned at a car wash on the way.

Left-When everything fits, clean with a grinder and paint. Again, a flexitive two-part paint works well.

The engine block was given obligatory cleaning and machine operations. Edges of cam bearings were beveled prior to installation of hot cam.

Crankshaft was polished, oil holes beveled, everything balanced, etc.

Since this is a hot street engine, the four-bolt mains are not necessary. Still, the crank was positioned, caps carefully checked with Plasti-gage, before final torquing.

Right-Forged pistons were installed, and each ring fit to the piston carefully.

Far Right-Each ring was squared in the cylinder bore, end gap checked and honed larger if necessary. It's the little things that make a difference.

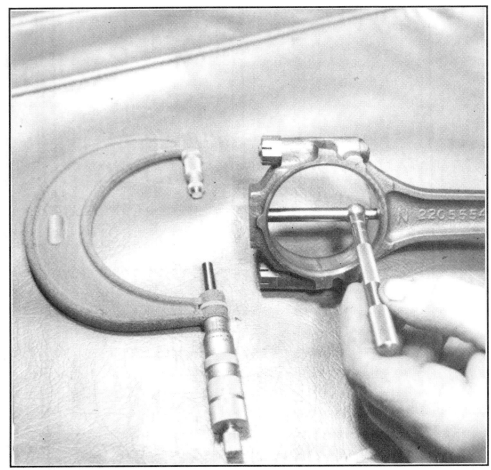

Above-Rod/piston assembly installed, then clearance of skirt around welded crank counterbalances were checked.

Left-Rods were cleaned, peened, checked for straightness, balanced, and big ends miked/honed if necessary.

Above-Weiand top end equipment installed, freeze plugs set in place, and the engine is getting ready for shipment.

Right-A polished/finned aluminum oil pan with increased capacity was installed first. Later it was replaced with a high-capacity steel pan.

Above- The crew at Dragmaster, with Dode Martin at left and Jim Nelson on right, shows off the finished project which was done in just one day.

Right- Back home in the driveway, a tripod holds the engine/trans combination as it is positioned to see where new mounts will fit.

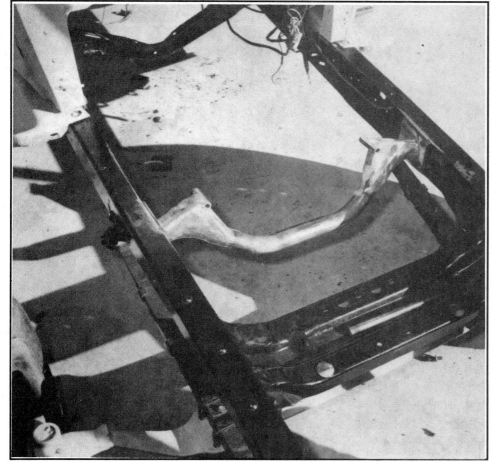

Above-Stock transmission crossmember has perch welded on front to accept Turbo 350.

Left-Front engine mount crossmember was fashioned from bent tubing, and mounts to frame pad via four bolts. Lower portion of tubing is swayed toward front crossmember for pan clearance.

Above-Mike Conte shows off the billet independent front suspension he designed for the re-born coupe.

Left-And like so many homegrown rod projects, there it sits for awhile as a room addition takes place, kids go to college, etc. Nothing more happened for the next 10 years.

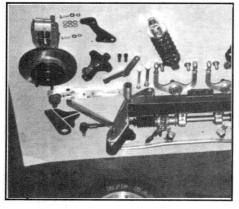

The Chevy IFS includes all the hi-tek whistles and bells, such as JFZ brakes, Aldan coil/over springs/shocks, rack & pinion steering, etc.

Work on the IFS starts by measuring a production item for another car, to see how close it comes to fitting the Chevy. Since most cars of any era are very similar, often very small changes are needed.

Front sheetmetal is removed from the coupe, and measurements of frame width are made.

Right-Since there was an engine mount crossmember and a front frame horn spreader bar in place, the stock front crossmember could be cut out.

Far right-Note the spreader bar is a length of angle iron to keep frame in correct stock position. Original crossmember mount flanges of rails are cut off (arrow).

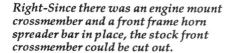

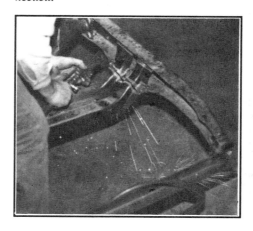

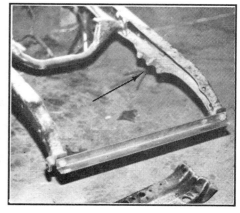

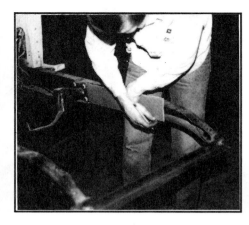

Above-Cardboard is used to make pattern for frame boxing plate, which is necessary for added strength when IFS is installed.

Right-Frame boxing plates are welded in place and edges ground for appearance. Critical measurements are marked directly on the frame for later reference.

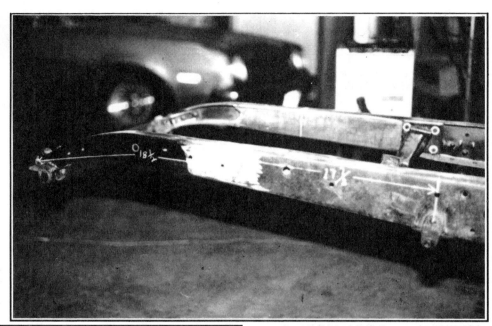

Above-The crossmember is welded in place, and the A-arms temporarily bolted in place with spring/wheels, etc.

Left-Locater bracket for the lower trailing arm is tack welded to the frame.

After checking everything for fit, the brackets are finish welded.

The radiator support and fender braces are set on the new crossmember and a bracket made off the crossmember front as a mount.

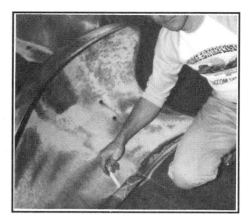

A small portion of inner fender material had to be removed to accommodate the new crossmember towers.

So, here is Cedric after nearly two decades, with new legs up front and an older author hanging on.

Which is where things were when new owner Jack Foulk gathered all the pieces for shipment to Pennsylvania. By now, engine needed to be pulled apart and light rust was attacking metal.

Enter Martz Chassis with a new frame made especially for the Experimetal 1932 Chevy roadster body. While similar to the old Cedric frame, it is worlds different.

Note difference in front suspension, with longer upper A-arms located lower on the tower, tubing center crossmember.

Rearend is positioned with 4-bars and a panhard bar, suspension is now coil/overs.

Anyone wanting a duplicate of this Chevy frame need only ring up Martz and give requirements. As well as some extra cash. But it is really a neat one. So, now you've seen Cedric progress from a typical driveway project clear through a hi-tek transformation, with various levels of low-tek/hi-tek in between.

by Mike Mushman   photos by Scott Smith

One Bad '32

Vehicle: 1932 Chevrolet 5-window coupe
Owner: Bob Binder, Elkridge, Maryland

In 1932 Chevrolet changed the appearance of their cars by using a longer hood, deep crown front fenders, door type vents in the hood and a built in radiator grille. Total production for the 5-window coupe was 34,796 units. Bob's goal was to create a vehicle that was an unmistakable hot rod. Judging by the finished product we would say his goal has been accomplished.

Bob Binder got his first car at the tender age of 10, and has been building them ever since. After a passionate affair with drag racing, Bob laid eyes on this '32 Chevy 5-window, and it was love at first sight.

Being a mechanic by trade, Bob did most of the work himself. But as with most street rodders, friends like Charlie Greger helped out along the way.

Ron Healy chopped the top 2-1/2 inches and then filled the insert. The red and black lacquer is owner sprayed.

To get it down the road rapidly a 4-bolt main Chevrolet mouse motor is employed. Bored .060" over it uses flat top pistons, a General Kinetics cam, LT-1 heads, roller rockers and Rhoads lifters. The fuel is delivered to this mouse that roars via an Edelbrock tunnel ram with a Holley carb perched atop.

Next in line is a 400 turbo with a shift kit, B&M Super Hole Shot 10" converter and a Gennie Shifter. Out back is a narrowed 9" Ford fitted with 4.30 gears, positraction and overdrive. A rare Hone 3rd member mounted overdrive lowers revs by 30% for highway cruising.

Suspension chores are handled by coilovers with ladder bars keeping averting in place. The ponies are delivered to 15 inches of Mickey Thompson hides.

Up front is a mere 4-inches of M.T. rubber, with a dropped I-beam axle mounted to parallel leaf springs. Steering is handled by a cross steer Vega box (an update made after the pictures were taken).

Stopping power for this pro-street rocket is supplied by disc brakes all the way around.

Inside, the coupe has all the necessary creature comforts. Included in the array of goodies are an AM/FM-CB, Classic instruments, and a tilt-telescoping steering column topped by a Grant wheel.

The black and grey velour interior is patterned after the original. Bob took the '32s upholstery apart and used the pieces as patterns to cut out new material. He had the necessary stitching done, and then reinstalled the completed pieces.

Next in line to come out of the Binder garage is a '32 Chevy Vicky, which will hold the wife and two small girls. Seems the whole family is smitten with street rodding.

Right-Making this coupe a real runner is a small block Chevrolet equipped with all the goodies. Note the neat carb cover and the radiator overflow tank.

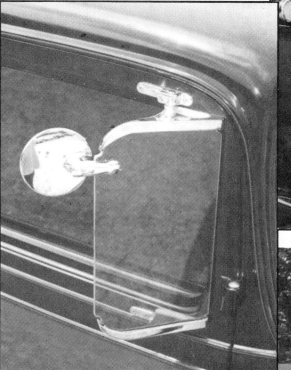

Above-Accessory wind wings keep the wind noise and buffeting to a minimum.

Right-Bob has his coupe sitting and looking good, with bigs 'n littles, and contrasting black and red paint. To top it off this Chevy can put you in the crease of the seat with its acceleration.

Below-With disc brakes all the way around, this car will stop. The early Chevrolet steering has recently been given the heave-ho and replaced by a Vega unit.

Right-The interior has all the comforts of home, and plenty of leg room too.

QUAD
Thirty-Four

Vehicle: 1934 Chevrolet 3-window coupe
Owner: Buddy Pastor, Melrose, Florida

Buddy Pastor called upon the latest in chassis and engine technology in the development of his chopped '34 coupe. Although the technical challenges were sometimes frustrating, in true hot rod fashion he kept on until the project came to life.

The neat thing about hot rodding these days is the tremendous variety of engines that can be selected to power a rod. Nowadays, you can choose from venerable V8s, inline sixes, V6s, or even a bunch of 4-cylinder powerplants. The choices are almost endless, and the wrecking yards are full of every kind of engine imaginable.

Buddy Pastor decided he wanted to drop the very latest technology under the hood of his '34 coupe. Even though he wasn't about to find such fresh technology laying around a wrecking yard, everything he had heard about the Oldsmobile Quad 4 made him want to get this engine. After test driving a few cars powered by the Quad 4, he ordered one from a dealer.

But Buddy took his project one step farther down the road to late model technology. He searched around until he came up with a 1984 Chevy S-10 pickup chassis as a foundation for the '34 coupe. You see, the '34 coupe has a stock wheelbase of 107 inches. The S-10 pickup wheelbase is a very close 108 inches. The track is also very close to the same, and the front and rear tires fit under the '34 with no modification to track width whatsoever.

The front of the S-10 frame was cut and a section removed, then a straight section welded in. It had to be notched at the front of the rear springs so it would follow the angle of the coupe body. Also, the rear kick-up angle was changed to match that of the '34. The right rear shock absorber had to be mounted toward the front so the gas tank would fit.

Stock S-10 disc front and drum rear brakes work perfectly for this car, and the S-10 fuel tank has replaced the '34 unit. The pickup's 10-bolt rearend was retained, and the independent front suspension adds modern ride and handling characteristics to this early car. Also scavenged from the S-10 were the hanging pedals, although they were shortened and rewelded to fit under the '34 dash.

The '89 Oldsmobile Quad 4 is a fuel injected engine, and this particular one is followed by a Muncie 4-speed transmission of '70s vintage. An '85 Camaro V6 or 4-cylinder bellhousing was modified to be compatible with the Quad 4. One of the biggest challenges of working with the Quad 4 engine was building the wiring harness. It was very difficult for Buddy to come up with the harness connectors. He found some from wrecking yards, got some from GM, and had the help of friends to locate the rest.

Then there was the question of the cooling system. The solution was finally found in a MoPar K car. The radiator was the perfect size, but it needed to be turned on its side to fit in the grille of the '34. Of course, this necessitated relocation of the hose fittings. The top fitting was moved down 3 inches and became the bottom fitting when the radiator was stood upright. A 90-degree filler was made from a section of brass pipe from a sink drain. The old filler was silver soldered to the new one so the pressure cap could be used. The upper fitting was another piece of brass drain pipe. Then, Buddy made brackets to hold an electric fan in place.

Other modifications to the coupe include a top chop of 3-5/8", and the installation of electric windows, with '86 Buick switches. A trunk latch and solenoid from an '86 Buice was added. The tilt steering column is out of an '84 Pontiac, and an '84 Buick Skyhawk contributed the parking brake mechanism and cables (the cables were shortened to fit). VDO gauges fill the dash. Bumpers are from an early VW. Taillights are '41-'48 Chevrolet, and headlights are Dietz units.

Buddy runs P185/75R14 General tires up front and eventually wants to have P235/75R15 in the rear. The rear was lowered 3 inches via lowering blocks, and the front springs were cut and lowered approximately 4 inches.

Buddy's car is not intended to be a show car, although it is a very nice looking ride. He is the kind of guy who loves to look at show cars, but wants to drive his cars. And judging from this one, who can blame him.

An '84 Chevrolet S-10 pickup truck was the donor of this chassis. As it turns out, the difference between the S-10 wheelbase and the '34 coupe wheelbase was only an inch. Track width was close to perfect, so no modification was necessary to get the tires to fit beneath the fenders.

In order to make the chassis conform more closely to the contours of the '34 coupe floor, a couple of modifications were needed. This section at the front of the frame was cut out and replaced by a straight section of frame.

One of the advantages of using the S-10 chassis was the acquisition of rack and pinion steering and front disc/rear drum brakes. This, plus the late model independent front suspension, gives the '34 great ride and handling characteristics.

The Quad 4 engine fits perfectly under the hood of the '34 coupe. A lot of headaches were brought on by trying to build an engine harness for this powerplant, but hot rodders like Buddy know how to solve problems. Note the chrome coolant pipe. This is a section of brass sink drain pipe from Ace Hardware.

Taillights are vintage '41-'48 items, and they seem to fit nicely on the rear fenders of this '34. The top chop brought the overall height of the car down 3-5/8".

A MoPar K car radiator was chosen for the cooling system. To make it fit, it had to be turned sideways and have all the hose connections modified, but with the addition of an electric fan, it keeps the Quad 4 cool.

'34 Master Coupe

Let's deal with reality here. Sometimes it simply isn't possible for an owner to build a whole car all by himself — at least not in one lifetime. The problem may be time (lack thereof) or talent (nobody knows everything), so the obvious solution is to invite the participation of outside help, and just keep your hand in the building process as much as possible.

That's what John Goodman did, and you can see the results on these pages. In all, this '34 Chevy Master 5-window coupe took over three years to complete. During the building process, John collaborated with several others to do work he couldn't do himself, for one reason or another. But along the way he never lost touch with the project, and that gives him something the turn-key buyer never has — personal, intimate knowledge of the car.

Preparing the body involved chopping the top 4 inches overall and filling it with the roof from a '65 Mustang. The back window was cut free of the body and chopped only 2-1/2 inches to keep from losing very much visibility to the rear. All of the stock chrome and stainless steel trim pieces and handles were removed. Then custom stainless steel and aluminum pieces were designed and made by Ron Healey and John.

Working from front to rear, the front bumper and brackets were removed and turn signal lights were installed in place of the brackets. Custom headlight bars were made to hold the Dietz lights. These were formed from five separate pieces of aluminum, welded together then sanded and polished to a finished piece. The radiator shell is filled with a custom-made aluminum trim ring. The stock hood was made into a three-piece top-open style. A gas strut rod lifts the hood after push button solenoid release. When the hood is pushed down, a Cadillac trunk closing mechanism closes the unit.

Wipers have been moved to the bottom of the windshield, using a VW motor with custom-made drive. The cowl vent has been filled, and the vent windows were removed and one piece of glass was installed. Stock door latch mechanisms were replaced by Mitsubishi units which are actuated by radio-controlled GM door lock solenoids. The hidden hinges are completely scratch-built, with pockets built into the door pillars,

1934 Chevrolet 5-window coupe
Owner: John W. Goodman, Westminster, Maryland

braced back to the firewall.

Trunk entry is by solenoid release. A GM automatic antenna for AM/FM and CB has been installed on top of the trunk deck. Taillights have been removed from the fenders and Mercury Cougar lenses formed to fit the rear panel. Custom trim rings were made of stainless steel for surrounding the lenses. The stock gas filler was covered and a new recessed gas filler was installed, hidden behind the rear license plate. The gas tank is a custom-built unit. Rear bumpers were removed and the original bracket areas smoothed over.

Power for the '34 comes from a '65 Daimler 2500 V8 hemi. The engine features polished aluminum heads, water pump, oil pan and intake that has been modified to accept a 4-barrel carburetor. Owner-made aluminum brackets secure the alternator and Sankyo air conditioner compressor. A stainless steel firewall sets off the engine compartment and a custom-made air cleaner (designed by John and milled by Rick Woodward) tops off the carburetor. Cooling is handled by a Walker radiator.

Torque is transmitted via a Borg Warner 3-speed automatic transmission to the Daimler rear axle, with 4.10:1 gears. The rear axle is set up in panhard rod mode and TCI coil-over shocks. Front suspension is out of a '67 Jaguar XKE. Brakes utilize J.F.Z. calipers, actuated by a Corvette master cylinder with the aid of a Datsun

B210 booster. Front tires are Michelin 165-15, and the rear skins are BFGoodrich P255-70SR15, and all the tires ride Weld Wheel Super Slots.

VDO cockpit gauges fill the stock dash, and a Vintage Air unit is mounted below. Overhead is a stainless steel console, housing the radio, interior light and switches. A tilt column from an '83 Oldsmobile has been dressed up with a LeCarra steering wheel. Radio speakers are positioned in the rear package shelf. Be-

neath the shelf is a Ron Francis electric panel. Electric window motors are GM belt-driven type with switches and door handles from a Chevy Blazer set in custom stainless trim. Rankin Upholsterers finished off the interior and trunk in red fabric.

John worked with Mike Gist on the completion of the bodywork. Flame red R&M Miracryl acrylic enamel with urethane clear was applied by Dave Cunningham. The graphics were designed and painted by Butch Nieves.

Headlight supports were handmade from five individual pieces of aluminum that were welded together then sanded and polished to a finished product.

Mercury Cougar taillights were made to fit the south end of the car, and the license plate is tucked neatly in a recess.

The radiator shell was filled with a custom-made aluminum trim ring, and the hood was transformed into a three-piece top-open style.

Power for the '34 five-window coupe comes from a '65 Daimler 2500 V8 hemi featuring polished aluminum heads and a custom-built air filter housing.

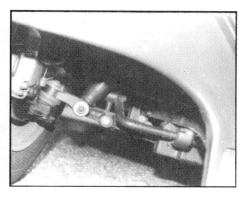
Front suspension is out of a '67 Jaguar, with J.F.Z. disc brakes being powered by a Corvette master cylinder and a Datsun booster.

Dual exhaust tucks neatly up out of the way, and turbo mufflers mellow out the exhaust notes.

Hidden behind the recessed license plate is the locking gas filler.

Smooth exterior is enhanced by removal of stock door handles, which were replaced by Mitsubishi interior units. Scratch-built hidden door hinges employ reinforced pockets built into the door pillars.

167

Pure Slick

Bill Batchelor is an ex-Air Force type who liked western Idaho so much that he decided to settle there, much to the delight of area rodders who seem to congregate around his shop by the dozens. Back in 1984, Bill found this 1935 Chevy Standard Coupe in a local farm barn, but it took a month of negotiating and $1750 to get the car. "I thought that was a ton of money," says Bill.

Vehicle: 1935 Chevrolet Standard Coupe
Owner: Bill Batchelor, Mountain Home, Idaho

The car sat in storage for a year, while Batchelor considered the things to do, and while he spent time gathering parts. Finally, in 1985, he started the project. First on the agenda was a 3-inch top chop and filled roof. The body came off the chassis to allow more room to work on the frame, so friend Jim Bledsoe used the time to build a 331-inch small block Chevy engine and TH350 (which trans case Bill had conned his wife Pam into polishing!).

The chassis got a front end from Sbarbaro Hot Rods, beneath a highly modified front crossmember. The stock X-member was removed, and a crossmember fabricated for the motor mounts, then a K-member with removable transmission mount was installed. Also from Sbarbaro came a crossmember with driveshaft loop and mounting for the rear 4-bar setup. Brackets for the 8-inch Ford rearend are also Sbarbaro.

After a stint with the Air Force, Bill Batchelor settled in Mountain Home, Idaho and stirred up the local hot rod scene by building this slick '35 Standard Coupe.

The frame was painted with Martin Senour Ureglow Red, with some components chrome plated. Stainless bolts were used wherever possible. After the chassis was completed, the body was installed, powertrain dropped in and wired, and the car driven about 300 miles as a checkout. It was then disassembled, the body set on a homemade body dolly, and finishing bodywork/paint took place. The body was painted Ford Fleet Red, using Ditzler lacquer. Interior work was done in leather and cloth by Mel Eggleston of Boise, Idaho. And the Rocky Mountains haven't been the same since.

Fenders and running boards came from Superior Glass Works. Dietz headlights are lowered to tuck in against the fenders. Side mirrors are from Squeegs.

The engine includes an Edelbrock intake to accommodate a trio of 2-barrel carburetors. A Crane cam, Magoo pulleys, Squeegs valve covers, TCI tuck-in headers, and a homebuilt A/C bracket finish off the powerplant.

Vent windows were eliminated, so fresh air interior comfort is via Airtique air conditioner through homebuilt vents. The dash panel is from Carriage Works, and is filled with VDO gauges. Seats are from a 1984 Celica Supra. Steering is Vega, with a 1968 Grand Prix column.

A shorty windshield wiper was installed to keep the chopped glass clear on moist days.

The 3-inch top chop brought the roof down just the right amount. A purely slick appearance was created by filling the top and removing the door handles.

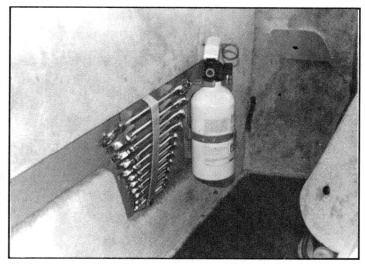

Special tool rack and fire extinguisher are immediately behind the driver's seat, an idea that others should probably copy.

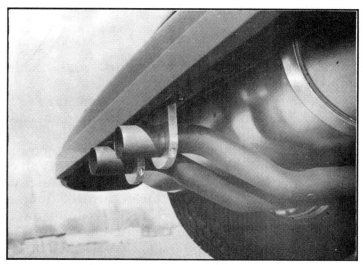

Twice pipes are supported directly beneath the rear bumper by a pair of nifty brackets.

High-Tech '37

Manny Schatz wanted a car with the classic lines of yesterday and the mechanical technology of today. Then he happened upon a certain '37 Chevy 2-door sedan with a "for sale" sign prominently displayed. That is simply too much temptation for some people to handle, and Manny ended up striking the deal that left him with the pink slip.

As the project began, the '37 was stripped all the way down, and Mickey Galloway was delegated the chore of perfecting the body. Among other things, that involved replacing the lower 6 inches of sheetmetal all the way around, as well as taking care of rust and ding removal. Holes were filled, the cowl vent was filled, hood side panel louvers were removed and filled, and the false louvers on top of the hood were hammered flat.

While all that was going on, numerous automobile cadavers were cannibalized to come up with specific high-tech components. A Mustang II contributed the front end. The rear axle lived previously in a Chevy Nova. A '75 Caprice donated the steering column and the power window units. Vent window handles are out of a Volvo. Seatbelt and shoulder harness units are from an S-10 Blazer and the four bucket seats were salvaged from an '82 Honda Accord. An internal-release unit from a Toyota replaced the stock hood release mechanism. A Toyota also contributed the door handles and opening/locking mechanisms, giving the car a clean, modern appearance. A VW Bug sacrificed its locking gas door for the '37. Sideview mirrors are Chevette units,

and the ralley wheels are stock Camaro in front and Corvette in the rear.

Exterior dress up includes custom-built front and rear bumpers that were designed to complement the flowing lines of the body style. Brown tinted glass is an accent to the two tone brown paint scheme. Both the darker topaz and the lighter beige are stock '77 Mercedes Benz colors, applied by Mickey Galloway in DuPont Centauri acrylic enamel.

Running gear includes a Target Master 350 V8 with an Edelbrock Performer intake manifold and Holley 650 cfm carb. Corvette aluminum valve covers, a custom air cleaner housing, and Ram Horn exhaust manifolds (painted with Eastwood's stainless paint) dress up the engine. Gear changing is handled by a TH350.

The dash was reworked by Mickey. He built a steel roll pan under the dash with three removable panels that flow from the dash to the firewall. This pan covers the air conditioner/heater unit and houses the light switch and power window switches. On the dash is an aluminum panel dotted with VDO gauges.

So, just how good is this car? Well, at the '89 Oakland Roadster Show, it garnered the coveted First Place award for Custom Rod Sedan as well as the Overall Custom Rod award.

When people ask Manny how much the whole project cost, he responds, "The dollars are many, the hours are probably more, but the rewards far outweigh any expense."

Vehicle: 1937 Chevrolet 2-door sedan
Owner: Manny Schatz, Danville, California
According to Manny's vision, this is how Chevrolet would have built their cars back in '37 if they had the advantage of today's technology.

Front fenders, running boards and pads, and the 2" wider rear fenders are from Old Chicago Fiberglass. Rear bumper is aluminum homebuilt, and the taillights are '39 Pontiac via the swap meet.

Locking fuel door is from a VW Bug, and was modified to conform to the body contour. Access to the cable to open the door is located in the trunk.

The upholstered trunk includes hidden storage for the floor jack and the small spare tires as well as spare hoses and belts. Cleaning supplies are organized, leaving plenty of room for luggage.

A Target Master 350 cid V8 tucks nicely under the hood, fed by the combined efforts of a Holley 650 and Edelbrock Performer. Front disc and rear drum brakes are power assisted.

Complete with fuzzy dice, the interior features a custom-built dash with a steel pan below that hides the air conditioner/heater unit.

Front bucket seats, from an '82 Honda Accord were located in a wrecking yard in Concord, California. These reclining seats utilize the complete Honda track for front-to-rear movement.

by James Handy

'37 Coupe

Being a regional safety inspector for NSRA, Bob Poer knows how to build a right-on street rod. A few years back, his 1937 Chevy sedan was the envy of every rod builder on the west coast, even though it had more miles on the odometer than a New York taxi. But Poer always wanted a coupe, same vintage, and it took him 14 years of gathering parts from backyards all over the Sacramento area. The biggest hassle of all? Trying to be patient while one body shop sat on the project for 22 months. He alleviated that problem by taking the car to friend Dave Dolman.

The stock 1937 chassis has been modified by the addition of a '74 Pinto front suspension and '74 Nova rearend with 3.08:1 gears. The front rides near the weeds, 6 inches lower than stock, by using the Pinto springs. Steering is a Pinto power rack. Enkei wheels with machined center caps carry Bridgestone radials. The entire chassis and running gear (as well as the underside of the body) are painted and chromed. The Pinto front end is adapted to the frame via a Progressive Automotive kit, steering shafts, and new rotors drilled to Chevy bolt pattern. The power steering pump is from a '72 Chevelle, 2-inch lowering blocks are used between the Nova rearend and stock '37 springs.

While this is no quarter-mile terror, it can get the highway numbers done, what with the '72 Chevy 307 cid V8 that has been bored .030". The small block runs a Chevrolet 300 horsepower 327 cam and GM lifters, as well as an Edelbrock manifold with 6510 Carter carbu-

Vehicle: 1937 Chevrolet coupe
Owner: Bob Poer, Yuba City, California

With 2-inch lowering blocks in the back, and cut Pinto coils in front, the car has that just-right stance without being too low to drive comfortably. Note the smooth running boards and hood sides.

retor. Ben Collins cleaned up the '73 TH350 automatic transmission with column shifter, and Poer mounted the combination using Chassis Engineering brackets. A shortened '71 Chevelle driveshaft connects power to the rearend.

Although it appears nearly stock, the body on this jewel has received massive massaging. The top is chopped 2 inches in front and 1-1/2 inches in back. Door hinges are hidden, using Body Coddington units, and the rear pan has been rolled and filled. Old Chicago furnished rear fenders that are 2 inches wider, and '39 Ford teardrop taillights are flush fit. The running boards are smooth, leading to the mildly reworked front end. Headlights are lowered 2-3/5 inches, and the grille bottom is bobbed to blend smoothly with the fenders. Hood sides are smoothed, with trick handles. The cowl vent has been filled and the windshield is butted and glued.

Light grey Cadillac velour interior by Frank Martinez of Live Oak, California contrasts nicely with the vivid Deltron red paint by Golden Valley Auto Body, of Yuba City. The molded dash holds a Fat Jack insert and VDO instruments, all connected by a Ron Francis wiring harness. Air conditioning is Vintage Air. Arm rests are Valley Auto, steering column is '74 Pontiac tilt above the modified '84 Chevy Celebrity bench seat.

Right-In the early stages of construction, the coupe awaits its sheetmetal covering in Bob Poer's small, but well-equipped garage.

Above-Installation of the transmission cooler is typical of the cleanliness of the work throughout this car.

Right-The Pinto master cylinder is mounted next to the Chevy TH350 automatic transmission, using a Chassis Engineering kit. Note the attention to detail.

Above-Progressive Automotive products were used to mount the Pinto front suspension into the early Chevy chassis. Those early Corvette rams horn factory headers are a rare commodity in California.

Right-The Chevy Nova rearend is mounted on stock '37 leaf springs with 2-inch lowering blocks.

Left-Now this is clean! The wider rear fenders have been bobbed and blended in with the rear rolled pan, and the trunk lid bottom. Taillights are '39 Ford.

Above-Those megaphone exhausts look pretty mean from this angle. Rear tires are 275-60R15 Bridgestones.

Left- Interior has all the creature comforts, including arm rests from Valley Auto, and an instrument cluster from Fat Jack. The column is a '74 Pontiac tilt unit.

Above-Only a '37 fanatic would notice the lowered headlights. Grille is N.O.S. and the pan beneath it has been molded and recontoured.

Left-Engine compartment is super clean and easy to keep that way, with adequate amounts of painted and chromed surfaces. This is no show car, just a super sanitary street rod.

175

'38 Special

Vehicle: 1938 Chevy Coupe
Owners: Charles and Adair Svoboda, New Prague, Minnesota

Back in 1973 Charles Svoboda picked up this 1938 Chevy and started to restore it. The engine was rebuilt and miscellaneous parts were purchased but as the years passed enthusiasm for his project waned. The coupe sat untouched for some time.

Charles began attending car shows and rod runs and found the desire to work on his car returning. But he wanted to make his Chevy different, something that would stand out in a crowd. So what does he do? With no welding, body work, or painting experience Charles decides to take a 4-inch section out of his coupe!

Armed with little more than a few old '50s magazine articles on sectioning for reference, the job was begun. A reciprocating air saw was used to make the cut that starts under the top door hinges and extends up and over the rear fenders. When the top of the body was reunited with the bottom, the fenders remained in their original location. The next step was to reshape the area between the deck lid and the fenders; a modification that is so subtle it can only be appreciated by comparing this car to a stocker. A rolled rear pan with lighting from modified GM pickup side markers finish off the rear.

Up front the hood was cut down to size by removing the louvered portion, and the grille was sectioned and recontoured to fit.

Door handles were taken off and smooth glass running boards were installed. When the body was done to his satisfaction, Charles covered it in Matador Red.

A '79 Buick V6 is used for power, modifications are limited to a mild cam. A Turbo 300 transmission and a '70 Nova rearend mounted to stock '38 springs complete the drive train. Front suspension is by an owner installed Nova clip. Rare Spyder wheels are wrapped with Goodyear Eagles.

After a year and a half of body work, painting, and running gear modifications, the '38 was turned over to Unique Upholstery for a grey cloth interior. The Chevy was finished just in time to be part of the Svobodas' wedding ceremony. Now that's the way to start a relationship.

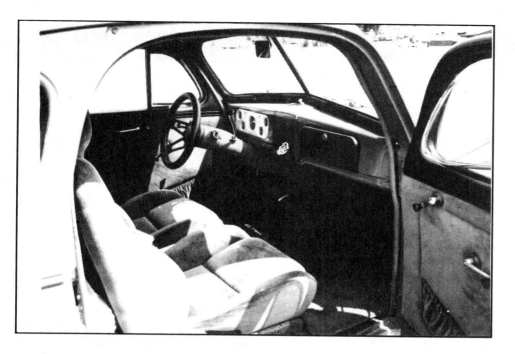

Interior features Fiero seating, tilt column, and an aluminum dash insert. Heating and air conditioning are recent additions.

Maintaining the proportions of a sectioned vehicle can be difficult. Charles pulled it off like a pro on his first try.

A basically stock Buick V6 provides reliable cruising power. Drum brakes are activated by a firewall mounted vacuum booster and master cylinder.

by Ron Ceridono

Finders, Keepers

We've all heard rumors of garages or barns with forgotten early iron hidden away inside. Cars that were under piles of junk just waiting to be discovered and rescued. As the stories were told and retold, the cars usually became better and better. Some had the keys in the ignition switch, a signed "pink" in the glove box. Others were in perfect condition, just bring a fresh battery, and it could be driven off. Well, here's proof at least one of those stories is true.

This 1939 Chevrolet was stashed away when it was only 5-years old. It wasn't exactly mint, having been crunched in an accident in 1944. But its odometer showed a mere 42,921 miles. Repairing the damage would have been easy, but there was a shortage of parts during WWII. Instead of being fixed the sedan was stored. When peace time came again, all the necessary parts were ordered and received, but never installed. Somewhere along the line the engine was removed, and sold. So, there it sat, under an increasing pile of debris.

Chuck Newbury had heard his share of rumors too, and one of them turned out to be true. In 1960 he discovered the real thing in a building in downtown Centralia, Washington.

His early attempts to buy the car failed, but he didn't give up. In 1986, after a 26 year pursuit, the owner gave in and agreed to sell the Chevy. Included were all the new parts (still in the factory wrappers), to repair the collision damage. There was a condition, however. The car would be Chuck's only if he promised to put a six back in it.

Vehicle: 1939 Chevrolet Master Deluxe
Owner: Chuck Newbury, Centralia, Washington

After a 42 year stint in storage, the Chevy again saw the light of day.

In June of '86 the body was stripped to bare metal, the damage repaired, and then painted black as it was originally. The interior, a near perfect original, was left as it was.

The missing engine was replaced by a late model 6-cylinder. A Powerglide transmission and a '66 Nova rearend finished off the drive train.

In August of '86 the Chevy was on the road again. It was driven to runs and even to Disneyland during the next couple of years, getting 23 miles to the gallon all the while. The odometer now showed 48,000 miles.

But then taking care of a black car began to get a little old, and a little more horsepower sounded appealing too. Plans for some changes started to take shape. In November of '88 the Chevy was dismantled again. Chuck painted the car orange, but it wasn't quite right. It was stripped to bare metal again. The next color to come out of the gun was turquoise.

Underneath the new color are lots of body modifications. Forty Chevy headlights were molded into the fenders, separated by a stainless steel grille. The doors now swing on hidden hinges and are opened electrically. Smooth steel running boards have replaced the originals. Out back custom taillights replace the stockers and the trunk lid has been smoothed and had hidden hinges installed. A vacuum operated 1939 license appears below the rolled rear pan when it's time to hit the streets.

The plan for more horsepower was addressed by the installation of a 461 cubic inch big block Chevrolet. The Rat motor has been balanced and contains enough go-fast goodies to make keeping up with traffic, nooo problem. A 350 turbo with a 2600 rpm stall speed converter delivers the ample torque to a '79 Lincoln rearend.

Up front suspension is now provided by a Mustang II unit. In the rear an Art Morrison 4-bar and slider kit was used. Disc brakes are found at all four corners.

Inside updates to match all the other changes were made. A two-tone grey interior replaced the original. Classic gauges fill the dash, and the windows are power operated. Sounds are provided by an overhead console housed stereo.

The '39 has been back on the street in its current form for a short period of time, and has already gathered more awards than we have space to list. Not bad for a former warehouse recluse.

We don't know about you, but we're going to check out the next rumor we hear about an old car that's stashed away, and maybe we'll take a battery along just in case.

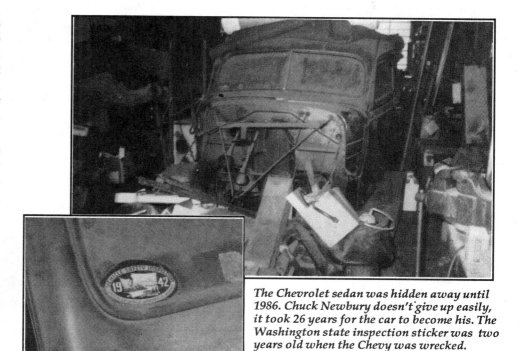

The Chevrolet sedan was hidden away until 1986. Chuck Newbury doesn't give up easily, it took 26 years for the car to become his. The Washington state inspection sticker was two years old when the Chevy was wrecked.

Dash and gauges are cherry, the steering wheel lacks the usual cracks and missing pieces. Note the accessory defroster fan. And yes, the odometer says 42,921.3 miles.

The Chevy comes to its new home. Check the new fenders still in factory wrappers.

The first rebuild featured a late Chevy 6 and a Powerglide. Suspension and brakes remained stock in the front. A Nova rearend was used. Mild mannered 6 delivered great gas mileage and reliable, if uninspired, performance.

The second rebuild featured a little more muscle under the hood. A 461 cid big block is equipped with a 750 Edelbrock carb, Weiand manifold, and roller rockers operated by a Competition Cams 280H 'shaft. Ignition is by Mallory, cooling by the Brassworks.

The original front suspension was replaced with Mustang II components, while out back 4-bars from Art Morrison position the disc brake equipped Lincoln 9-inch.

The body also had its share of changes this time around. 1940 Chevy headlights have been molded into the '39 fenders, giving the sedan a much smoother look.

Before the two-tone grey interior was installed a Ron Francis wiring kit went in, along with a healthy dose of Kool Kar insulation. Lots of aluminum in the form of a tilt column, pedals, dash inserts, and arm rests can be found.

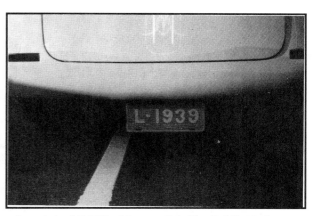

An original '39 Washington "Golden Jubilee" plate is flanked by two huge exhaust tips.

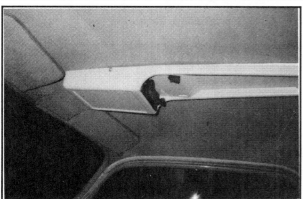

An overhead console contains the stereo. All the garnish moldings have been painted the same turquoise that covers the exterior. The upholstered trunk contains a spare, the battery, and the fuel filler.

The electrically opened trunk lid has been smoothed and swings on hidden hinges. Custom rectangular taillights and a rolled rear pan finish off the rear.

by Harvey Mushman   photos by Tim Frazier

'42 Salt Sedan

Vehicle: 1942 Chevy Aerosedan   Owner: Gary Cope, Auburn, California

You can't tell now, but the Chevy's name came about from the condition of the Aerosedan body. During a late night construction session one of the crew members commented that the body looked like it had gangrene. When the laughter stopped, its name was Gang Green.

Some cars lead a charmed life. This Chevy was scheduled to be crushed on three separate occasions but scrap yard owner Gary Cope just couldn't let it happen, he saved it at the last moment each time. Knowing he didn't want to destroy it, but not really sure why he was saving it, the rusty Stovebolt was stored behind his shop.

A trip to Bonneville in 1985 got Gary hooked on the salt, and on his return home the question of what to do with the car he had rescued was answered. The decision was made to run the Chevy at SpeedWeek the

following year. Thirty short days after beginning, the car was assembled, built after hours by a volunteer crew with full time jobs.

The plan was to build the car Gary and crew chief Tim Tenold wanted in high school, but couldn't afford as kids. What else could power the sedan in that case than a 302 GMC, the engine they lusted after in their youth. Bored to 318 cubic inches, the Jerry Weigt built six-cylinder features a rare cast iron Wayne head, one of fifteen thought to have been made. Four Stromberg 97s feed fuel to valves operated by a Howard flat tappet

Practically every piece on this car came from the scrap yard, including the accessory bumper tips, a rare '42 only option. The Chevy makes the transition from Bonneville to the 1/4 mile with little more than a gear change.

cam. To solve some of the inherent vibration problems in these early sixes a viscous vibration damper from a 6-71 Detroit Diesel is used. Hedders were built by fellow Bonneville competitors Jim and Chris Hill at Specialty Products Design. A Chevy 4-speed, and a Ford nine-inch rearend complete the drive train.

Up front is a Dodge axle mounted on '37 Chevy springs, stock steering, and '51 Chevy pickup brakes. Camaro mono-leaves and traction bars are used in the rear.

L.B. Howell was called on to transform the body, actually a '47, into a '42 by substituting earlier front sheetmetal and trim. Lots of hours and numerous patch panels later, an original two tone green combination was applied in acrylic enamel. Not done in some luxurious bondo emporium, the paint was shot in a barn at 4:00 am by the light of a drop cord.

Since completion the Aerosedan has seen double duty as a nostalgia drag racer and a straightaway campaigner. The Chevy has clicked off a 13.50 elapsed time at 104 mph at the drags weighing 3500 pounds in Bonneville trim. At SpeedWeek 1990 the Gang Green crew upped their own XXV/ALT record to an amazing 150.549 with Gary's son, Garrett, driving the car for the first time. Not bad for a rusty old Chevy that was crusher bound.

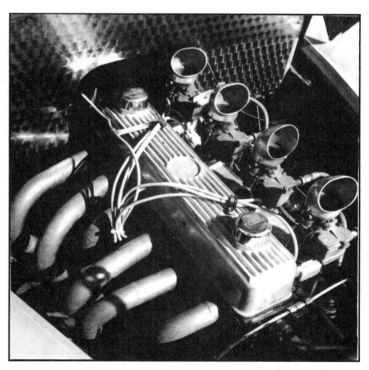

The Dave Riolo designed fuel system features a unique fuel log/regulator designed to deliver enough volume for sustained high speeds, with low pressure to keep the 97s from flooding. Cast iron Wayne head is a rare item, as most were aluminum.

by Rich Johnson

Old Style
Stylemaster

Post-war Chevys (1946-'48) have really started to gain popularity among the hot rodding ranks over the past few years. All kinds of wild paint schemes, hot motors, and body modifications are showing up. While Steve Hardwick thought about really doing a hot number on his '46 Chevy Stylemaster coupe, in the end he chose to keep it simple. And that was a great decision.

Vehicle: 1946 Chevrolet Stylemaster coupe
Owner: Steve Hardwick, Mountain Home, Idaho

The 1946 Stylemaster coupe was Chevrolet's first car to come off the assembly line after the war. It was basically a warmed over '42, with a total production number of 14,642.

Steve liked the body style, but didn't want to really go all out, so he dropped in a 235 cid straight six Chevy engine, equipped with a McGurk tri-power intake system and split exhaust.

The body was lowered, painted with Deltron and flamed by Steve and friend Doug Kriebs. Brown and

Deltron paint and flames were applied by Steve and friend Doug Kriebs. The car sits pleasingly lower than stock, but is far from being in the weeds, which means that it is still able to be driven without fear of damage to the undercarriage.

tan velour interior work was performed by Steve and his friends at Robin's Nest Upholstery. Note that Steve was able to participate in the building of this car both inside and out. And that is an important component to hot rodding.

Steve is the kind of rodder who's back yard serves as storage for such items as a '49 Merc, '55 rag top Ford, '32 Ford 5-window coupe, '33 Plymouth coupe, '26 Buick roadster and other precious parts and pieces. All of this constitutes projects to come. That, after all, is why there is a future.

There is rumored to be a '49 Plymouth in the building process, with work being done by Steve's wife, Gail, and friends. The car is supposed to be Gail's when it's finished, but Steve says, "We'll see."

Right, Steve! Nice guy!

Brown and tan velour upholstery material was stitched by Steve and his friends at Robin's Nest Upholstery. Fuzzy dice and a barefoot accelerator pedal mark this as a car typical of the period.

This is a fine example of a modestly done rod. Clean and beautiful, with flames and good looking wheels, but not overdone. This is the kind of ride that we either had or wanted to have back in the good old days.

Below-Tri-power atop a McGurk intake manifold is one of the hop-up items installed on the 235 inline six. A split exhaust system gets rid of the gasses most efficiently.

Garfield rides back bumper patrol on Steve's '46 Stylemaster coupe, and has watched as more than 60,000 miles have passed beneath this car in the past several years. This is a driver, not to be confused with those not so hot rods that never see the street.

With all the trim still on the car, and the body looking basically stock, Steve and Gail make appearances at car shows whenever they can. Here is a car everyone can appreciate for its simple beauty and the way it was built with a relative lack of overspending.

by Ron Ceridono

Purple Pickup

Vehicle: 1948 Chevy Pickup
Owner: George and Vicki Arbuckle Elwood, Indiana

George and Vicki Arbuckle wanted a ride that would get people's attention. What better way to accomplish that than a chopped, purple, '48 Chevy pickup.

The project had been started by the Arbuckles' neighbor, Bob Gillum. Bob had begun to build a work truck when his buddy, Dave Kinnaman, suggested they chop the top. That sounded like a neat idea but after the lid was lowered other priorities, like a new baby, put the Chevy on hold.

One year had passed with the truck sitting in a barn, when Bob decided to sell. A deal was made and George hauled the pickup home in pieces, convincing himself on the way that this would be a quick project. One thing led to another, as they often do with hot rods, and 2-1/2 years later the truck was on the road.

As the top had been chopped 4 inches it was decided to continue the fat 'n smooth look. The door handles were removed, hood corners were rounded, and the headlights frenched. Up front a Studebaker

grille was used because it was hanging in the garage and needed a home. Louvers were punched in the hood and the tailgate, and the rear was finished off with inverted Trans-Am taillights. The folks at East Side Parts in Elwood, Indiana mixed up their version of purple to cover the exterior.

Inside, seating is provided by Chevelle bucket seats separated by a hand crafted console. To aide in cruising comfort a GM tilt column, power windows, and air conditioning were added. Stewart-Warner gauges supply necessary information.

Under the hood we find a stock 400 cu. in. small block Chevy. Power is delivered to the leaf spring suspended Pontiac rearend by a Turbo 400.

To get the front down and still provide the desired ride, a frame clip from a 1973 Pontiac Ventura was grafted to the original rails. Disc brakes and power steering are another benefit of the chassis update.

The Arbuckles' goal was to build a rod that attracted attention, we think they've succeeded.

Right-The purple '48 rides on 14 x 8 ET mags shod with 60 series rubber. The floor of the pickup bed was done with yellow poplar planks and stainless steel strips. A race type fuel cell is mounted below the bed. A unique adaptation of Trans-Am lights was used at the rear.

Below-The interior is done in light and dark gray velour. Climate control is by way of a Superior heating and cooling unit. Gauges are installed in a custom aluminum panel.

Right-A GM power brake unit and tandem master cylinder mounts to a handmade aluminum firewall. Chrome valve covers and air cleaner along with lots of paint detailing complete the under hood scene.

Above-George spent many hours in the garage to get this Chevy to its present condition. Dave Kinnaman, Bob Gillum, and wife Vicki provided valuable help.

Right-Use of a Studebaker grille causes lots of double takes. Turn signals are mounted in the grille, driving lights below. A small chin spoiler is molded into the lower pan.

Blue
Flame

When he was thirteen years old, Frank Zaversnik would thumb through the small-size Custom Rodder and dream of the day he would sit behind the wheel of his own low-down cruiser. It took a couple of decades before Frank realized his dream. In 1976, he bought this 1950 Chevrolet 2-door sedan, and in the years since, the Blue Flame has become well known at street machine runs and ISCA car shows.

Vehicle: 1950 Chevy 2-door sedan
Owner: Frank Zaversnik, Roy, Utah

This custom has 108 louvers punched in the hood. Hood corners have been rounded in the best traditional fashion, and a pair of '54 Buick portholes were added. Headlights are frenched with '53 Ford rings, and the stock top grille bar has been molded to the fenders and painted. This serves to support the original center grille bar, which has thirteen '54 Chevy teeth. License plate guards from a '49 Chevy bumper are employed. All side trim, emblems, and door handles were removed. The gas filler is relocated to inside the trunk. Tail-

Timeless in form, this 1950 Chevy 2-door sedan fulfilled the desire of young Frank Zaversnik, who spend his youth wearing out the pages of early Custom Rodder magazines and dreaming of the day when he would have such a car for his own.

lights (with blue dots) are from a Rambler, mounted to the panel below the deck lid. Ribbed lakes pipes are nostalgia items that seem style-timeless. Frank found them in the attic of a still-operating muffler shop.

Tom Davis and Bob Myers applied the Cadillac Firemist acrylic enamel with a light pearl overcoat for depth. Flames are by Steve Stanford. Rocky Schmalz did the white tuck 'n roll upholstery, which is carried over into the trunk. Lowering is via coil work in front and lowering blocks at the rear. Wide whites are genuine Port-A-Walls.

The engine is in keeping with the old timey flavor. With friend Bob Rasmussen, Frank scoured the swap meets for old speed and dress-up equipment for the rebuilt 235 six. The head was shaved, high-lift rocker arms and solid lifters added to the valvetrain, and an Edelbrock twin-carb manifold installed. The Fenton headers lead directly to dual exhausts. All this is topped with a Sharp alloy valve cover.

Here is a car from another place and another time. But it is just as much in style today as it was more than four decades ago.

A single '54 Buick porthole graces each side of the hood, while 108 louvers vent heat from the engine compartment. Fuzzy dice and Appleton spots lend an air of '50s nostalgia.

Below-An Edelbrock dual-carb intake manifold tops the 235 cid six. The head was shaved and high-lift rockers incorporated for use with solid lifters. Fenton headers channel fumes through dual exhausts.

Custom grille has a molded and painted top bar. The original center bar has thirteen teeth from a '54 Chevy. Frenched headlights are surrounded by '53 Ford rings.

Below-Tuck 'n roll interior was stitched by Rocky Schmalz. Matching upholstery is carried over into the trunk. Basically stock dashboard is accented by nostalgia items such as the fuzzy dice and floor shifter.

The trunk is well organized with all the tools and supplies having their own place. Note that the gas filler has been moved to the inside of the trunk to clean up the exterior.

Hot Licks

by Rich Johnson

The controversy is ageless, and it is represented in excellent manner by the car on these pages. Can a 4-door be a hot rod, or must all hot rods be 2-door models? Ask that question aloud at any rod run, and you'll incite near riots of argument. However, ask that question of the editors at the headquarters of Tex Smith Publishing, and you'll receive a smile and a knowing nod. This type of question, cloaked in many forms, arouses emotions among the nouveau-rodder who has formed opinions based upon the vocalizations of someone else. The essence of real hot rodding has always been that you work with whatever car you have, regardless of vintage or body style.

In this case, fins and flames, and everything else that Dennis A. Oliveira of San Mateo, California did to build Hot Licks into a hot rod, speak much louder than the fact that the car has 4 doors. In fact, here is perhaps the quintessential Fifties hot rod for a family.

Predominant body color is '86 Chevy IROC blue iridescent. Flames blend from pearl white through pearl yellow, into orange, culminating in scallops of pearl white with orange pinstriping at the rear. The car has been nosed and decked, and a custom license plate housing was frenched into the deck lid. Clear '59 Cadillac bullet taillights replace the stock gunsights on the hood, bluedot taillights have their place out back, and Appleton spots and lakes pipes complete the exterior.

Vehicle: 1957 Chevy 4-door hardtop
Built by: Dennis A. Oliveira, San Mateo, California
Owner: Leonard J. Rutman, Bellmore, Long Island, New York

Flames and fins make this one dynamite example of a Fifties hot rod. Hot Licks gets the once-over by a fireman at the San Mateo, California fire station.

Pleated interior is done in contrasting dark and lighter blue iridescent vinyl, with the trunk upholstered to match. Stitch work was performed by Ray Camacho of Classic Interiors in south San Francisco.

Under the hood is a 275 horsepower 327 V8 of '67 vintage, coupled to a TH350 automatic transmission. The drivetrain was built and installed by Phil Brown of San Bruno, California.

Two years of work went into the building of Hot Licks. Much of the assembly work was done by owner Leonard Rutman of New York. And in the spirit of true hot rodding, this example should lay the old controversy to rest once and for all.

Classic rear view of the '57 Bel Air is enhanced by twin antennae and bluedot taillights. License plate has been recessed into the deck lid.

Below-This '57 has been nosed and decked, has Appleton dummy spots on each front fender, and is ready for the show. The engine is clearly visible in the reflective surface beneath the hood.

Middle Right-Go power is generated by this '67 vintage 275 horse 327 V8, complete with Corvette valve covers. A TH350 automatic transmission backs up the engine.

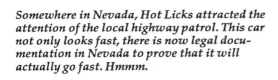

Somewhere in Nevada, Hot Licks attracted the attention of the local highway patrol. This car not only looks fast, there is now legal documentation in Nevada to prove that it will actually go fast. Hmmm.

Kooool '58

The '58 Impala has long been a favorite with hot rodders, but an Impala custom? There aren't many. That's what makes Greg Beck's 1958 Impala hardtop so unique.

Before Nissan Hot Red was laid on the car, Greg did a few minor body modifications, such as frenching the antenna, extending the front fender eyebrows 1/2", installing '59 Cadillac taillights, shaving the deck lid, and shaving and peaking the hood.

Inside, Greg installed a pair of '63 Ford Galaxie buckets up front. The '63 Ford console was installed and then equipped with a trio of VDO "Night Design" gauges, and a switch to operate the power antenna. Both the console and the face of the dash were covered with engine-turned aluminum panels. Upholstery work (red pleats on white) was done by the craftsmen at Jerry's Auto Upholstery in Greeley, Colorado. A Kenwood sound system booms out the tunes.

Under the hood is a Racing Head Service (RHS) series 268 high energy 350 small block Chevy engine that can really get this ride down the road in a hurry. Behind the mouse motor is a T.C.I. prepped TH350 automatic transmission with an 11-inch converter to get the ponies to the rear.

Rock 'N Roll rides on chrome wheels with baby moons, wrapped in a set of BFGoodrich T/A radials. To help stop this beauty, Greg installed an E.C.I. front disc brake kit and a Camaro master cylinder. To ease it through the corners with a minimum of body roll, a larger diameter front sway bar replaced the stock unit, and a rear sway bar was installed as well. Gas shocks at each corner keep the suspension system under control.

1958 was a very good year for Chevrolet, and if they had built a few Impalas like Greg Beck's, it would have been even better.

Vehicle: 1958 Chevrolet Impala hardtop
Owner: Greg Beck, Greeley, Colorado

Greg has done a ton of subtle body modifications, such as extending the fender eyebrows 1/2", shaving and peaking the hood, and shaving the deck lid. Note that the grille was painted to give it a tube type appearance.

Bucket seats and console came from a '63 Ford Galaxie. A trio of VDO "Night Design" gauges found a home on the console. Engine-turned aluminum panels add snap to the face of the dashboard and the console.

Below-Inside this beautifully detailed engine compartment is a Racing Head Service series 268 high energy 350 cid V8. It's the kind of mouse motor that will definitely let this car haul the mail.

With the lake pipes and frenched antenna, this '58 has a great mild custom look to it. Most of the side trim on the '58 Impala was aluminum, and Greg left it in place.

Below-For rear taillights, Greg installed '59 Cadillac units. With the chrome wheels and baby moons, lake pipes, Cadillac taillights, and everything else that Greg did to it, this custom looks like it was built in the early '60s.

Tasmanian *Devil*

In 1960, Chevrolet introduced the Corvair, and as they say, the rest is history. But at the same time, the Impala was introduced with a few updated features such as a new oval grille with enclosed headlamps, and missile-inspired side trim. The 1960 Impala sports coupe is the last of the '50s fin cars, with its downsized "seagull wings."

While the '60 Impala sports coupe had the '50s look, there was an option available which made the Impala a real screamer. It was the 335 horsepower 348 cubic inch big block with tri-power intake. This was the forerunner to the '64 Impala with the famous 409 motor, which is still a much sought-after car and motor.

But John and Christine Boyd didn't care about all the history behind their '60 Impala hardtop. They just like 'em. And since they like customs, they decided to build one, and a nice one at that.

Dubbed the Tasmanian Devil, this Impala has received all the custom tricks, such as a tube grille front and rear, '59 Chevy headlights and '61 Pontiac taillights. The doors and hood have been rounded, door handles shaved, and a vacuum trunk release installed. Air scoops were added to the sides, the antennas were frenched and surrounded by a molded lip. Lake pipes are in place, and a wild paint job of bright red with purple scallops captures everyone's attention.

Being the owner of Precision Automotive, John didn't want to settle for a stocker engine. He dropped in a healthy LT1 Corvette motor that has been treated to a Pete Jackson gear drive and Edelbrock high-rise manifold. Right behind the engine is a Muncie 2+2 transmission.

So, if this particular '60 Impala catches your eye, you better look fast, 'cause this is one custom that can move in a hurry.

Vehicle: 1960 Chevrolet Impala
Owner: John and Christine Boyd, St. Louis, Missouri

Full custom treatment was given to the rear view of this '60 Impala. The classic "seagull wings" are still there, but that's about the only stock feature. A rear bar grille has been added, along with a set of '61 Pontiac taillights.

Right-Wire wheels, lake pipes, and molded scoops highlight each side of the Tasmanian Devil. This is a custom that attracts attention from every angle.

Below-The bar grille for the front of the car carries over the same theme as was employed in the rear. Headlights are '59 Chevy, turned on a steep diagonal angle. Purple scallops contrast dramatically against the bright red paint.

Right-The custom interior is complete with fuzzy dice, under dash air conditioner unit, and floor shift. Upholstery is reminiscent of the era represented by this car.

Above-A pair of antennae has been frenched into the horizontal surface of the passenger side fin. Note the screen covering the antenna tunnel, and the lip that has been molded around it.

Right-Under the hood lives a healthy LT1 Corvette powerplant which has been treated to a few goodies to make it even stronger. Transmission duties are performed by a Muncie 2+2.

by John Lee

Grandma's
Kool Custom

Work around custom cars long enough and it'll get in your blood. Just ask Dan Becklehimer. In his job at Jon's Body Shop in Lafayette, Indiana, Dan had a hand in building a radical '53 F-100 and a chopped '79 Dodge Li'l Red Express for customers, plus lending a hand on Jon's pro-street '36 Plymouth.

With that exposure and experience, he rolled the '68 Impala hardtop he'd bought from his grandfather into the shop and started cutting. After spending more than 1000 hours on it over the next year, the smooth pieces you see here rolled out into the daylight.

His first stop was at Grandpa and Grandma's to show them what he'd done with the car they bought new. "They were very impressed," said Dan.

Judges have also been very impressed. The Impala has gathered up awards at every show, including Koolest Late Model at the KKOA Leadsled Spectacular.

The transformation started with cutting the top off and dropping it five inches, making it more of a fastback while retaining the stock rear window and basic side window shape. Then Dan welded up the trunk lid and molded the rear bumper to the body. Access to the rear storage compartment is now through a fold-down seat back.

The front clip is also one piece, with the bumper tips and double face bars molded to the body. The rectangular openings are filled with stainless steel grille bars, stock turn signal lenses and one-piece headlight lenses from an '88 Caprice. The shaved doors are opened with electric remote controls.

All emblems and the side markers have been removed, and Dan made the teardrop fender skirts out of quarter-inch rod and the roof skin from a '76 Ford. Along with the stock taillights, a third brake light was tunneled into the former deck lid key hole. The power

antennas are also frenched.

Dan sprayed the smooth, integrated body in Ford Shenandoah Green with a very subtle dry-brush graphic in light blue on the top edge of the doors. Red painted wheel rims, black General XP 2000 tires and stock wheel

Vehicle: 1968 Chevrolet Impala hardtop
Owner: Dan Becklehimer, Lafayette, Indiana

covers set off the monochrome finish.

In keeping with the modern theme, the engine and compartment are painted green and blue. The 327 V8 and Powerglide transmission are stock.

The color scheme carries over to the interior, where Bob and Mike Lyons of Brookville, Ohio sculptured modern designs into a foam base and covered it with blue and green tweed fabric with red accents. Front seats came from a '78 Datsun and the back seat is from an '89 Cavalier. A '76 Camaro console provides tape storage for a Nakamichi stereo, hooked up to an Alpine amplifier and 150-watt speakers.

Dan thinks his boss, Jon Hicks, was very generous in allowing him to take up space in the shop to build this custom. Jon, in return, doesn't mind having an employee driving to shows in a knock-out custom — and telling people where it was built!

A profile view of Dan's '68 Impala hardtop shows just how sleek and low it is, after the 5-inch top chop and a full menu of other custom tricks, including molding front and rear bumpers into the body.

All stock side trim, door handles and emblems were removed, and Dan made teardrop skirts by using quarter-inch steel rod and the roof skin from a '76 Ford.

Smooth and tasteful front end treatment is a combination of stainless steel bar grille and one-piece headlight lenses from an '88 Caprice, as well as molding the front bumper into the body.

Along with the stock taillights, a third brake light was tunneled into the former deck lid key hole. The smooth, bumperless appearance with recessed license plate adds a flavor of aerodynamics.

Stock 327 V8 and Powerglide transmission provide more than enough performance for this type of car. To match the overall paint scheme, the engine and underhood area are painted blue and green.

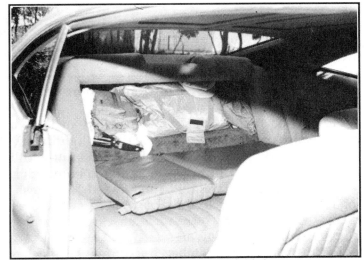

Access to the trunk storage space is via a fold-down rear seat back, since the deck lid was welded shut to create a seamless body. The rear seat was originally in an '89 Cavalier.

by John Lee

Late Model *Nomad*

Chevrolet started something with the '55 Nomad, namely a trend toward station wagons with style that you wouldn't mind being seen in at the country club.

Vehicle: 1979 Chevrolet Nomad
Owner: Jim Ebenhoh, Fenton, Missouri

Trouble is, once they started it, they didn't keep it going. Chevy dropped the 2-door hardtop style Nomad in '57, just when other manufacturers began to pick up on the concept.

Jim Ebenhoh of Fenton, Missouri is one who lamented the passing of the original concept and decided to create his own late model version of the Nomad theme.

A '79 Caprice 4-door wagon, purchased for $1800, was the starting point. Jim threw away the doors, and substituted the doors and rear quarter panel front sections from a Caprice coupe to create a 2-door wagon.

He ditched the roof rack and installed an Impala front header panel and headlights. Plastic lighting fixture grillework, painted flat black, fills the full-width grille opening. Stock bumpers are painted body color.

To customize the taillights, Jim applied 1/4" masking tape in strips spaced 1/4" apart, then painted over them with body color. The result is lenses that appear to be covered with a grillework.

To finish off the eye-catcher, Jim dumped it 4 inches in front and installed painted 7x15" spoke wheels from an '82 vintage Z-28. The knockout paint scheme is Porsche Guards Red with bold scallops in custom-mixed hot pink. Pinstriping was done by Rotten Ron, and window moldings are flat black.

The interior, upholstered in tan vinyl, uses the stock Caprice wagon rear seat and a split front seat with Pontiac Bonneville door panels. A modified '87 Cavalier steering wheel mounts on the tilt column. Cruise control, Sanyo AM/FM stereo, power windows, seats and door locks are all included. The stock 4-barrel equipped 350 V8 has over 100,000 miles on it.

Jim did all the work himself at Donovan Auto Body in St. Louis, where he builds customs in the back room while everyone else is rebuilding wrecks. Without counting his six months of spare time work, he got the late model Nomad on the road for under five grand!

Front treatment includes the installation of an Impala front header panel and headlights. Full-width grillework is made of plastic lighting fixture material that has been painted flat black. Stock bumpers are painted body color.

Taillights were customized by applying 1/4" strips of masking tape at 1/4" intervals, then painting over them with body color. When removed, the tape left body color stripes across the lenses, giving the impression of a grillework.

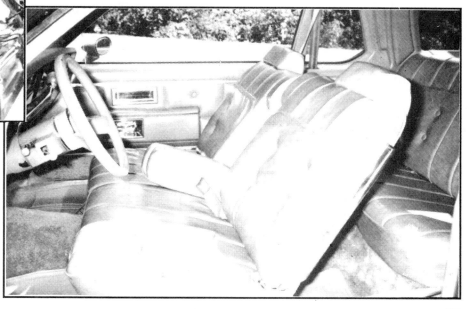

Above-The engine is a stock 350 V8 that breathes through a 4-barrel. Still running fine, the engine has more than 100,000 miles on it.

Interior consists of a stock Caprice wagon rear bench seat and a split front bench out of a Pontiac Bonneville. A modified '87 Cavalier steering wheel is mounted to the tilt column.

Sources

Following are names, addresses, and phone numbers of folks who are involved in Chevrolet-related hot rod stuff. If these guys don't have it, they can undoubtedly give you some leads to help you find what you're looking for.

Air-Tique
915-H North Nolan River Rd.
Cleburne, TX 76031
(817)641-6933

Antique Auto Parts Cellar
P.O. Box 3
So. Weymouth, MA 02190
(617)335-1579

Bitchin' Products
10707 Airport Dr.
El Cajon, CA 92020
(619)449-2837

Bob's Classic Auto Glass
430 Morrill Ave.
Reno, NV 89512
(702)322-8887

Bob's Super Chevy Parts
15361 Kinsman Road
P.O. Box 175
Middlefield OH 44062
(216)632-1080

Borgeson Universal Co. Inc.
1050 South Main St.
Torrington, CT 06790
(203)482-8283

Bow-Tie Engineering
P.O. Box 422
Palo Cedro, CA 96073

Brodix Cylinder Heads
P.O. Box 1347
Mena, AR 71953
(501)394-1075

Butch's Rod Shop
2853 Northlawn Ave.
Dayton, OH 45439
(513)298-2665

C.A.R.S. Inc.
1964 West 11 Mile Road
Berkley, MI 48072
(313)398-7100

Chassis Engineering
119 N. 2nd St.
West Branch, IA 53358
(319)643-2645

Classic Instruments, Inc.
1678-P Beavercreek Road
Oregon City, OR 97045
(503)655-3520

Classic Sales
Hwy 71, P.O. Box 65
West Point, TX 78963
(409)242-3716

Chev's Of The 40's
18409 NE 28th St. #T
Vancouver, WA 98682
(206)254-CHEV

Chicago Camaro & Firebird
900 S. 5th Ave.
Maywood, IL 60153
(708)681-2187

Conte Enterprises
28002 110th Ave. E.
Graham, WA 98338
(206) 847-4666

David J. Entler Restorations
RD #2 Box 479C
Glen Rock, PA 17327
(717)235-2112

Experi-Metal Inc.
6345 Wall St.
Sterling Heights, MI 48077
(313)977-7800

Dick's Chevy Parts
4358 Bosart Road
Springfield, OH 45503
(513)325-7861

Fat Man Fabrications
8621-C Fairview Rd. Hwy 218
Charlotte, NC 28227
(704)545-0369

Fiberglass and Wood
Rt 3 Box 118
Nashville, GA 31639
(912)686-3838

Hart Enterprises
1475 W. Bullard
Fresno, CA 93711
(209)435-7109

Headers by Ed
2710 16th Ave. So.
Minneapolis, MN 55407
(612)729-2802

Hot Rod Carbureting
812 E. 120 St.
Kansas City, MO 64146
(816)942-7419